HOSPITALITY FINANCIAL MANAGEMENT

HOSPITALITY FINANCIAL MANAGEMENT

M. C. METTI

ANMOL PUBLICATIONS PVT. LTD.
NEW DELHI - 110 002 (INDIA)

ANMOL PUBLICATIONS PVT. LTD.

H.O.: 4374/4B, Ansari Road, Darya Ganj,
New Delhi-110 002 (India)
Ph.: 23278000, 23261597

B.O.: No. 1015, Ist Main Road, BSK IIIrd Stage
IIIrd Phase, IIIrd Block
Bangalore - 560 085 (India)
Visit us at: www.anmolpublications.com

Hospitality Financial Management

ISBN 978-81-261-3241-6

PRINTED IN INDIA

Printed at Mehra Offset Press, Delhi.

Contents

Preface

Managers have to develop at least basic skills in financial management. Expecting others in the hotels to manage finances is clearly asking for trouble. Basic skills in financial management start in the critical areas of cash management and bookkeeping, which should be done according to certain financial controls to ensure integrity in the bookkeeping process. A budget depicts what you expect to spend (expenses) and earn (revenue) over a time period. They are useful for projecting how much money you'll need for a major initiative, for example, buying a facility, hiring a new employee, etc. They also help track whether you're on plan or not. There are yearly (or annual or operating) budgets, cash budgets, capital budgets (for major assets, such as equipment, buildings, etc.) and proposal budgets (for fundraising), etc.

Usually, there are two major types of costs to consider: indirect costs and direct costs. Indirect costs are what we sometimes call "administrative" or "overhead" costs, for example, costs to run the central facility. Direct costs are those that fund resources which directly produce services to clients. Usually, the lower your administrative costs, the more it looks like your resources are going directly to services to clients. In addition, you may have restricted grants (that is, grants that are dedicated for certain programs), which require you to report monies spent on overhead and directly on the programme. Therefore, it's wise to track carefully how much money each of your programs requires to operate and how much revenue it generates, as well. A major challenge is to analyze how much of the indirect costs are associated with each programme.

As a new or small nonprofit, your biggest challenge is likely to be managing your cash flow probably the most important financial statement for a hotel business is the cash flow statement. The overall purpose of managing your cash flow is to make sure that you have enough cash to pay current bills. Businesses of hotels can manage cash flow by examining a cash flow statement and cash flow projection. Basically, the cash flow statement includes total cash received minus total cash spent. Cash management looks primarily at actual cash transactions.

New leaders and managers should soon go on to learn how to generate financial statements and analyze those statements to really understand the financial condition of the hotel business. Financial analysis shows the "reality" of the situation of a business seen as such, financial management is one of the most important practices in management. This book will help you understand basic practices in financial management, and build the basic systems and practices needed in a healthy hotel business.

Author

Chapter 1

Nature and Scope of Financial Management

FINANCIAL MANAGEMENT

Management of funds is an important aspect of financial management. Management of funds act as the primary concern whether it may be in a business undertaking or in an educational institution. Financial management, which is simply meant dealing with management of money matters. A financial institution acts as an agent that provides financial services for its clients. Financial institutions generally fall under financial regulation from a government authority. Common types of financial institutions include banks, building societies, credit unions, stock brokerages, asset management firms, and similar businesses.

Financial institutions provide a service as intermediaries of the capital and debt markets. They are responsible for transferring funds from investors to companies, in need of those funds. The presences of financial institutions facilitate the flow of monies through the economy. To do so, savings accounts are pooled to mitigate the risk brought by individual account holders in order to provide funds for loans. Such is the primary means for depository institutions to develop revenue. Should the yield curve become inverse, firms in this arena will offer additional fee-generating services including securities underwriting, sales and trading, and prime brokerage.

MEANING OF FINANCIAL MANAGEMENT

By Financial Management we mean efficient use of economic resources namely capital funds. According to Phillippatus, "Financial management is concerned with the managerial decisions that result in the acquisition and financing of short term and long term credits for the firm". Here it deals with the situations that require selection of specific assets (or combination of assets), the selection of specific problem of size and growth of an enterprise. Here the analysis deals with the expected inflows and outflows of funds and their effect on managerial objectives.

Most acceptable definition was given by S.C. Kuchhal is that;"Financial Management deals with Procurement of funds and their effective utilization in the business". So the analysis simply states two main aspects of financial management like procurement of funds and an effective use of funds to achieve business objectives.

Procurement of Funds

As funds can be obtained from different sources so procurement of funds is considered as an important problem of business concerns. Funds procured from different sources have different characteristics in terms of risk, cost and control. Funds issued by the issue of equity shares are the best from risk point of view for the company as there is no question of repayment of equity capital except when the company is under liquidation. From the cost point of view equity capital is most expensive source of funds as dividend expectations of shareholders are normally higher than prevalent interest rates. Financial management constitutes risk, cost and control. The cost of funds should be at minimum for a proper balancing of risk and control. In the globalised competitive scenario mobilization of funds plays a very significant role. Funds can be raised either through domestic market or from abroad. Foreign Direct Investment (FDI) as well as Foreign Institutional Investors (FII) are two major sources of raising funds. The mechanism of procurement of funds has to be modified in the light of requirements of foreign investors. From time to time it is seen that many firms have been liquidated not because their technology was obsolete or because their products were not in demand or their labour was not skilled and motivated but there was a complete mismanagement of financial affairs. Even in a boom period, when a company make high profits there is also a fear of liquidation because of bad financial management.

Financial management optimizes the output from the given input of funds. In the country like India where resources are scarce and the demand for funds are many, the need of proper financial management is required. In case of newly started companies with a high growth rate it is more important to have sound financial management since finance alone guarantees their survival. Financial management is very important in case of non-profit organizations, which do not pay adequate attentions to financial management. How ever a sound system of financial management has to be cultivated among bureaucrats, administrators, engineers, educationalists and public at a large.

Utilization of Funds

Effective utilization of funds as an important aspect of financial management avoids the situations where funds are either kept idle or proper uses are not being made. Funds procured involve a certain cost and risk. If the funds are not used properly then running business will be too difficult. In case of dividend decisions we also consider this. So it is crucial to employ the funds properly and profitably.

Scope of Financial Management

A sound financial management is essential in all types of organizations whether it may be profit or non-profit. Financial management is essential in a planned Economy as well as in a capitalist set-up as it involves efficient use of the resources.

Objectives of Financial Management

Efficient Financial management requires the existence of some objectives, which are as follows:

1. *Profit Maximization*

Objective of financial management is same as the objective of a company that is to earn profit. But profit maximization cannot the sole objective of a company. It is a limited objective. If profits are given undue Importance then problems may arise as discussed below.

- The term profit is vague and it involves much more contradictions.
- Profit maximization has to be attempted with a realization of risks involved. A positive relationship exists between risk and profits. So both risk and profit objectives should be balanced.
- Profit Maximization does not take into account the time pattern of returns.
- Profit maximization fails to take into account the social considerations

2. *Wealth Maximization*

It is commonly agreed that the objective of a firm is to maximize value or wealth. Value of a firm is represented by the market price of the company's common stock. The market price of a firm's stock represents the focal judgement of all market participants as to what the value of the particular firm is. It takes in to account present and prospective future earnings per share, the timing and risk of these earning, the dividend policy of the firm and many other factors that bear upon the market price of the stock. Market price acts as the performance index or report card of the firm's progress.

Prices in the share markets are largely affected by many factors like general economic outlook, outlook of particular company, technical factors and even mass psychology. Normally this value is a function of two factors as given below,

- The anticipated rate of earnings per share of the company
- The capitalization rate.

The likely rate of earnings per shares (EPS) depends upon the assessment as to how profitably a company is growing to operate in the future. The capitalization rate reflects the liking of the investors for the company.

Methods of Financial Management

In the field of financing there are various methods to procure funds. Funds may be obtained from long-term sources as well as from short-term sources. Long-term funds may be availed by owners that are shareholders, lenders by issuing debentures, from financial institutions, banks and public at large. Short-term funds may be availed from commercial banks, public deposits, etc. Financial leverage or trading on equity is an important method by which a finance manager may increase the return to common shareholders.

At the time of evaluating capital expenditure projects methods like average rate of return, pay back, internal rate of returns, net present value and profitability index are used. A firm can increase its profitability without affecting its liquidity by an efficient utilization of the current resources at the disposal of the firm. A firm can increase its profitability without affecting its liquidity by an efficient management of working capital. Similarly for the evaluation of a firm's performance there are different methods. Ratio analysis is a popular technique to evaluate different aspects of a firm. An investor takes in to account various ratios to know wheather investment in a particular company will be profitable or not. These ratios enable him to judge the profitability, solvency, liquidity and growth aspect of the firm.

Financial Management In India

In the country like India there is a changing scenario of financial management. As the economy is opening up and global participation is increasing very fast, the opportunities have no limits. Presently financial management passes through an era of experimentation as a larger part of finance activities are carried out.

A few highlights in this context:

- Interest rates are free from regulations.
- Rupee is fully convertible in current account.
- Optimum debt equity mix is possible.
- Maintaining share prices are also crucial. In liberalized scenario the capital market is an important avenue of funds for business.
- Ensuring management control is vital especially in the light of foreign participation.

Corporate Valuation

Use Equity Multiples (as opposed to Enterprise Multiples). In order to consider how valuing a Financial Institution's balance sheet is different from a non-Financial firm. Consider how an industrials firm wields capital machinery (asset) and the loans it used to finance that asset (liabilities). The line is blurred in Financial Institutions, which must hold deposit accounts (assets) to fuel the issuance of loans. The same accounts are considered loans as they are held in ownership not of the bank, but of the individual client.

Discounted Cash Flow (DCF) Model

You'll need the FCFE (Free Cash Flow for Equity), which is the amount of money that is returned to shareholders. Calculate a FCFF (Free Cash Flow to the Firm): EBIT(1-tax rate)-Capital Expenditures+(Depreciation & Amortization) - (Net increase in working capital)= FCFF

FCFF-Debt+Cash=FCFE

Use the Capital Asset Pricing Model, not the Weighted Average Cost of Capital (for the same reasons one uses Equity Multiples in relative valuation) to determine the cost of equity (the return required by shareholders in order to make the decision to invest in a financial institutions)

Bank

The First Provincial Bank of Taiwan in Taipei, Republic of China was formerly the central bank of the Republic of

China and issued the New Taiwan dollar. A bank is a business that provides banking services for profit. Traditional banking services include receiving deposits of money, lending money and processing transactions. Some banks (called Banks of Issue) issue banknotes as legal tender. Many banks offer ancillary financial services to make additional profit; for example: selling insurance products, investment products or stock broking.

Currently in most jurisdictions the business of banking is regulated and banks require permission to trade. Authorisation to trade is granted by bank regulatory authorities and provide rights to conduct the most fundamental banking services such as accepting deposits and making loans. There are also financial institutions that provide banking services without meeting the legal definition of a bank . Banks have a long history, and have influenced economies and politics for centuries.

The word bank comes from the early modern English banke, from French banque, an adaptation of Italian banca feminine, "used side by side," and in same sense, with banco masculine; adaptation of Teutonic bank, banc, "bench." The double form and gender in Romanic, cf. Italian, Spanish, Portuguese banco, banca, Provençal banc, banca, French banc, banche, are apparently original (cf. medieval Latin bancus, banca), and due to the double gender of the German: Old High German der, diu banch, Middle High German der, die banc, early modern and dialect German der, die bank. The original meaning "shelf, bench" was extended in Italian to that of "tradesman's stall, counter, money-changer's table, mensa argentaria, whence "money-shop, bank," a use of the word which passed, with the trade of banking, from Italy into other countries. In this sense, Italian uses both banco and banca, Spanish and Portuguese the masculine banco; but in French the Italian feminine banca was adapted as banque, whence English banke, bank. The word is thus ultimately identical with Bench and Bank.

Italian, monte "mount, heap, amount, stock," was used in some of the senses of "bank," the notion that the name banco, banca, originated in a German rendering of monte is erroneous: German bank had no such sense as "mount, heap," only that of "bench, shelf." Rather is it the fact, that in the development of banking, the banco of the money-changer, and the monte or "joint-stock capital" were at length combined, and bank applied in English to both. The terms bankrupt and "broke" are similarly derived from banca rotta, which refers to an out-of-business bank, having its bench physically broken. Money lenders in Northern Italy originally did business in open areas, or big open rooms, with each lender working from his own bench or table.

Traditionally, a bank generates profits from transaction fees on financial services and from the interest it charges for lending. In recent history, with historically low interest rates limiting banks' ability to earn money by lending deposited funds, much of a bank's income is provided by overdraft fees and riskier investments.

Services Typically Offered by Banks

Although the type of services offered by a bank depends upon the type of bank and the country, services provided usually include:

- Taking deposits from their customers and issuing checking and savings accounts to individuals and businesses
- Extending loans to individuals and businesses
- Cashing cheques
- Facilitating money transactions such as wire transfers and cashiers checks
- Issuing credit cards, ATM cards, and debit cards
- Storing valuables, particularly in a safe deposit box
- Cashing and distributing bank rolls

Financial transactions can be performed through several different channels:

- Branch
- ATM
- Mail
- Telephone banking
- Online banking

Types of Banks

Banks' activities can be characterised as retail banking, dealing directly with individuals and small businesses, and investment banking, relating to activities on the financial markets. Most banks are profit-making, private enterprises. However, some are owned by government, or are non-profit making.

In some jurisdictions retail and investment activities are, or have been, separated by law.

Central banks are non-commercial bodies or government agencies often charged with controlling interest rates and money supply across the whole economy. They act as Lender of last resort in event of a crisis.

Types of Retail Banks

- Commercial bank, is the term used for a normal bank to distinguish it from an investment bank. After the great depression, the U.S. Congress required that banks only engage in banking activities, whereas investment banks were limited to capital markets activities. Since the two no longer have to be under separate ownership, some use the term "commercial bank" to refer to a bank or a division of a bank that mostly deals with deposits and loans from corporations or large businesses.
- Community Banks are locally operated financial institutions that empower employees to make local decisions to serve their customers.
- Community development bank are regulated banks that provide financial services and credit to underserved markets or populations.
- Postal savings banks are savings banks associated with national postal systems.
- Private banks manage the assets of high net worth individuals.

- Offshore banks are banks located in jurisdictions with low taxation and regulation. Many offshore banks are essentially private banks.
- Savings bank In Europe, savings banks take their roots in the 19th or sometimes even 18th century. Their original objective was to provide easily accessible savings products to all strata of the population. In some countries, savings banks were created on public initiative, while in others socially committed individuals created foundations to put in place the necessary infrastructure. Nowadays, European savings banks have kept their focus on retail banking: payments, savings products, credits and insurances for individuals or small and medium-sized enterprises. Apart from this retail focus, they also differ from commercial banks by their broadly decentralised distribution network, providing local and regional outreach and by their socially responsible approach to business and society.
- Building societies and Landesbanks both conduct retail banking.
- Ethical banks are banks that prioritize the transparency of all operations and make only social-responsible investments.

Types of Investment Banks

- Investment banks "underwrite" (guarantee the sale of) stock and bond issues, trade for their own accounts, make markets, and advise corporations on capital markets activities such as mergers and acquisitions.
- Merchant banks were traditionally banks which engaged in trade financing. The modern definition, however, refers to banks which provide capital to firms in the form of shares rather than loans. Unlike Venture capital firms, they tend not to invest in new companies.

Both Combined

- Universal banks, more commonly known as a financial services company, engage in several of these activities. For example, First Bank (a very large bank) is involved in commercial and retail lending, and its subsidiaries in tax-havens offer offshore banking services to customers in other countries. Other large financial institutions are similarly diversified and engage in multiple activities. In Europe and Asia, big banks are very diversified groups that, among other services, also distribute insurance, hence the term bancassurance.

Other Types of Banks

- Islamic banks adhere to the concepts of Islamic law. Islamic banking revolves around several well established concepts which are based on Islamic canons. Since the concept of interest is forbidden in Islam, all banking activities must avoid interest. Instead of interest, the bank earns profit (mark-up) and fees on financing facilities that it extends to the customers. Also, deposit makers earn a share of the bank's profit as opposed to a predetermined interest.

Banks in the Economy

Role in the Money Supply

A bank raises funds by attracting deposits, borrowing money in the inter-bank market, or issuing financial instruments in the money market or a capital market. The bank then lends out most of these funds to borrowers. However, it would not be prudent for a bank to lend out all of its balance sheet. It must keep a certain proportion of its funds in reserve so that it can repay depositors who withdraw their deposits. Bank reserves are typically kept in the form of a deposit with a central bank. This behaviour is called fractional-reserve banking and it is a central issue of monetary policy. Some governments (or their central banks) restrict the proportion of a bank's balance sheet that can be lent out, and use this as a tool for controlling the money supply. Even where the reserve ratio is not controlled by the government, a minimum figure will still be set by regulatory authorities as part of bank regulation.

Size of Global Banking Industry

Worldwide assets of the largest 1,000 banks grew 15.5% in 2005 to reach a record $60.5 trillion. This follows a 19.3% increase in the previous year. EU banks held the largest share, 50% at the end of 2005, up from 38% a decade earlier. The growth in Europe's share was mostly at the expense of Japanese banks whose share more than halved during this period from 33% to 13%. The share of US banks also rose, from 10% to 14%. Most of the remainder was from other Asian and European countries.

The US had by far the most banks (7,540 at end-2005) and branches (75,000) in the world. The large number of banks in the US is an indicator of its geographical dispersity and regulatory structure resulting in a large number of small to medium sized institutions in its banking system. Japan had 129 banks and 12,000 branches. In 2004, Germany, France, and Italy had more than 30,000 branches each—more than double the 15,000 branches in the UK.

Bank Crises

Banks are susceptible to many forms of risk which have triggered occasional systemic crises. Risks include liquidity risk (the risk that many depositors will request withdrawals beyond available funds), credit risk (the risk that those that owe money to the bank will not repay), and interest rate risk (the risk that the bank will become unprofitable if rising interest rates force it to pay relatively more on its deposits than it receives on its loans), among others.

Banking crises have developed many times throughout history when one or more risks materialize for a banking sector as a whole. Prominent examples include the U.S. Savings and Loan crisis in 1980s and early 1990s, the Japanese banking crisis during the 1990s, the bank run that occurred during the Great

Depression, and the recent liquidation by the central Bank of Nigeria, where about 25 banks were liquidated.

Regulation

The combination of the instability of banks as well as their important facilitating role in the economy led to banking being thoroughly regulated. The amount of capital a bank is required to hold is a function of the amount and quality of its assets. Major banks are subject to the Basel Capital Accord promulgated by the Bank for International Settlements. In addition, banks are usually required to purchase deposit insurance to make sure smaller investors are not wiped out in the event of a bank failure.

Another reason banks are thoroughly regulated is that ultimately, no government can allow the banking system to fail. There is almost always a lender of last resort—in the event of a liquidity crisis (where short term obligations exceed short term assets) some element of government will step in to lend banks enough money to avoid bankruptcy.

Public Perceptions of Banks

In United States history, the National Bank was a major political issue during the presidency of Andrew Jackson. Jackson fought against the bank as a symbol of greed and profit-mongering, antithetical to the democratic ideals of the United States. Currently, many people consider that various banking policies take advantage of customers. Specific concerns are policies that permit banks to hold deposited funds for several days, to apply withdrawals before deposits or from greatest to least, which is most likely to cause the greatest overdraft, that allow backdating funds transfers and fee assessments, and that authorize electronic funds transfers despite an overdraft.

In response to the perceived greed and socially-irresponsible all-for-the-profit attitude of banks, in the last few decades a new type of banks called ethical banks have emerged, which only make social-responsible investments (for instance, no investment in the arms industry) and are transparent in all its operations. In the US, Credit unions have also gained popularity as an alternative financial resource for many consumers. Also, in various European countries, cooperative banks are regularly gaining market share in retail banking.

Profitability

Large banks in the United States are some of the most profitable corporations, especially relative to the small market shares they have. This amount is even higher if one counts the credit divisions of companies like Ford, which are responsible for a large proportion of those companies' profits. For example, the largest bank, Citigroup, which for the past 3 years has made more profit than any other company in the world, has only a 5% market share. If Citigroup were to be as dominant in its industry as a Home Depot, Starbucks, or Wal Mart in their respective industries, with a 30% market share – and if its profit margins scaled up proportionally – it would make more money than the top ten non-banking U.S. industries combined.

In the past 10 years in the United States, banks have taken many measures to ensure that they remain profitable while responding to ever-changing market conditions. First, this includes the Gramm-Leach-Bliley Act, which allows banks again to merge with investment and insurance houses. Merging banking, investment, and insurance functions allows traditional banks to respond to increasing consumer demands for "one stop shopping" by enabling cross-selling of products (which, the banks hope, will also increase profitability). Second, they have moved toward risk-based pricing on loans, which means charging higher interest rates for those people who they deem more risky to default on loans.

This dramatically helps to offset the losses from bad loans, lowers the price of loans to those who have better credit histories, and extends credit products to high risk customers who would have been denied credit under the previous system. Third, they have sought to increase the methods of payment processing available to the general public and business clients. These products include debit cards, pre-paid cards, smart-cards, and credit cards. These products make it easier for consumers to conveniently make transactions and smooth their consumption over time (in some countries with under-developed financial systems, it is still common to deal strictly in cash, including carrying suitcases filled with cash to purchase a home). However, with convenience there is also increased risk that consumers will mismanage their financial resources and accumulate excessive debt. Banks make money from card products through interest payments and fees charged to consumers and companies that accept the cards. The banks' main obstacles to increasing profits are existing regulatory burdens, new government regulation, and increasing competition from non-traditional financial institutions.

CORPORATE GOVERNANCE

Corporate governance is the set of processes, customs, policies, laws and institutions affecting the way a corporation is directed, administered or controlled. Corporate governance also includes the relationships among the many players involved (the stakeholders) and the goals for which the corporation is governed. The principal players are the shareholders, management and the board of directors. Other stakeholders include employees, suppliers, customers, banks and other lenders, regulators, the environment and the community at large.

Corporate governance is a multi-faceted subject. An important theme of corporate governance deals with issues of accountability and fiduciary duty, essentially advocating the implementation of guidelines and mechanisms to ensure good behaviour and protect shareholders. Another key focus is the economic efficiency view, through which the corporate governance system should aim to optimize economic results, with a strong emphasis on shareholders welfare. There are yet other sides to the corporate governance subject, such as the stakeholder view, which calls for more attention and accountability to players other than the shareholders (e.g.: the employees or the environment). Recently there has been considerable interest in the corporate governance practices of modern corporations, particularly since the high-profile collapses of large US firms such as Enron Corporation and Worldcom.

Definition

The term corporate governance has come to mean two things.

- The processes by which companies are directed and controlled.
- A field in economics, which studies the many issues arising from the separation of ownership and control.

Relevant rules include applicable laws of the land as well as internal rules of a corporation. Relationships include those between all related parties, the most important of which are the owners, managers, directors of the board, regulatory authorities and to a lesser extent employees and the community at large. Systems and processes deal with matters such as delegation of authority. The corporate governance structure spells out the rules and procedures for making decisions on corporate affairs. It also provides the structure through which the company objectives are set, as well as the means of attaining and monitoring the performance of those objectives.

Corporate governance is used to monitor whether outcomes are in accordance with plans and to motivate the organisation to be more fully informed in order to maintain or alter organisational activity. Corporate governance is the mechanism by which individuals are motivated to align their actual behaviours with the overall participants.

History

In the 19th century, state corporation law enhanced the rights of corporate boards to govern without unanimous consent of shareholders in exchange for statutory benefits like appraisal rights, in order to make corporate governance more efficient. Since that time, and because most large publicly traded corporations in America are incorporated under corporate administration friendly Delaware law, and because America's wealth has been increasingly securitized into various corporate entities and institutions, the rights of individual owners and shareholders have become increasingly derivative and dissipated. The concerns of shareholders over administration pay and stock losses periodically has led to more frequent calls for Corporate Governance reforms.

In the 20th century in the immediate aftermath of the Wall Street Crash of 1929 legal scholars such as Adolf Augustus Berle, Edwin Dodd, and Gardiner C. Means pondered on the changing role of the modern corporation in society. Berle and Means' monograph "The Modern Corporation and Private Property" continues to have a profound influence on the conception of corporate governance in scholarly debates today.

From the Chicago school of economics, Ronald Coase's "Nature of the Firm" introduced the notion of transaction costs into the understanding of why firms are founded and how they continue to behave. Fifty years later, Eugene Fama and Michael Jensen's "The Separation of Ownership and Control" (1983, Journal of Law and Economics) firmly established agency theory as a way of understanding corporate governance: the firm is seen as a series of contracts. Agency theory's dominance was highlighted in a 1989 article by Kathleen Eisenhardt.

American expansion after World War II through the emergence of multinational corporations saw the establishment of the managerial class. Accordingly, the following Harvard Business School management professors published influential monographs studying their prominence: Myles Mace (entrepreneurship), Alfred D. Chandler, Jr. (business history), Jay Lorsch (organizational behaviour) and Elizabeth MacIver (organizational behaviour). According to Lorsch and MacIver "many large corporations have dominant control over business affairs without sufficient accountability or monitoring by their board of directors."

Current preoccupation with corporate governance can be pinpointed at two events: The East Asian Crisis of 1997 saw the economies of Thailand, Indonesia, South Korea, Malaysia and The Philippines severely affected by the exit of foreign capital after property assets collapsed. The lack of corporate governance mechanisms in these countries highlighted the weaknesses of the institutions in their economies. The second event was the American corporate crises of 2001-2002 which saw the collapse of two big corporations: Enron and WorldCom, and the ensuing scandals and collapses in other corporations such as Arthur Andersen, Global Crossing and Tyco.

Role of Institutional Investors

Many years ago, worldwide, buyers and sellers of corporation stocks were *individual* investors, such as wealthy businessmen. Over time, markets have become more *institutionalized*; buyers and sellers are largely institutions (e.g., pension funds, insurance companies, mutual funds, hedge funds, investor groups, and banks). The rise of the institutional investor has brought with it some increase of professional diligence which has tended to improve regulation of the stock market (but not necessarily in the interest of the small investor or even of the naïve institutions, of which there are many). Note that this process occurred simultaneously with the direct growth of individuals investing in the market (for example individuals have twice as much money in mutual funds as they do in bank accounts). However this growth occurred primarily in individuals turning over their funds to professionals to manage, such as in mutual funds. In this way, the majority of investment now is described as "institutional investment" even though the vast majority of the funds are for the benefit of individual investors.

Unfortunately, there has been a concurrent lapse in the oversight of large corporations, which are now almost all owned by large institutions. The Board of Directors of large corporations used to be chosen by the principal shareholders, who usually had an emotional as well as monetary investment in the company (think Ford), and the Board diligently kept an eye on the company and its principal executives (they usually hired and fired the President, or Chief executive officer – CEO). Nowadays, if the owning institutions don't like what the President/CEO is doing and they feel that firing him will be costly (think "golden handshake") and/or time consuming, they will simply sell out their interest. Also, nowadays, the Board is mostly chosen by the President/CEO, and may be made up primarily of his cronies (or, at least, officers of the corporation, who owe their jobs to him, or fellow CEOs from other corporations). Since the (institutional) shareholders rarely object, the President/CEO generally takes the Chairman of the Board position for himself (which makes it much more difficult for the institutional owners to "fire" him). Finally, the largest pools of invested money (such as the mutual fund 'Vanguard 500', or the largest investment management firm for corporations, State Street) are designed simply to invest in a very large number of companies with sufficient liquidity, based on the idea that this strategy will largely eliminate individual company or financial risk and, therefore, these investors have even less interest in what a particular company is doing.

Since the marked rise in the use of Internet transactions in the 1990s, both individual and professional stock investors around the world have emerged as a potential new kind of major (short term) force in the ownership of corporations and in the markets: the casual participant. Even as the purchase of individual shares in any one corporation by individual investors diminishes, the sale of derivatives (e.g., exchange-traded funds (ETFs), Stock market index options, etc.) has soared. So, the interests of most investors are now increasingly rarely tied to the fortunes of individual corporations.

But, the ownership of stocks in markets around the world varies; for example, the majority of the shares in the Japanese market are held by financial companies and industrial corporations (there is a large amount of cross-holding among Japanese keiretsu corporations and within S. Korean chaebol 'groups'), whereas stock in the USA or the UK and Europe are much more broadly owned, often still by large individual investors. In the latter half of the 1990s, during the Asian financial crisis, a lot of the attention fell upon the corporate governance systems of the developing world, which tend to be heavily into cronyism and nepotism.

In the first half of the 1990s, the issue of corporate governance in the U.S. received considerable press attention due to the wave of (belated?) CEO dismissals (e.g.: IBM, Kodak, Honeywell) by their boards. Calpers led a wave of institutional shareholder activism (something only very rarely seen before), as a way of ensuring that corporate value would not be destroyed by the now traditionally cozy relationships between the CEO and the board of directors. In the early 2000s, the massive bankruptcies (and criminal malfeasance) of Enron and Worldcom, as well as lesser corporate debacles, such as Adelphia Communications, AOL, Arthur Andersen, Global Crossing, Tyco, and, more recently, Freddie Mac and Fannie Mae, led to increased shareholder and governmental interest in corporate governance, culminating in the passage of the Sarbanes-Oxley Act of 2002. Since then, the stock market has greatly recovered, and shareholder zeal has waned accordingly.

Parties to Corporate Governance

Parties involved in corporate governance include the regulatory body (e.g. the Chief Executive Officer, the board of directors, management and shareholders. Other stakeholders who take part include suppliers, employees, creditors, customers and the community at large. In corporations, the shareholder delegates decision rights to the manager to act in the principal's best interests. This separation of ownership from control implies a loss of effective control by shareholders over managerial decisions. Partly as a result of this separation between the two parties, a system of corporate governance controls is implemented to assist in aligning the incentives of managers with those of shareholders. With the significant increase in equity holdings of investors, there has been an opportunity for a reversal of the separation of ownership and control problems because ownership is not so diffuse.

A board of directors often plays a key role in corporate governance. It is their responsibility to endorse the organisation's strategy, develop directional policy, appoint, supervise and remunerate senior executives and to ensure accountability of the organisation to its owners and authorities. All parties to corporate governance have an interest, whether direct or indirect, in the effective performance of the organisation. Directors, workers and management receive salaries, benefits and reputation, while shareholders receive capital return. Customers receive goods and services; suppliers receive compensation for their goods or services. In return these individuals provide value in the form of natural, human, social and other forms of capital.

A key factor in an individual's decision to participate in an organisation e.g. through providing financial capital and trust that they will receive a fair share of the organisational returns. If some parties are receiving more than their fair return then participants may choose to not continue participating leading to organisational collapse.

Principles

Key elements of good corporate governance principles include honesty, trust and integrity, openness, performance orientation, responsibility and accountability, mutual respect, and commitment to the organisation. Of importance is how directors and management develop a model of governance that aligns the values of the corporate participants and then evaluate this model periodically for its effectiveness. In particular, senior executives should conduct themselves honestly and ethically, especially concerning actual or apparent conflicts of interest, and disclosure in financial reports.

Commonly accepted principles of corporate governance include:

- Rights and equitable treatment of shareholders: Organisations should respect the rights of shareholders and help shareholders to exercise those rights. They can help shareholders exercise their rights by effectively communicating information that is understandable and accessible and encouraging shareholders to participate in general meetings.

- Interests of other stakeholders: Organisations should recognise that they have legal and other obligations to all legitimate stakeholders.
- Role and responsibilities of the board: The board needs a range of skills and understanding to be able to deal with various business issues and have the ability to review and challenge management performance. It needs to be of sufficient size and have an appropriate level of commitment to fulfill its responsibilities and duties. There are issues about the appropriate mix of executive and non-executive directors. The key roles of chairperson and CEO should not be held by the same person.
- Integrity and ethical behaviour: Organisations should develop a code of conduct for their directors and executives that promotes ethical and responsible decision making. It is important to understand, though, that systemic reliance on integrity and ethics is bound to eventual failure.
- Disclosure and transparency: Organisations should clarify and make publicly known the roles and responsibilities of board and management to provide shareholders with a level of accountability. They should also implement procedures to independently verify and safeguard the integrity of the company's financial reporting. Disclosure of material matters concerning the organisation should be timely and balanced to ensure that all investors have access to clear, factual information.

Issues involving corporate governance principles include:

- Oversight of the preparation of the entity's financial statements
- Internal controls and the independence of the entity's auditors

- Review of the compensation arrangements for the chief executive officer and other senior executives
- The way in which individuals are nominated for positions on the board
- The resources made available to directors in carrying out their duties
- Oversight and management of risk
- Dividend policy

Mechanisms and Controls

Corporate governance mechanisms and controls are designed to reduce the inefficiencies that arise from moral hazard and adverse selection. For example, to monitor managers' behaviour, an independent third party (the auditor) attests the accuracy of information provided by management to investors. An ideal control system should regulate both motivation and ability.

Internal Corporate Governance Controls

Internal corporate governance controls monitor activities and then take corrective action to accomplish organisational goals. Examples include:

- Monitoring by the board of directors: The board of directors, with its legal authority to hire, fire and compensate top management, safeguards invested capital. Regular board meetings allow potential problems to be identified, discussed and avoided. Whilst non-executive directors are thought to be more independent, they may not always result in more effective corporate governance and may not increase performance. Different board structures are optimal for different firms. Moreover, the ability of the board to monitor the firm's executives is a function of its access to information. Executive directors possess superior knowledge of the decision-making process and therefore evaluate top management on the basis of the quality of its decisions that lead to financial performance outcomes, *ex ante*. It could be argued, therefore, that executive directors look beyond the financial criteria.

- Remuneration: Performance-based remuneration is designed to relate some proportion of salary to individual performance. It may be in the form of cash or non-cash payments such as shares and share options, superannuation or other benefits. Such incentive schemes, however, are reactive in the sense that they provide no mechanism for preventing mistakes or opportunistic behaviour, and can elicit myopic behaviour.
- Audit committees

External Corporate Governance Controls

External corporate governance controls encompass the controls external stakeholders exercise over the organisation.

Examples include:

- Debt covenants
- External auditors
- Government regulations
- Media pressure
- Takeovers
- Competition
- Managerial labour market

Systemic Problems of Corporate Governance

- Supply of accounting information: Financial accounts form a crucial link in enabling providers of finance to monitor directors. Imperfections in the financial reporting process will cause imperfections in the effectiveness of corporate governance. This should, ideally, be corrected by the working of the external auditing process.
- Demand for information: A barrier to shareholders using good information is the cost of processing it,

especially to a small shareholder. The traditional answer to this problem is the efficient market hypothesis (in finance, the efficient market hypothesis (EMH) asserts that financial markets are efficient), which suggests that the shareholder will free ride on the judgements of larger professional investors.

- Monitoring costs: In order to influence the directors, the shareholders must combine with others to form a significant voting group which can pose a real threat of carrying resolutions or appointing directors at a general meeting.

Role of the Accountant

Financial reporting is a crucial element necessary for the corporate governance system to function effectively. Accountants and auditors are the primary providers of information to capital market participants. The directors of the company should be entitled to expect that management prepare the financial information in compliance with statutory and ethical obligations, and rely on auditors' competence

Current accounting practice allows a degree of choice of method in determining the method of measurement, criteria for recognition, and even the definition of the accounting entity. The exercise of this choice to improve apparent performance (popularly known as creative accounting) imposes extra information costs on users. In the extreme, it can involve non-disclosure of information.

One area of concern is whether the accounting firm acts as both independent auditor and management consultant to the firm they are auditing. This may result in a conflict of interest which places the integrity of financial reports in doubt due to client pressure to appease management. The power of the corporate client to initiate and terminate management consulting services and, more fundamentally, to select and dismiss accounting firms contradicts the concept of an independent auditor.

The Enron collapse is an example of misleading financial reporting. Enron concealed huge losses by creating illusions that a third party was contractually obliged to pay the amount of any losses. However, the third party was an entity in which Enron had a substantial economic stake. In discussions of accounting practices with Arthur Andersen, the partner in charge of auditing, views inevitably led to the client prevailing.

However, good financial reporting is not a sufficient condition for the effectiveness of corporate governance if users don't process it, or if the informed user is unable to exercise a monitoring role due to high costs.

REGULATION

Rules Versus Principles

Rules are typically thought to be simpler to follow than principles, demarcating a clear line between acceptable and unacceptable behaviour. Rules also reduce discretion on the part of individual managers or auditors.

In practice rules can be more complex than principles. They may be ill-equipped to deal with new types of transactions not covered by the code. Moreover, even if clear rules are followed, one can still find a way to circumvent their underlying purpose - this is harder to achieve if one is bound by a broader principle.

Enforcement

Enforcement can affect the overall credibility of a regulatory system. They both deter bad actors and level the competitive playing field. Nevertheless, greater enforcement is not always better, for taken too far it can dampen valuable risk-taking. In practice, however, this is largely a theoretical, as opposed to a real, risk.

Corporate Governance Models Around the World

Anglo-American Model

There are many different models of corporate governance around the world. These differ according to the variety of capitalism in which they are embedded. The liberal model that is common in Anglo-American countries tends to give priority to the interests of shareholders. The coordinated model that one finds in Continental Europe and Japan also recognizes the interests of workers, managers, suppliers, customers, and the community. Both models have distinct competitive advantages, but in different ways. The liberal model of corporate governance encourages radical innovation and cost competition, whereas the coordinated model of corporate governance facilitates incremental innovation and quality competition.

In the United States, a corporation is governed by a board of directors, which has the power to choose an executive officer, usually known as the chief executive officer. The CEO has broad power to manage the corporation on a daily basis, but needs to get board approval for certain major actions, such as hiring his/her immediate subordinates, raising money, acquiring another company, major capital expansions, or other expensive projects. Other duties of the board may include policy setting, decision making, monitoring management's performance, or corporate control.

The board of directors is nominally selected by and responsible to the shareholders, but the bylaws of many companies make it difficult for all but the largest shareholders to have any influence over the makeup of the board; normally, individual shareholders are not offered a choice of board nominees among which to choose, but are merely asked to rubberstamp the nominees of the sitting board. Perverse incentives have pervaded many corporate boards in the developed world, with board members beholden to the chief executive whose actions they are intended to oversee. Frequently, members of the boards of directors are CEOs of other corporations, which some see as a conflict of interest.

Non Anglo-American Model

In East Asian countries, family-owned companies dominate. A study by Claessens, Djankov and Lang (2000) investigated the top 15 families in East Asian countries and found that they dominated listed corporate assets. In countries such as Pakistan, Indonesia and the Philippines, the top 15 families controlled over 50% of publicly owned corporations through a system of family cross-holdings, thus dominating the capital markets. Family-owned companies also dominate the Latin model of corporate governance, that is companies in Italy, Spain, France (to a certain extent), Brazil, Mexico and other countries in South America.

Codes and Guidelines

Corporate governance principles and codes have been developed in different countries and issued from stock exchanges, corporations, institutional investors, or associations (institutes) of directors and managers with the support of governments and international organizations. As a rule, compliance with these governance recommendations is not mandated by law, although the codes linked to stock exchange listing requirements may have a coercive effect.

For example, companies quoted on the London and Toronto Stock Exchanges formally need not follow the recommendations of their respective national codes. However, they must disclose whether they follow the recommendations in those documents and, where not, they should provide explanations concerning divergent practices. Such disclosure requirements exert a significant pressure on listed companies for compliance.

In the United States, companies are primarily regulated by the state in which they incorporate though they are also regulated by the federal government and, if they are public, by their stock exchange. The highest number of companies are incorporated in Delaware, including more than half of the Fortune 500. This is due to Delaware's generally business-friendly corporate legal environment and the existence of a state court dedicated solely to business issues (Delaware Court of Chancery). Most states' corporate law generally follow the American Bar Association's Model Business Corporation Act. While Delaware does not follow the Act, it still considers its provisions and several prominent Delaware justices, including former Delaware Supreme Court Chief Justice E. Norman Veasey, participate on ABA committees.

One issue that has been raised since the Disney decision in 2005 is the degree to which companies manage their governance responsibilities; in other words, do they merely try to supersede the legal threashold or should they create governance guidelines that ascend to the level of best practice. For example, the guidelines issued by associations of directors, corporate managers and individual companies tend to be wholly voluntary. For example, The GM Board Guidelines reflect the company's efforts to improve its own governance capacity. Such documents, however, may have a wider multiplying effect prompting other companies to adopt similar documents and standards of best practice.

One of the most influential guidelines has been the 1999 OECD Principles of Corporate Governance. This was revised in 2004. The OECD remains a proponent of corporate governance principles throughout the world. The World Business Council for Sustainable Development WBCSD has also done substantial work on corporate governance, particularly on accountability and reporting, and in 2004 created an Issue Management Tool: Strategic challenges for business in the use of corporate responsibility codes, standards, and frameworks.This document aims to provide general information, a "snap-shot" of the landscape and a perspective from a think-tank/professional association on a few key codes, standards and frameworks relevant to the sustainability agenda.

Corporate Governance and Firm Performance

In its 'Global Investor Opinion Survey' of over 200 institutional investors first undertaken in 2000 and updated in 2002, McKinsey found that 80% of the respondents would pay a premium for well-governed companies. They defined a well-governed company as one that had mostly out-side directors, who had no management ties, undertook formal evaluation of its directors, and was responsive to investors' requests for information on governance issues. The size of the premium varied by market, from 11% for Canadian companies to around 40% for companies where the regulatory backdrop was least certain (those in Morocco, Egypt and Russia).

Other studies have linked broad perceptions of the quality of companies to superior share price performance. In a study of five year cumulative returns of Fortune Magazine's survey of 'most admired firms', Antunovich et al found that those "most admired" had an average return of 125%, whilst the 'least admired' firms returned 80%. In a separate study Business Week enlisted institutional investors and 'experts' to assist in differentiating between boards with good and bad governance and found that companies with the highest rankings had the highest financial returns. On the other hand, research into the relationship between specific corporate governance controls and firm performance has been mixed and often weak. The following examples are illustrative.

Board Composition

Some researchers have found support for the relationship between frequency of meetings and profitability. Others have found a negative relationship between the proportion of external directors and firm performance, while others found no relationship between external board membership and performance. In a recent paper Bagahat and Black found that companies with more independent boards do not perform better than other companies. It is unlikely that board composition has a direct impact on firm performance.

Remuneration/Compensation

The results of previous research on the relationship between firm performance and executive compensation have failed to find consistent and significant relationships between executives' remuneration and firm performance. Low average levels of pay-performance alignment do not necessarily imply that this form of governance control is inefficient. Not all firms experience the same levels of agency conflict, and external and internal monitoring devices may be more effective for some than for others.

Some researchers have found that the largest CEO performance incentives came from ownership of the firm's shares, while other researchers found that the relationship between share ownership and firm performance was dependent on the level of ownership. The results suggest that increases in ownership above 20% cause management to become more entrenched, and less interested in the welfare of their shareholders.

Firm performance has been found to be positively associated with share option plans. These plans direct managers' energies and extend their decision horizons toward the long-term, rather than the short-term, performance of the company.

Attention to Corporate Governance

Corporate governance issues are receiving greater attention in both developed and developing countries as a result of the increasing recognition that a firm's corporate governance affects both its economic performance and its ability to access long-term, low-cost investment capital. In response to calls by OECD ministers, a revised version of its "Principles of Corporate Governance" was produced in 2004.

Numerous high-profile cases of corporate governance failure have focused the minds of governments, companies and the general public on the threat posed to the integrity of financial markets, although it is not clear that any system will or should prevent business failures, or that it is possible to provide a guarantee against fraud.

Corporate Governance concerns have been widely studied. For the United States, an analysis of these concerns has been published by the New York Society of Securities Analysts in their 2003 Corporate Governance Handbook. What constitutes good and bad corporate governance is an on-going debate in politics, civil society, and academia. For an international survey of the scientific literature see Becht, Bolton and Roell 2002.

The OECD publishes an annual paper on corporate governance. First issued in 1999, this paper has provided the framework for regional corporate governance roundtables in cooperation with the World Bank around the world. It has been endorsed as one of the Financial Stability Forum's 12 key standards, and form the basis for the World Bank's Review of Observance of Standards and Codes.

Principal-agent Problem

In economics, the principal-agent problem treats the difficulties that arise under conditions of incomplete and asymmetric information when a principal hires an agent. Various mechanisms may be used to try to align the interests of the agent with those of the principal, such as piece rates/ commissions, profit sharing, efficiency wages, the agent posting a bond, or fear of firing. The principal-agent problem is found in most employer/employee relationships, for example, when stockholders hire top executives of corporations.

Overview

In economics, the problem of motivating one party to act on behalf of another is known as 'the principal-agent problem'. The principal-agent problem arises when a principal compensates an agency for performing certain acts that are useful to the principal and costly to the agent, and where there are elements of the performance that are costly to observe. This is the case to some extent for all contracts that are written in a world of information asymmetry, uncertainty and risk. Here, principals do not know enough about whether (or to what extent) a contract is or has been satisfied. The solution to this information problem - closely related to the moral hazard problem - is to ensure (as far as possible) the provision of appropriate incentives so that agents act in the way principals wish. In terms of game theory, it involves changing the rules of the game so that the self-interested rational choices that the principal predicts the agent will make coincide with the choices the principal desires. Even in the limited arena of employment contracts, the difficulty of doing this in practice is reflected in a multitude of compensation mechanisms ('the carrot') and supervisory schemes ('the stick'), as well as in critique of such mechanisms as e.g. Deming expresses in his Seven Deadly Diseases of management.

Employment Contract

In the context of the employment contract, individual contracts form a major method of restructuring incentives, by connecting as closely as is optimal the information available about employee performance, and the compensation for that performance. Because of differences in the quantity and quality of information available about the performance of individual employees, the ability of employees to bear risk, and the ability of employees to manipulate evaluation methods, the structural details of individual contracts vary widely, including such mechanisms as "piece rates, options, discretionary bonuses, promotions, profit sharing, efficiency wages, deferred compensation, and so on." Typically, these mechanisms are used in the context of different types of employment: salespeople often receive some or all of their remuneration as commission, production workers are usually paid an hourly wage, while office workers are typically paid monthly or semimonthly (and if paid overtime, typically at a higher rate than the hourly rate implied by the salary). The way in which these mechanisms are used is different in the two parts of the economy which Doeringer and Piore called the "primary" and "secondary" sectors. The secondary sector is characterised by short-term employment relationships, little or no prospect of internal promotion, and the determination of wages primarily by market forces. In terms of occupations, it consists primarily of low or unskilled jobs, whether they are blue-collar (manual-labour), white-collar (e.g. filing clerks), or service jobs (e.g. waiters). These jobs are linked by the fact that they are characterized by "low skill levels, low earnings, easy entry, job impermanence, and low returns to education or experience."

Non-financial Compensation

Part of this variation in incentive structures and supervisory mechanisms may be attributable to variation in the level of intrinsic psychological satisfaction to be had from different types of work. Sociologists and psychologists frequently argue that individuals take a certain degree of pride in their work, and that introducing performance-related pay can destroy this "psycho-social compensation", because the exchange relation between employer and employee becomes much more narrowly economic, destroying most or all of the potential for social exchange. Evidence for this is inconclusive - Deci, and Lepper, Greene and Nisbett find support for this argument; Staw suggests other interpretations of the findings.

Team Production

On a related note, Drago and Garvey use Australian survey data to show that when agents are placed on individual pay-for-performance schemes, they are less likely to help their coworkers. This negative effect is particularly important in those jobs that involve strong elements of 'team production', where output reflects the contribution of many individuals, and individual contributions cannot be easily identified, and compensation is therefore based largely on the output of the team. In other words, pay-for-performance increases the incentives to free-ride, as there are large positive externalities to the efforts of an individual team member, and low returns to the individual. The negative incentive effects implied are confirmed by some empirical studies, eg Newhouse for shared medical practices (costs rise and doctors work fewer hours as more revenue is shared), and Leibowitz and Tollison find that larger law partnerships typically result in worse cost containment. As a counter, peer pressure can potentially solve the problem, but this depends on peer monitoring being relatively costless to the individuals doing the monitoring/censuring in any particular instance (unless one brings in social considerations of norms and group identity and so on). Studies suggest that profit-sharing, for example, typically raises productivity by 3-5%, although there are some selection issues (Prendergast).

Empirical Evidence

There is however considerable empirical evidence of a positive effect of compensation on performance (although the studies usually involve "simple" jobs where aggregate measures of performance are available, which is where piece rates should be most effective). In one study, Lazear saw productivity rising by 35% (and wages by 12%) in a change from salary to piece rates, with a third of the productivity gain due to worker selection effects. Paarsch and Shearer also find evidence supportive of incentive and productivity effects from piece rates, as do Banker, Lee, and Potter , although the latter do not distinguish between incentive and worker selection effects. Fernie and Metcalf find that British jockeys perform significantly better when offered prizes for winning races compared to being on fixed retainers. McMillan, Whalley and Zhu and Groves et al look at Chinese agricultural and industrial data respectively and find significant incentive effects. Kahn and Sherer find that better evaluations of white-collar office workers were achieved by those employees who had a steeper relation between evaluations and pay. Nikkinen and Sahlstrom find empirical evidence that agency theory can be used, at least to some extent, to explain financial audit fees internationally.

Four principles of Contract Design

Milgrom and Roberts identify four basic principles of contract design:

- The Informativeness Principle,
- The Incentive-Intensity Principle,
- The Monitoring Intensity Principle, and
- The Equal Compensation Principle.

Informativeness Principle

In the absence of a world of perfect information, Holmstrom developed what became known as the Informativeness Principle. This essentially states that any measure of performance that (on the margin) reveals information about the effort level chosen by the agent should be included in the compensation contract. This includes, for example, Relative Performance Evaluation - measurement relative to other, similar agents, so as to filter out some common background noise factors, such as fluctuations in demand. By removing some exogenous sources of randomness in the agent's income, a greater proportion of the fluctuation in the agent's income falls under his control, increasing his ability to bear risk. If taken advantage of, by greater use of piece rates, this should improve incentives.

Incentive-Intensity Principle

However, setting incentives as intense as possible is not necessarily optimal from the point of view of the employer. The Incentive-Intensity Principle states that the optimal intensity of incentives depends on four factors: the incremental profits created by additional effort, the precision with which the desired activities are assessed, the agent's risk tolerance, and the agent's responsiveness to incentives. According to Prendergast, "the primary constraint on performance-related pay is that provision imposes additional risk on workers."

A typical result of the early principal-agent literature was that piece rates tend to 100% (of the compensation package) as the worker becomes more able to handle risk, as this ensures that workers fully internalize the consequences of their costly actions. In incentive terms, where we conceive of workers as self-interested rational individuals who provide costly effort (in the most general sense of the worker's input to the firm's production function), the more compensation varies with effort, the better the incentives for the worker to produce.

Monitoring Intensity Principle

The third principle - the Monitoring Intensity Principle - is complementary to the second, in that situations in which the optimal intensity of incentives is high correspond to situations in which the optimal level of monitoring is also high. Thus employers effectively choose from a "menu" of monitoring/incentive intensities. This is because monitoring is a costly means of reducing the variance of employee performance, which makes more difference to profits in the kinds of situations where it is also optimal to make incentives intense.

Equal Compensation Principle

The final principle is the Equal Compensation Principle, which essentially states that activities equally valued by the employer should be equally valuable (in terms of compensation, including non-financial things such as pleasantness) to the employee. This relates to the problem that employees may be engaged in several activities, and if some of these are not monitored or are monitored less heavily, these will be neglected, as activities with higher marginal returns to the employee are favoured. This can be thought of as a kind of "disintermediation" - targeting certain measurable variables may cause others to suffer. For example, teachers being rewarded by test scores of their students are likely to tend more towards teaching 'for the test', and de-emphasise less relevant but perhaps equally or more important aspects of education; while AT&T's practice at one time of rewarding programmers by the number of lines of code written resulted in programs that were longer than necessary - i.e. Programme efficiency suffering.

Following Holmstom and Milgrom (1990) and Baker (1992), this has become known as "multi-tasking" (where a subset of relevant tasks is rewarded, non-rewarded tasks suffer relative neglect). Because of this, the more difficult it is to completely specify and measure the variables on which reward is to be conditioned, the less likely that performance-related pay will be used: "in essence, complex jobs will typically not be evaluated through explicit contracts." Where explicit measures are used, they are more likely to be some kind of aggregate measure, for example, baseball and American Football players are rarely rewarded on the many specific measures available, but frequently receive bonuses for aggregate performance measures such as Most Valuable Player.

The alternative to objective measures is subjective performance evaluation, typically by supervisors. However, there is here a similar effect to "multi-tasking", as workers shift effort from that subset of tasks which they consider useful and constructive, to that subset which they think gives the greatest appearance of being useful and constructive, and more generally to try to curry personal favour with supervisors. (One can interpret this as a destruction of organizational social capital - workers identifying with, and actively working for the benefit of, the firm - in favour of the creation of personal social capital - the individual-level social relations which enable workers to get ahead.

A linear model

The four principles can be summarised in terms of the simplest (linear) model of incentive compensation:

$$w = a + b(e + x + g \times y)$$

where w stands for the wage, e for (unobserved) effort, x for unobserved exogenous effects on outcomes, and y for observed exogenous effects; while g and a represent the weight given to y, and the base salary, respectively. The interpretation of b is as the intensity of incentives provided to the employee.

Nonlinearities

The above discussion on explicit measures assumed that contracts would create the linear incentive structures summarised in the model above. But while the combination of normal errors and the absence of income effects yields linear contracts, many observed contracts are nonlinear. To some extent this is due to income effects as workers rise up a tournament/hierarchy: "Quite simply, it may take more money to induce effort from the rich than from the less well off." In addition, the marginal return to effort may increase: it is more important for a CEO to work hard than for a shop floor worker (eg Murphy 1998 highlights the importance of bonuses for executives). Similarly, the threat of being fired creates a nonlinearity in wages earned versus performance.

Moreover, many empirical studies illustrate inefficient behaviour arising from nonlinear objective performance measures, or measures over the course of a long period (eg a year), which create nonlinearities in time due to discounting behaviour. This inefficient behaviour arises because incentive structures are varying: for example, when a worker has already exceeded a quota or has no hope of reaching it, versus being close to reaching it - eg Healy (1985), Oyer (1997), Leventis (1997). Leventis shows that New York surgeons, penalised for exceeding a certain mortality rate, take less risky cases as they approach the threshold. Courty and Marshke (1997) provide evidence on incentive contracts offered to agencies, which receive bonuses on reaching a quota of graduated trainees within a year. This causes them to 'rush-graduate' trainees in order to make the quota.

Objective and subjective performance evaluation

Objective Performance Evaluation

The major problem in measuring employee performance in cases where it is difficult to draw a straightforward connection between performance and profitability is the setting of a standard by which to judge the performance. One method of setting an absolute objective performance standard - rarely used because it is costly and only appropriate for simple repetitive tasks - is time-and-motion studies, which study in detail how fast it is possible to do a certain task. These have been used constructively in the past, particularly in manufacturing. More generally, however, even within the field of objective performance evaluation, some form of relative performance evaluation must be used. Typically this takes the form of comparing the performance of a worker to that of his peers in the firm or industry, perhaps taking account of different exogenous circumstances affecting that

Subjective Performance Evaluation

Subjective performance evaluation allows the use of a subtler, more balanced assessment of employee performance, and is typically used for more complex jobs where comprehensive objective measures are difficult to specify and/or measure. Whilst often the only feasible method, the attendant problems with subjective performance evaluation have resulted in a variety of incentive structures and supervisory schemes.

One problem, for example, is that supervisors may under-report performance in order to save on wages, if they are in some way residual claimants, or perhaps rewarded on the basis of cost savings. This tendency is of course to some extent offset by the danger of retaliation and/or demotivation of the employee, if the supervisor is responsible for that employee's output. As an example, there have been numerous cases where net profits were apparently underreported on successful Hollywood films, where actors or writers had been promised a percentage of net profits - Cheatham, David, and Cheatham.

Another problem relates to what is known as the "compression of ratings". Two related influences - centrality bias, and leniency bias - have been documented (Landy and Farr 1980, Murphy and Cleveland 1991). The former results from supervisors being reluctant to distinguish critically between workers (perhaps for fear of destroying team spirit), while the latter derives from supervisors being averse to offering poor ratings to subordinates, especially where these ratings are used to determine pay, not least because bad evaluations may be demotivating rather than motivating. However, these biases introduce noise into the relationship between pay and effort, reducing the incentive effect of performance-related pay. Milkovich and Wigdor (1991) suggest that this is the reason for the common separation of evaluations and pay, with evaluations primarily used to allocate training.

FINANCIAL MANAGEMENT GOALS AND POLICIES

Financial management goals and policies provide the framework for financial planning and decision making by the school board, budget committee, and district staff. They are designed to help ensure the financial integrity of the district which, along with prudent management of its financial resources, is necessary if the district is to provide the educational services, support services and facilities that address the needs and desires of our students, their parents, and the community.

The following goals and policies for the school district are intended to guide the district in its financial matters. The goals are broad statements of board philosophy for financial management of the district. The policies provide more specific direction for consistent financial management decisions.

Financial Management Goals

1. The district will establish a financial base sufficient to support high quality and innovative educational programs which meet community needs.
2. The district will follow prudent and professional financial management practices in order to achieve and maintain long-term financial stability.
3. The district will demonstrate to the taxpayers of the district and the financial community that its schools are well managed.
4. The district will provide cost-effective services to citizens by cooperating with other educational, government, and nonprofit agencies.
5. The district will have an adequate capital improvement Programme that maintains existing district assets, provides for student and employee safety, maintains a quality instructional environment, and allows for enhancements that are necessary to meet changes in enrollment.
6. The district will continually review and improve its formal budget document and other financial information so that it clearly and openly communicates its resources, expenditures, and financial position.
7. The district will communicate, as permitted by law, with its employees and the community so that they understand the district's Programme requirements and financial status.

Valuing diversity is a core value of Financial Management. Financial Management uses a very broad definition of diversity. In addition to the categories identified by the steering committee (race, gender, disability, class, sexual identity/orientation, religion, age, ethnicity, culture, region/ geography and indigenous statue), Financial Management also values variety in work styles, personality types and education levels.

Approximately one third of the Financial Management (FM) staff members are immigrants and non-native English speakers. Specific efforts are made to address issues of diversity within the division in order to maximize employee performance and customer satisfaction. Our diversity initiative complements other work being done on campus to support the UW's mission of creating a comfortable educational environment that will attract and retain the best and the brightest from all backgrounds.

Current Financial Management Efforts in the Interest of Diversity:

- Biennial employee surveys to gauge satisfaction in the workplace and answer specific questions about diversity
- Measure on the Operational Performance Dashboard that gauges "% of staff who agree that making FM more diverse will make the organization better overall (top two ratings on the 7 point scale). Current measure is 72%; target is 90%.
- Formal on-going diversity initiative
- Two teams focus specifically on diversity; one has created a mentoring Programme with an emphasis on diversity, and the other helps to educate and make the division more aware and appreciative of diversity
- Development and presentation of mandatory diversity training
- Additional training for supervisors and managers
- Ongoing Programme for diversity-related presentations

- A diversity calendar on the web
- A roster of internal interpreters
- A roster of conversation coaches for improving English skills
- A set of measurements that reflect the importance of cultural competence
- Accountability to cultural competence
- An ongoing English Skills in the Workplace Programme for non-native speakers, offered through UW English Skills Programs
- Educational outreach Programme to students, parents, prospective students and campus staff, many of which are in partnership with or by request from Office of Minority Affairs
- Employee development plans for all staff that include financial support and release time for training and other developmental activities

THE NATURE OF FINANCIAL MANAGEMENT

Financial management is that part of total management which is concerned primarily with the financial affairs of an organization and the translation of actions, both past and proposed, into meaningful and relevant information for use in the management process. It includes the functions of budgeting, accounting, reporting, and the analysis and interpretation of the financial significance of past events and future plans. It sometimes also includes other related functions such as internal auditing, management analysis, and others. It is not primarily concerned with the technical procedures and methodology of those individual functions. Rather, it is characterized by the coordination and correlation of those functions into an effective and broad system of financial control that will assure that they, collectively more than individually, become an integral part of the management of the organization.

Financial management involves the art of interrelating data to obtain a perspective of the total financial situation that will assist managers in Programme planning and decision-making. A very simple operating Programme may require only a minimum of financial management, and this, in some cases, can be provided by the manager himself. However, many Federal agencies with complex programs have a need for broad financial advice and know-how – advice that can only be furnished following a synthesis, analysis, and interrelating of meaningful financial data with programming and planning information by an organization and officials particularly adept and capable in financial matters.

More fully, financial management may be described as—

Designing, establishing, and maintaining an integrated financial management system, including at least budgeting, accounting, and managerial-financial reporting, which will furnish timely data that are used in the direction, evaluation, and control of operations at the various levels of management. Such a system must be compatible with the requirements of the Bureau of the Budget, the General Accounting Office, and the Treasury Department, and should provide accountability for agency funds and assets and full disclosure of the financial results of agency operations.

This involves responsibility for proper and economic management of all financial resources under jurisdiction of the agency, in accordance with a wide variety of laws and regulations. To accomplish this, a suitable financial management organization must be established and maintained, and must be staffed with appropriate, competent personnel. Rather than being limited to supervision of separate entities such as the budgetary system, the accounting system, the financial reporting system, etc., financial management consists of the integration and coordination of those operations into a comprehensive financial system that is compatible with management needs.

Such an Integrated System Necessarily Includes:

(a) Developing an integrated financial planning and reporting process that involves both long-range plans and the annual budget as a segment of those plans. Such a planning and reporting process must be designed to provide both broad and specific financial policies that will facilitate achievement of the Programme goals and objectives of the agency, form an effective basis for formulation and justification of budget requests, and provide reliable financial and managerial data for management and control in execution of the budget and long-range plans;

(b) Using the end-products of the budgeting, accounting, and managerial-financial reporting organizations (by analyzing, evaluating, and synthesizing the data) to compare actual performance with planned objectives; interpreting and interrelating Programme plans, budget proposals, costs of operations, and Programme accomplishments; and accepting responsibility for the financial soundness of the agency – not only in terms of current year financial operations, but in terms of the soundness of financial planning for future operations. This requires the chief financial officer's involvement, on an advisory basis, in the fundamental elements of Programme development, Programme execution, and Programme review and evaluation. It also involves furnishing integrated advice to the responsible Programme manager on the financial aspects of managing the agency's resources – so that the manager can maintain a balance between requirements and available resources that will permit the attainment of Programme objectives with minimum costs and maximum efficiency.

THE COMPONENTS OF THE WORK OF FINANCIAL MANAGERS

In general, the work of the financial manager may be divided into two categories; viz., that which must be included to meet the minimum requirements for this series and that which may be included in addition. These are as follows:

A. Functions which must be included:

1. Accounting – typically includes:
   (a) Planning the Programme within delegated limits;
   (b) Developing, revising, and/or adapting accounting systems;
   (c) Executing day-to-day ledger maintenance and related operations for the classification and other recording of financial transactions;
   (d) Analyzing the results and interpreting the effects of transactions upon the financial resources of the organization;
   (e) Applying accounting concepts to solve problems, render advice, or to meet other needs of management; and
   (f) Managing the total accounting Programme, including supervision of subordinate accountants, accounting technicians, voucher examiners, payroll clerks, and other similar supporting personnel.
2. Budgeting – typically includes:
   (a) The formulation – developing instructions, calls for estimates, preparing estimates, reviewing and consolidating estimates;
   (b) The presentation either within the organization or at hearings (within the agency, at the budget bureau, or subcommittee); and
   (c) The execution – funds control, Programme adjustments, review of reports and preparation of reports.
3. Managerial-Financial Reporting – typically includes not only the recurring budget, accounting, and financial reports but also Programme operation evaluation and statistical reports and other work performance type reports, both regular and one-time in nature.

Managerial-financial reporting is the process of providing appropriate data to key officials at all levels of management for the purpose of helping to achieve the most effective Programme and financial management. Stress is placed on aiding in the making of management decisions. Normally, much of such data will be of a financial character, developed from the accounting and the budget systems; however, frequently data will be a combination of both financial and non-financial information and, in some cases, the data may be entirely non-financial in nature. In its ideal form, the data are so integrated as to represent a single total data system. Since in good managerial-financial reporting, concern is given to the development of the systems that will provide the essential data, one of the normal responsibilities of the Financial Manager is the development, revision and/or adaptation of the managerial-financial reporting system.

4. Advice to Management – typically includes: advising from a financial point of view and serving as the technical expert on the financial aspects of all matters.

B. Functions directly related to the management of Financial Resources and Which **may** ***be Included:***

1. Management Analysis

   –Typically includes: administering, supervising, or performing study, analysis, evaluation, development or improvement of managerial policies, practices, methods, and procedures;

2. Records or Paperwork Management

   – Typically includes: operating, maintaining, or administering one or more administrative control systems, services, processes or functions such as those for forms control, the handling of correspondence, directives control, the disposition of records;

3. Auditing

   – Typically includes: the establishment and improvement of audit policies, programs, methods, and procedures, and the achievement of a high standard of auditing; the proper timing and coverage of audits; the disposition of technical accounting questions developed in audits, including disposition through negotiations and conferences with affected business establishments or other interested organizations; responsibility for all auditing and related activities in connection with payments and cost analyses; and shaping, directing, and administering the audit activities;

4. Statistics
   – Typically includes: administering or performing professional work, or providing professional consultation in the application of statistical theories, techniques, and methods to the gathering and/or interpretation of quantified information; or advising on, administering, supervising, or performing work involved in collecting, editing, computing, compiling, analyzing; and presenting statistical data, where the work requires knowledge and application of statistical methods and procedures, and techniques, but does not require professional knowledge of the mathematical or statistical theories, assumptions, or principles upon which they are based;

5. Digital Computer, Electric Accounting Machines, and Other Machine Systems
   – Typically includes: supervising or administering overall digital computer systems activities, including combined digital computer-tabulating equipment organizations; performing staff planning and administrative work in administering a machine system organization, whether EAM, ADP, or other.

Distinguishing Among Financial Manager, Other Managerial, Budget and Accounting Officer, and Administrative Officer Positions

Because there is a considerable degree of overlapping of functions among the above types of positions, the lines of demarcation are not clearly drawn. It is seldom feasible to determine the proper series and/or title on the sole basis of the subordinate functions (e.g., accounting, budgeting, personnel, etc.). The following material highlights the essential features which characterize each of the positions.

Administrative Officer and Assistant

Administrative officer or assistant positions that do not include responsibility for accounting, budgeting, *and* managerial-financial reporting are easily distinguished from financial management positions.

Many administrative officers or assistants are, however, responsible for financial management as one aspect of the total Programme of administrative or managerial services and functions that they provide. Such positions must be distinguished from financial management positions on the basis of the paramount qualifications required. If ability to manage a variety of administrative, managerial, and supportive services and controls is the paramount qualification requirement, rather than knowledge of financial management, then the position is that of an administrative officer or assistant. Contrarily, if the primary qualification requirement of the position is knowledge and ability in the field of financial management, then the position is classifiable in this series even though it may include responsibility for additional types of administrative or managerial service or control functions.

Budget and Accounting Officer

The key to distinguishing budget and accounting positions from financial manager positions is the presence in the latter type of position of a "comptrollership" concept of financial management. Although the budget and accounting officer exercises a high degree of expertise, competence, and knowledge of the organization and its functions and operations, the requirements of his position are to supervise the accounting operation and the budget operation. The financial manager provides the management officials of the organization he/she serves with authoritative accounting advice and authoritative budget advice and interprets the results and needs of each of these functions to those officials. The financial manager is the technical expert in both fields for the organization's management staff. He/she assures the coordination of these two separate functions within his subordinate staff to the extent that is required for the effective conduct of each of these two functions.

The financial manager, too, supervises the accounting and budget operations and provides (personally or otherwise) technical expertise in the budget and in the accounting functions. In this respect and to this extent his position is similar to the position of budget and accounting officer. The financial manager, however, has further substantial responsibilities. He/she is responsible for developing and executing a comprehensive Programme of financial policy and financial control which constitutes a major and integral component of the organization's total management concept and practice. Both accounting and budgeting are essential ingredients of such a Programme of financial management, but, either separately or jointly, are no more than some of the raw material from which the financial manager builds his broad Programme of financial management. (This additional responsibility inherent in financial management positions is described in detail in the section of this standard titled "The Nature of Financial Management".)

Financial Manager

The financial manager's role is characterized by responsibility for serving as a financial advisor to management. He/she does not manage (except for his own Programme). Through this *advisory service role,* the financial manager provides valuable assistance to top management in its task of managing and in reaching decisions. The financial manager's

Programme is aimed at utilizing accounting and fund control systems to maintain proper financial balance and to assure that management obtains maximum benefit from *financial* resources without sacrificing efficiency or violating rules or regulations. The financial manager is responsible for examining and reporting upon work progress and Programme accomplishments in financial terms.

Other Managerial and Executive Positions

In general, managerial and executive positions are easily distinguished from financial manager positions. Normally, managers direct one or more operating programs (defined in footnote on page 3). However, some positions are not so easily classified. For example, the functional responsibilities may be similar to or include those which are typical of financial manager positions, but there may also be present a more active and direct role in the overall management of the organization served. (Such positions sometimes result from the increment of additional responsibility to an especially competent financial manager.) Differences such as these must be taken into account in assigning positions of these types to both series and grade. Generally speaking, the presence in a position of characteristics such as the following to a significant degree excludes a position from this series:

1. Serving in a determinative rather than an advisory capacity in the management of operating programs or functional areas (other than those identified in this standard as of a financial management nature);
2. Direct, rather than recommendatory, involvement in the management of significant agency resources not of a financial nature;
3. Emphasis in the qualifications required on broad managerial ability rather than on financial management acumen. Exclusion paragraph No. 3 is applicable to positions which are excludable from this series on these bases.

HOW TO USE THIS STANDARD

The grade-level portion of this standard consists of three broad factors used to determine the grade levels of these positions. These are: Factor I – Characteristics of the Operating Programme; Factor II – Characteristics of the Financial Management Programme; and Factor III – Characteristics of the Advisory Service Provided to Management.

Factors I and II also include three sub factors for each of which three degrees of intensity are identified. The discussions of factors I and II include simple instructions for determining the overall factor level through the use of the subfactor degree evaluations. A grade- level conversion table is provided so that the levels of the three factors can be converted into grade levels. In addition, positions of overall assistants to financial managers may be evaluated by reference to the following factors and grade conversion table, provided due consideration is given to the lesser responsibility which is normally inherent in the assistant role. Normally, the position of full assistant is classified one grade below the financial manager position.

CLASSIFICATION FACTORS

With the exception of the factor "qualifications required" which is discussed below, the material covering the factors which must be used to differentiate grades among positions in this series is embedded in the factor discussions which follow. Discussion of other factors which are not meaningful in fixing grades for individual positions have been omitted.

QUALIFICATIONS REQUIRED

Financial management requires a positive and imaginative outlook, a depth of experience and training across and beyond specialty lines, and an understanding of varied skills that can provide broadly-based financial advice which will facilitate the conduct of Federal programs in accordance with the conditions of our times. It also requires an understanding of the programme and organization of the agency served and the ability to devise and/or operate a system of financial management suited to that agency's Programme and organization. Following are the required knowledges, abilities, and other qualities. (Note that detailed knowledge of the individual financial management functions is *not* listed, since the breadth of these positions precludes a requirement for competence on the part of most financial managers in *all* of the individual functions. Most financial managers rely on subordinate staff specialists to provide technical know-how in certain functions; however, in some positions in this series the duties require that the incumbent be a professionally-qualified accountant. (Such a requirement does not remove the position from this series.)

Financial managers must have:

1. A broad knowledge of and ability to utilize principles, methods, techniques, and systems of financial management;
2. Ability to plan, direct, and coordinate difficult and complex programs;
3. Ability to develop, apply, and adjust financial plans and policies to attain agency objectives;
4. Ability to select, develop, and supervise a subordinate staff;
5. Ability to establish and maintain effective working relationships, not only with subordinate staff, but with all levels of key management officials, the latter particularly requiring the exercise of tact, ingenuity and resourcefulness;
6. Ability to make oral and written presentations in a clear and concise manner;
7. Ability to apply a high level of sound, independent judgment in the solution of financial problems and in the administration of a financial management Programme;
8. A broad knowledge of agency operating programs.

Factor I – Characteristics of the Operating Programme

The nature, scope, impact, complexity, and characteristics of the operating Programme served provide both the arena and the boundaries for the work of the financial official. While for any particular operating Programme there is a very wide range within which a financial management Programme can fluctuate, it is necessary that the total setting of the position be measured and comprehended before it is feasible to appraise the grade-level worth of any specific financial manager's position. This factor, through its three subfactors, provides an evaluation of the setting in which the financial management Programme operates.

This factor is divided into three subfactors:

A. Scope of Operating Programme Served

B. Type of Operating Programme Served

C. Management Level of the Operating Programme

Each subfactor is in turn subdivided into three broadly defined degrees each of which encompasses a wide range of Programme characteristics.

Subfactor A – Scope of operating Programme served

This subfactor is concerned with the extent to which the Programme and actions of the financial manager affect such things as the general economy, defense, international relations, health and welfare, natural resources, government operations, the public health, etc.

Degree A. – The operating Programme served is among the largest and most critical of the Government's many programs and is characterized by paragraph 1 and two or more of paragraphs 2 through 5:

1. The Programme is nationwide or worldwide in its operations and impact;
2. The Programme is critical to the operations of a number of large and important Government agencies or of other programs of comparable size, impact, and national significance;

3. The Programme has a critical impact on a wide variety and number of the most important industries which function on a national or close to national basis; or otherwise has a critical impact on the total financial economy of the nation;
4. The Programme and its financial management are frequently or continually very much in the public eye and are subject to an unusually high degree of attention by the Congress, the press, and in the arena of public debate and discussion.
5. The Programme is multipurpose or multi-function *and* consists of a large number and wide variety of subordinate "programs" many of which individually are equivalent to degree B of this subfactor.

Degree B. – The operating Programme served is substantial in size and impact and is normally characterized by one or more of the following:

1. The Programme is nationwide or worldwide in its operations;
2. The Programme constitutes a substantial aspect of the Programme or operations of several departments or independent agencies; or is a significant aspect of Governmentwide operations;
3. The Programme has a substantial impact on a number and variety of substantially nationwide industries, or on a few of the largest nationwide industries;
4. The Programme and its financial management are from time to time (but significantly less constantly and frequently than is true for Degree A) prominently in the public eye and are subject at such times to more than usual attention by the Congress, the press, and in the arena of public debate and discussion;
5. The Programme is multipurpose, multi-function, or consists of a number and variety of subordinate "programs" when several of these purposes,

functions, or programs are themselves substantial in scope, e.g., comparable to Degree C of this factor.

Degree C. – The operating Programme served is characterized by or does not significantly exceed the following: for situations which do not meet this lower limit.)

1. The Programme is substantially local or regional in scope;
2. The Programme is in or affects only a single department, bureau, or independent agency Programme although similar programs may exist in other agencies;
3. The Programme has a significant impact primarily on local industries or local segments of industries; or has a limited impact on a national scale;
4. The Programme and its financial management are the subject of attention (on a national, regional, or local basis) by the press, the Congress, and the public to the degree which is normal or usual for most governmental activities, with more intense interest occurring only rarely and then often only on a limited geographic scale;
5. The Programme may consist of a number of subordinate functions or "programs" but few, if any, are of a scope and magnitude to require their own administrative support or financial management organizations.

Subfactor B – Type of Operating Programme Served

This subfactor reflects the type of organization served, considering the basic mission or purpose for which the organization exists. When there is a mixed Programme, a general characterization of the basic mission should be made and the appropriate degree assigned.

While all activities of the Government are important, there are situations where the mission of the organization places exceptional demands on the financial management machinery of the organization. Activities which are particularly "charged" from the standpoint of national security, or activities which must be geared to regular operation on a "crash" basis may involve special problems. The continually fluctuating or dynamic nature of the Programme may add to the complexity of the financial manager's position. Other examples of exceptional demands resulting from the mission of the organization may be situations in which the programs of the organization are subject to extreme fluctuations, requiring very large-scale seasonal or periodic adjustments of the financial plan, work force, or initiation of new and experimental programs, etc.

Special problems may also be involved in activities which are the subject of intense public interest and concern so that they are in the limelight of public discussion, political implications, or economic controversy. In general, the application of the following degrees to the organization's mission will in almost all instances result in an accurate appraisal of the position under this sub factor. When, however, factors such as those enumerated in this paragraph as of significantly greater or lesser impact than is normally the case for missions of the type and scope involved, this fact should be considered in resolving reasonable doubts as to which of the degrees is most appropriate.

Degree A. – The operating Programme or programs are highly complex and varied, involve an extraordinarily large budget, and/or are otherwise of a nature which affords the greatest scope and need for financial management and the greatest opportunity for a financial management Programme to have a critical impact on the operating Programme. Examples of such operating programs include:

1. Large-scale industrial, commercial, or financial operations;
2. Broad research and development programs which involve on individual research efforts the combined efforts of many contractors, subcontractors, laboratories; universities, or other appropriate organizations, as, for example, a project to develop a weapons systems.

Degree B. – The operating programs involve substantial need for financial management and afford substantial opportunity for a financial management Programme to function as a major participant or major tool of overall management. Examples of such operating programs include:

1. Programs which involve the expenditure of significant proportions of the Programme budget for purposes other than employee salaries and administrative support and service, e.g., programs of a public welfare, medical welfare, agricultural, educational, or comparable nature;
2. Research and development programs of sufficient magnitude and scope as to require their own administrative support and financial management organizations;
3. Industrial, commercial, or financial operations of lesser scope and magnitude than are characteristic of Degree A of this factor;
4. Programs with diversified personal service operations of such nature as to create substantially greater problems of scheduling, controlling, costing, etc. (e.g., as in providing substantial and varied services to other agencies, State and local governments, private enterprise, and the general public on a reimbursable basis) than are normally characteristic of programs described in paragraph 1 of Degree C of this subfactor.

Degree C. – The operating programs involve minimal current need for financial management and currently offer limited opportunity for the financial management Programme to function as a major participant or a major tool of overall management. Examples of such operating programs include:

1. Programs in which the Programme budget is primarily for employee salaries and administrative support and service;
2. Programs of any type or scope in which the Programme management plan or method of

operation does not include the use of a financial management Programme to more than a minimal degree.

Subfactor C – Management Level of the Operating Programme

Financial manager positions vary in organizational setting from the department or agency level to field installation or field activity levels. Differences in organizational levels carry very important differences in the level of delegated authority for setting policies, establishing procedures, and accomplishing objectives – both those of the overall agency and those of the financial management Programme. Associated with this delegated authority is the related responsibility for coordinating the financial management Programme and synthesizing data therefrom for management's use. This subfactor measures the overall effect of the managerial setting on the financial manager's position.

Degree A. – This is the "primary policy level" and is the level at which are determined – subject only to the framework of laws and to the regulations and policies issued by the President, the Congress, the Bureau of the Budget, the General Accounting Office, and similar control agencies having Governmentwide jurisdiction the programs, policies, and procedures which are to be the work and method of operation of the organizations. In most cases, this is the department or agency level of Government.

Degree B. – This is characterized as the "secondary policy level" at which there is a positive responsibility and a significant freedom for developing and adapting significant operating policies, procedures, programs, standards, operating goals, etc., within the overall framework established by the "primary policy level."

(*Note:* This degree is not used for all organizations which are immediately below the "primary policy level." If the organization is not materially and substantially concerned with the development of significant internal operating policies, procedures, or programs, or if little more is involved than the restatement of issuances from the "primary policy level", the Programme should be evaluated at Degree C rather than at this degree.)

Degree C. – This is characterized as the *"operating level"* at which the primary function is conducting operations in conformity with comprehensive policies, procedures, and specifically detailed programs established by a higher organizational echelon.

"Operating-level" programs have authority and opportunity to adapt the policies and procedures established by higher echelons to fit the local conditions and needs. However, this authority does not extend to changing the essential substance of the prescribed policies and procedures. (When authority to adopt policies and procedures to fit local needs and conditions is *not* present, the question of whether the position of head of the "financial" Programme is of the type classifiable in this series must be carefully considered)

(Note: Responsibility for reviewing, coordinating, and synthesizing the results of subordinate level organizations is included in many programs. This type of responsibility is usually, but not invariably, included in programs at the primary and secondary policy levels and may be found at the operating level in some instances. Since credit for this responsibility in specific reference to the financial manager's responsibility is provided elsewhere in this standard, the presence or absence of this responsibility should not be used to determine the appropriate degree under this subfactor.)

Procedure for Establishing the Overall Value of Factor I

1. Evaluate all three subfactors to determine the proper degree for each;
2. Make sure that successive borderline decisions are as evenly balanced as is feasible between conservative and liberal decisions;
3. Using the following criteria, assign a single overall level for the total factor.

Level 1 – At least 2 subfactors are evaluated at Degree A.

Level 2 – At least 2 subfactors are evaluated at Degree B.

Level 3 – At least 2 subfactors are evaluated at Degree C.

Factor II – Characteristics of the Financial Management *Programme*

This factor is concerned with the evaluation of the responsibility and difficulty involved in managing and directing the subordinate staff and subordinate functions (accounting, budgeting, reporting, etc.) which go toward making up the financial management Programme. In a sense, this factor is most concerned with the kind and value of the management responsibility with which each financial manager is vested over his own subordinate staff.

This factor is divided into three subfactors:

A. Volume of Special Staff Management Problems

B. Nature of the Staff Management Responsibility

C. Scope of Functional Coverage

Each subfactor is in turn subdivided into three broadly defined degrees.

Subfactor A – Volume of Special Staff Management Problems

This factor provides a means of appraising and giving credit for the existence in some positions of certain types of special problems which seriously complicate the management and direction of some financial management programs.

Degree A. – This degree is characterized by the presence, in a significant and substantial degree, of at least two elements of special difficulty which are comparable to the following (and which have not been credited under another factor or subfactor.

1. The operating Programme and consequently the financial management Programme is marked by both short-and long-term instability with the consequential need for frequent, extensive, and basic revisions of financial plans, programs, and operations.
2. The types of operating programs or the conditions of operation are such that the usual approaches to problems will not suffice. The financial manager must develop new approaches, work in areas where there is no adequate experience data, develop and/or work with broad new concepts, and possess exceptionally imaginative and creative abilities to develop, present, and execute effective financial plans.
3. The operating programs at the several subordinate echelons or installations are so numerous and so varied from one to another, and the local conditions are so basically divergent, that the financial management programs present an exceptional degree of complexity in synthesizing financial and managerial data and in developing and executing an effective coordinated financial plan.

Degree B. – This degree is characterized by the presence of one element of special difficulty comparable to those described in Degree A above.

Degree C. – This degree is characterized by the absence of an element of special difficulty comparable to the types discussed in Degree A above.

Subfactor B – Nature of the Staff Management Responsibility

This subfactor deals with the scope and nature of the management problem which is inherent in supervising and directing the day-to-day operations of the several functions included in the financial management Programme. It measures the complexity of the staff management responsibility in terms of the organizational complexity of the financial management staff and the problems involved in coordinating the programs of subordinate echelons. The terms "providing technical direction", etc., used in the following degrees, should not be construed to mean the financial manager must personally be technically skilled in all of the subordinate operations. Rather, it means that he is responsible for the provision of technical guidance, either from his own resources or through the capabilities of various specialists on his staff.

Degree A. – The financial manager's subordinate organization is extremely large and organizationally complex. In a decentralized situation, it consists of a large number of subordinate financial organizations at several subordinate organizational levels (e.g., bureau, region, district, field station) with widely varying operations, programs and financial management problems. When the financial management Programme is centralized, his staff is comparable in size and complexity, i.e., is very large and is organized into a large number of subordinate segments (e.g., functional divisions) most of which are further subdivided into several organizational layers or echelons, each of significant size. In either situation there are very substantial problems in coordinating the activities and output of the many subordinate segments and in providing technical direction, guidance, and control to an extremely large financial management Programme.

Degree B. – The financial manager's subordinate organization is large. When the financial management Programme is decentralized, it typically consists of a number of financial management organizations located at subordinate installations or stations. In a centralized Programme, the staff is comparable in size and normally is organized into a number of subordinate segments which are further subdivided, sometimes into two or more levels. In either situation, there are significant problems in coordinating the activities and output of the subordinate segments and in providing technical direction, guidance, and control to a large financial management Programme.

Degree C. – The financial manager's subordinate organization is divided into several subordinate segments, some of which may be further subdivided. The financial manager provides both technical and administrative direction, guidance, and control to his staff.

Subfactor C – Scope of Functional Coverage

This subfactor deals with the breadth or scope of the financial management Programme. It relates to the extent to which the Programme goes beyond the three basic functions of accounting, budgeting and managerial/financial reporting to include additional functional areas.

Degree A. – Characteristic of this degree are financial management programs of exceptional breadth and comprehensiveness which provide a wide variety of management support and control services to management. Programs characteristic of this degree are concerned with long-range planning on a broad base, with the solution of major management problems, and the development of new and improved management techniques, support procedures, and controls to achieve the agency goals. In addition, programs at this degree are marked by the exceptional breadth of their functional coverage and include, as significant and substantial segments of the total financial management Programme, several (typically at least three unless there are two of outstanding size, scope, and impact) additional functions such as those listed below (or others of comparable breadth and complexity).

1. Management Analysis.
2. Auditing (Internal and/or External).
3. Statistical Services (for operating programs).
4. Automatic (Electronic) Data Processing (for operating programs in addition to financial management functions).
5. Programme Analysis, Reporting, and Evaluation (of operating programs).

Degree B. – Financial management programs at this degree are comprehensive and are concerned with the provision of a substantially greater than minimum range of financial management and general management services. Thus, programs at this degree are marked by the breadth of their functional coverage and include, in addition to the three basic functions of accounting, budgeting, and managerial/ financial reporting, at least one additional function (such as is listed above in Degree A or of comparable breadth and complexity).

Degree C. – Financial management programs characteristic of this degree are those in which the three "basic" functions of accounting, budgeting, and managerial/financial reporting constitute the major substance of the Programme.

Procedure for Establishing the Overall Value of Factor II

The same procedure is used for this factor as is described for Factor I. The subfactors are separately evaluated and an overall level assigned as follows:

Level 1 – At least two subfactors at Degree A.

Level 2 – At least two subfactors at Degree B.

Level 3 – At least two subfactors at Degree C.

Factor III – Characteristics of the Advisory Service Provided to Management

This factor is used to measure the scope and responsibility in the financial manager's position for providing integrated and comprehensive financial advice and assistance to management. Inherent in evaluating this factor is the need to consider the circumstances under which financial advisory service is rendered and the consequent relationship of the advisory service to the overall managerial decision-making function.

Special Note: Except in rare situations the potential scope and impact of the advisory service rendered is directly related to the nature and scope of both the operating Programme served and the financial management Programme itself. This means that while it could be possible for a Financial Manager to render a minimum of advisory service although responsible for a broad functional financial management Programme and/ or although serving a great variety and complexity of operating programs reverse situations could seldom, if ever, occur. In other words, it is not normally possible for a Financial Manager to provide the highest level advisory service to management when he is responsible for a minimum of financial management functional coverage or when the operating programs offer limited opportunity for financial management to function as a tool of overall management. No sub factors have been provided for this factor; consequently, the overall levels provide the only evaluation required.

Level 1—This level exceeds Level 2 in that it represents an *unusual* degree of participation in the overall *general* management of the operating Programme served. The financial manager is a responsible member of the top management team and is relied on for authoritative advice on all aspects of financial management. In addition to the type of advisory services described at Level 2, he is a fully participating technical advisor in all or almost all significant management planning and policy and decision-making actions in his organization.

At Level I, the financial manager actively participates in formal and informal management sessions, including policy review and advisory boards or committees whose functions are not limited to financial management. The advisory services are significantly broader than those normally provided by a financial manager as described at Level 2. The significantly broader advisory role of a Level 1 financial manager involves *direct* participation (although in a staff advisory capacity) in all major aspects of the overall general management of the operating Programme served, including active participation in the making of management decisions that are related to general policy-setting matters and long-range Programme planning. (By contrast, the financial manager at Level 2 provides advice relating to those managerial planning, policy-formulation, and decision-making matters involving important financial considerations.)

Level 2—This level includes financial management advisory service relating to management plans, policies, and decisions involving important financial considerations. The financial manager participates in meetings, conferences, or other sessions concerning the general overall management of the operating programs for the purpose of representing the financial management Programme and for determining the significance of management decisions on financial plans and other financial matters.

Characteristic of Level 2 is the situation in which the financial manager regularly attends formal and informal management planning and policy and decision-making sessions concerning matters involving important financial considerations, in order to fulfill requests for financial data and advice. As the technical advisor in his field, the financial manager may be invited to contribute financial data, financial management advice, or recommendations based on his financial management expertise on a wide range of management problems.

He/she may also attend a wide variety of managerial meetings, sessions, conferences, etc., as an observer so that he will be fully aware at all times of operating programs appropriately related to current management needs. Financial management is accepted and used within the organization as a significant aspect and tool of overall management and the financial advice and data supplied by the financial manager plays a significant role in the handling of major management problems. The advisory service provided is broad in scope and consistently reflects all major facets of the financial management Programme of the organization.

Level 3—Characteristic of this degree is the situation in which the financial manager prepares and submits to various managerial levels a wide variety of financial reports, statements, and data of both a factual and analytical nature. While many of these are of a regularly recurring nature, others are prepared and supplied upon the initiative of the financial manager in order to bring actual or anticipated problems to the attention of the appropriate managerial levels.

In addition, the financial manager is required to prepare and submit (in any appropriate method) financial data, advice, and recommendations on specific proposals, problems, plans, policies, etc., which are or will be subject to managerial consideration. From time-to-time the financial manager may be requested to attend various managerial meetings or sessions either so that he will be available if technical financial advice is needed, or as an observer of particularly significant managerial events. In this situation financial management is accepted and used within the organization as a significant matter for managerial consideration when major decisions or policies are involved.

Chapter 2

Management Capital Investment

INVESTMENT

Investment or investing is a term with several closely-related meanings in business management, finance and economics, related to saving or deferring consumption. An asset is usually purchased, or equivalently a deposit is made in a bank, in hopes of getting a future return or interest from it. Literally, the word means the "action of putting something in to somewhere else" (perhaps originally related to a person's garment or 'vestment').

Types of investment

The major difference in the use of the term investment between the economics field and the finance field is that economists refer to a real investment (such as a machine or a house), while financial economists refer to a financial asset, such as money that is put into a bank or the market, which may then be used to buy a real asset.

Business Management

The investment decision (also known as capital budgeting) is one of the fundamental decisions of business management: managers determine the assets that the business enterprise obtains; these assets may be physical (e.g. buildings or machinery), intangible (e.g. patents, software, goodwill), or financial. Whatever the type of asset, the manager must assess whether the net present value of the investment to the enterprise is positive; the net present value is calculated using the enterprise's marginal cost of capital.

Economics

In Economics, investment means the purchase (and thus the production) and/or stock of capital goods and/or technology - goods which are not consumed but instead used in future production. Examples include building a railroad, or a factory, clearing land, or putting oneself through college. In measures of national income and output, investment is also a component of GDP given in the formula GDP = C + I + G + NX. The investment function in that aspect is divided into non-residential investment (such as factories, machinery etc) and residential investment (new houses).

Investment is often modeled as a function of income and interest rates, given by the relation I = (Y, i). An increase in income will encourage higher investment, whereas a higher interest rate may discourage investment as it becomes costlier to borrow money. Even if a firm chooses to use its own funds in an investment, the interest rate represents an opportunity cost of investing those funds rather than loaning them out for interest.

Finance

In finance, investment means buying securities or other monetary or paper (financial) assets in the money markets or capital markets, or in fairly liquid real assets, such as gold as an investment, real estate, or collectibles. Valuation is the method for assessing whether a potential investment is worth its price.

Types of financial investments include shares or other equity investment, and bonds (including bonds denominated in foreign currencies). These investments assets are then expected to provide income or positive future cash flows, but may increase or decrease in value giving the investor capital gains or losses.

Trades in contingent claims or *derivative securities* do not necessarily have future positive expected cash flows - so are not considered to be assets, or strictly speaking, securities or investments. Nevertheless, since their cash flows are closely related to (or derived from) those of specific securities, they are often studied as or treated as investments.

Investments are often made indirectly through intermediaries, such as banks, mutual funds, pension funds, insurance companies, collective investment schemes, or even investment clubs. Though their legal and procedural details differ, an intermediary generally makes an investment using money from many individuals, each of whom receives a claim on the intermediary.

Personal finance

Within personal finance, money used to purchase shares, put in a collective investment scheme or used to buy any asset where there is an element of capital risk is deemed an investment. Saving within personal finance refers to money put aside, normally on a regular basis. This distinction is important as investment risk can cause a capital loss when an investment is realised, unlike saving(s) where the more limited risk is cash devaluing due to inflation.

In many instances the term saving and investment are used interchangeably which confuses this distinction. For example many deposit accounts are labeled as investment accounts by banks for marketing purposes. To help establish whether an asset is saving(s) or an investment you should consider where your money is invested. If the answer is cash then it is savings, if it is a type of asset which can fluctuate in value then it is investment.

The term Capital Investment has two usages in business. Firstly, Capital Investment refers to money used by a business to purchase fixed assets, such as land, machinery, or buildings. Secondly, Capital Investment refers to money invested in a business with the understanding that the money will be used to purchase fixed assets, rather than used to cover the business' day-to-day operating expenses.

GOALS OF PROJECT PLANNING

Strategic planning involves defining objectives and developing strategies to reach those objectives. It may employ methods like SWOT analysis to help clarify objectives and strategies. Strategic planning uses "the big picture" to pursue large scale, long term objectives. This is in contradistinction to "tactical" planning, which has to focuss on short term, smaller objectives. "Long range" planning typically projects current activities and programs onto a model of the external world, thereby predicting likely results. "Strategic" planning tries to "create" more desirable future results by (a) influencing the outside world or (b) adapting current programs and actions so as to have more favourable outcomes in the external environment.

Within business, strategic planning may provide overall direction strategic management to a company or give specific direction in such areas as:

- Financial strategies
- Human resource/organizational development strategies
- Information technology deployments
- Marketing strategy

We want to do Strategic Planning to:

- Have the capability to obtain the desired objective
- Fit well both with the external environment and with an organization's resources and core competencies - it should appear feasible and appropriate
- Have the capability of providing an organization with a sustainable competitive advantage - ideally through uniqueness and sustainability
- Prove dynamic, flexible, and able to adapt to changing situations
- Suffice on its own - specifically providing favorable outcomes without the need for cross-subsidization

Most strategic planning methodologies depend on a three-step process (sometimes called the *STP* process):

- Situation - evaluate the current situation and how it came about

- Target - define goals and/or objectives (sometimes called ideal state)
- Path - map a possible route to the goals/objectives

An alternative approach is called *Draw-See-Think*

- Draw - what is the ideal image or the desired end state?
- See - what is today's situation? What is the gap from ideal and why?
- Think - what specific actions must be taken to close the gap between today's situation and the ideal state?
- Plan - what resources are required to execute the activities?

In general terms, strategic planning can proceed incrementally or revolutionarily.

Strategic Planning as a set of Logical and Creative Steps

1. Clarification of objective (end-state) to be pursued. The following terms have been used in the literature: desired end states, plans, policies, goals, objectives, strategies, tactics and actions. Definitions vary, overlap and fail to achieve clarity. The following concept has been found useful. The items listed above may be organized in a hierarchy of means and ends and numbered as follows: Top Rank Objective (TRO), Second Rank Objective, Third Rank Objective, etc. From any rank, the objective in a lower rank answers to the question "How?" and the objective in a higher rank answers to the question "Why?" The exception is the Top Rank Objective (TRO): there is no answer to the "Why?" question. That is how the TRO is defined. An example may help to clarify the concept presented above.
2. Information gathering and analysis. This includes an external assessment (such as environmental scanning), and an internal resource assessment. Morphological analysis may be applied to both

internal resource assessments and external assessments. SWOT (Strengths, Weaknesses, Opportunities, Threats) Analysis may be used to assess those aspects of the organization and the environment that are important to achieving the objective of the strategic plan.

3. Evaluation of the feasibility of the objective in view of the SWOTs.
4. Strategy-development. This is a creative step that answers these four questions: How can we use the Strengths, stop the Weaknesses, exploit the Opportunities and defend against the Threats in pursuit of the selected objetive.
5. Developing Action Programs for the more attractive strategies, covering: Name of the strategy, Benefits to be expected from implementing this Programme, Actions: What will be done? Responsible persons: Who will be in charge of the Programme? Timing: When will the Programme start? When will it be completed? Location(s): Where will the Programme be implemented? Resources: What will be needed: people, money, information, other resources? Control System: How will progress be measured and reported? Rewards for performance, if any. Contingency plans: What will be done if results fall short?

FINANCIAL MARKET

In economics a financial market is a mechanism which allows people to trade money for securities or commodities such as gold or other precious metals. In general, any commodity market might be considered to be a financial market, if the usual purpose of traders is not the immediate consumption of the commodity, but rather as a means of delaying or accelerating consumption over time.

Financial markets are affected by forces of supply and demand, and allocate resources over time through a price mechanism such as the interest rate. Typically financial markets use a market making or a bid and ask process.

Both general markets, where many commodities are traded and specialised markets (where only one commodity is traded) exist. Markets work by placing many interested sellers in one "place", thus making them easier to find for prospective buyers. An economy which relies primarily on interactions between buyers and sellers to allocate resources is known as a market economy in contrast either to a command economy or to a non-market economy that is based, such as a gift economy.

In Finance, Financial markets facilitate:

- The raising of capital (in the capital markets);
- The transfer of risk (in the derivatives markets); and
- International trade (in the currency markets).

They are used to match those who *want* capital to those who *have* it. Typically a borrower issues a receipt to the lender promising to pay back the capital. These receipts are *securities* which may be freely bought or sold. In return for lending money to the borrower, the lender will expect some compensation in the form of interest or dividends.

The term Financial markets can be a cause of much confusion. Financial markets could mean:

1. Organisations that facilitate the trade in financial products. i.e. Stock exchanges facilitate the trade in stocks, bonds and warrants.
2. The coming together of buyers and sellers to trade financial products. i.e. stocks and shares are traded between buyers and sellers in a number of ways including: the use of stock exchanges; directly between buyers and sellers etc.

In academia, students of finance will use both meanings but students of economics will only use the second meaning. Financial markets can be domestic or they can be international.

Types of financial markets

The financial markets can be divided into different subtypes:

- Capital markets which consist of:
  - Stock markets, which provide financing through the issuance of shares or common stock, and enable the subsequent trading thereof.
  - Bond markets, which provide financing through the issuance of Bonds, and enable the subsequent trading thereof.
- Commodity markets, which facilitate the trading of commodities.
- Money markets, which provide short term debt financing and investment.
- Derivatives markets, which provide instruments for the management of financial risk.
  - Futures markets, which provide standardised forward contracts for trading products at some future date.
- Insurance markets, which facilitate the redistribution of various risks.
- Foreign exchange markets, which facilitate the trading of foreign exchange.

The capital markets consist of primary markets and secondary markets. Newly formed (issued) securities are bought or sold in primary markets. Secondary markets allow investors to sell securities that they hold or buy existing securities.

Raising Capital

To understand financial markets, let us look at what they are used for, i.e. what is their purpose? Without financial markets, borrowers would have difficulty finding lenders themselves. Intermediaries such as banks help in this process. Banks take deposits from those who have money to save. They can then lend money from this pool of deposited money to those who seek to borrow. Banks popularly lend money in the form of loans and mortgages.

More complex transactions than a simple bank deposit require markets where lenders and their agents can meet borrowers and their agents, and where existing borrowing or lending commitments can be sold on to other parties. A good example of a financial market is a stock exchange. A company can raise money by selling shares to investors and its existing shares can be bought or sold. The following table illustrates where financial markets fit in the relationship between lenders and borrowers:

Lenders

Individuals do not think of themselves as lenders but they lend to other parties in many ways. Lending activities may be:

- Putting money in a savings account at a bank;
- Contributing to a pension plan;
- Paying premiums to an insurance company;
- Investing in government bonds; or
- Investing in company shares.

Companies tend to be borrowers of capital. When companies have surplus cash that is not needed for a short period of time, they may seek to make money from their cash surplus by lending it via short term markets called money markets.

There are a few companies that have very strong cash flows. These companies tend to be lenders rather than borrowers. Such companies may decide to return cash to lenders (e.g. via a share buyback.) Alternatively, they may seek to make more money on their cash by lending it (e.g. investing in bonds and stocks.)

Borrowers

Individuals borrow money via bank loans for short term needs or longer term mortgages to help finance a house purchase. Companies borrow money to aid short term or long term cash flows. They also borrow to fund modernisation or future business expansion.

Governments often find their spending requirements exceed their tax revenues. To make up this difference, they need to borrow. Governments also borrow on behalf of nationalised industries, municipalities, local authorities and other public sector bodies. In the UK, the total borrowing requirement is often referred to as the public sector borrowing requirement.

Governments borrow by issuing bonds. In the UK, the government also borrows from individuals by offering bank accounts and Premium Bonds. Government debt seems to be permanent. Indeed the debt seemingly expands rather than being paid off. One strategy used by governments to reduce the value of the debt is to influence inflation. Municipalities and local authorities may borrow in their own name as well as receiving funding from national governments. In the UK, this would cover an authority like Hampshire County Council.

Public Corporations typically include nationalised industries. These may include the postal services, railway companies and utility companies. Many borrowers have difficulty raising money locally. They need to borrow internationally with the aid of Foreign exchange markets.

Derivative Products

During the 1980s and 1990s, a major growth sector in financial markets is the trade in so called derivative products, or derivatives for short. In the financial markets, stock prices, bond prices, currency rates, interest rates and dividends go up and down, creating *risk*. Derivative products are financial products which are used to *control* risk or paradoxically *exploit* risk.

Currency markets

Seemingly, the most obvious buyers and sellers of foreign exchange are importers/exporters. While this may have been true in the distant past, whereby importers/exporters created the initial demand for currency markets, importers and exporters now represent only 1/32 of foreign exchange dealing, according to BIS.

The picture of foreign currency transactions today shows:

- Banks and Institutions
- Speculators
- Government spending (for example, military bases abroad)
- Importers/Exporters
- Tourists

Analysis of Financial Markets

Much effort has gone into the study of financial markets and how prices vary with time. Charles Dow, one of the founders of Dow Jones & Company and The Wall Street Journal, enunciated a set of ideas on the subject which are now called Dow Theory. This is the basis of the so-called technical analysis method of attempting to predict future changes. One of the tenets of "technical analysis" is that market trends give an indication of the future, at least in the short term. The claims of thc technical analysts are disputed by many academics, who claim that the evidence points rather to the random walk hypothesis, which states that the next change is not correlated to the last change.

The scale of changes in price over some unit of time is called the volatility. It was discovered by Benoît Mandelbrot that changes in prices do not follow a Gaussian distribution, but are rather modeled better by Lévy stable distributions. The scale of change, or volatiliy, depends on the length of the time unit to a power a bit more than 1/2. Large changes up or down are more likely that what one would calculate using a Gaussian distribution with an estimated standard deviation.

Financial Markets in Popular Culture

Only negative stories about financial markets tend to make the news. The general perception, for those not involved in the world of financial markets is of a place full of crooks and con artists. Big stories like the Enron scandal serve to enhance this view.

Stories that make the headlines involve the incompetent, the lucky and the downright skillful. The Barings scandal is a classic story of incompetence mixed with greed leading to dire consequences. Another story of note is that of Black Wednesday, when sterling came under attack from hedge fund speculators. This led to major problems for the United Kingdom and had a serious impact on its course in Europe. A commonly recurring event is the stock market bubble, whereby market prices rise to dizzying heights in a so called exaggerated bull market. This is not a new phenomenon; indeed the story of Tulip mania in the Netherlands in the 17th century illustrates an early recorded example.

Financial markets are merely tools. Like all tools they have both *beneficial* and *harmful* uses. Overall, financial markets are used by honest people. Otherwise, people would turn away from them *en masse*. As in other walks of life, the financial markets have their fair share of rogue elements.

Financial Markets Slang

- Big swinging dick, a highly successful financial markets trader. The term was made popular in the book *Liar's Poker*, by Michael Lewis
- Geek, a Quant
- Nerd, a Quant
- Quant, a quantitative analyst skilled in the *black arts* of PhD level (and above) mathematics and statistical methods
- Rocket scientist, a financial consultant at the zenith of mathematical and computer programming skill. They are able to invent derivatives of frightening complexity and construct sophisticated pricing models. They generally handle the most advanced computing techniques adopted by the financial markets since the early 1980s. Typically, they are physicists and engineers by training; rocket scientists do not necessarily build rockets for a living.

BALANCE SHEET

A balance sheet, in formal bookkeeping and accounting, is a statement of the book value of a business or other organization or person at a particular date, at the end of a period such as a "fiscal year," as distinct from an income statement, also known as a profit and loss account (P&L), which records revenue and expenses over a specified period of time.

A balance sheet is often described as a "snapshot" of the company's financial condition on a given date. Of the four basic financial statements, the balance sheet is the only statement which applies to a single point in time, instead of a period of time.

A simple business operating entirely in cash could measure its profits by simply withdrawing the entire bank balance at the end of the period, plus any cash in hand. However, real businesses are not paid immediately; they build up inventories of goods to sell and they acquire buildings and equipment. In other words: businesses have assets and so they could not, even if they wanted to, immediately turn these into cash at the end of each period. Real businesses also owe money to suppliers and to tax authorities, and the proprietors do not withdraw all their original capital and profits at the end of each period. In other words businesses also have liabilities.

A modern balance sheet usually has three parts: assets, liabilities and shareholders' equity. The main categories of assets are usually listed first and are followed by the liabilities. The difference between the assets and the liabilities is known as the 'net assets' or the 'net worth' of the company. The net assets shown by the balance sheet equals the third part of the balance sheet, which is known as the shareholders' equity. This balance is not a coincidence. Records of the values of each account in the balance sheet are maintained using a system of accounting known as double-entry bookkeeping.

Balance Sheet Structure

The following Balance Sheet structure is just an example. It does not show all possible kinds of assets, equity and liabilities, but it shows the most usual ones. Because it shows Goodwill it could be a consolidated balance sheet. Monetary values are not shown, summary (total) rows are missing as well.

Equity Valuation

The real value to a purchaser of the business or a shareholder may be different from the net assets shown by the balance sheet. This is because factors that affect the value of a business may not be recorded yet. For example, a purchaser will be interested in the future earnings of the business, whether assets such as property have been revalued recently, and whether there are potential liabilities in the future such as lawsuits. The value of the assets in the balance has also been based on the assumption that the business is a going concern, otherwise the break-up value of the assets may be far less than the value in the balance sheet.

Constructing a Balance Sheet

Case Study

1.1. A new business starts up as a limited company called Sunrise Ltd by raising $10,000 from the owners i.e. share holders. The money is put in to a new bank account. What would the assets, liabilities and equity be?

Assets:
Bank Balance 10,000
Equity and Liabilities:
Share Capital 10,000

1.2 They then use 6,000 of its bank account to buy a delivery van. Assets and liabilities after this transaction:

Assets:
Bank Balance 4,000
Delivery Van 6,000
Equity and Liabilities:
Share Capital 10,000

1.3 Sunrise Ltd then buys some inventory at 3,000 on credit. Assets and liabilities after this transaction:

Assets:
Bank Balance 4,000
Delivery Van 6,000
Inventory 3,000
Liabilities:
Accounts Payable 3,000 (to be paid to creditors)
Equity:
Share Capital 10,000

Total assets must always equal total liabilities (and equity). It is inevitable as the liabilities (and equity) are providing the funds that we are spending on these assets.

1.4 Shortly afterwards, after selling 1,000 of inventory for 2,500, payment of 2,600 of the accounts payable and the purchase of 2,200 of machinery financed by a 2,200 bank loan, the assets and liabilities change to the following:

Sunrise Ltd.
Balance Sheet
As of December 31, 2005

\- - - - - - - - - - - - - -

Fixed Assets
Delivery Van 6,000
Machinery 2,200

\- - - - - - - - - - - - - -

Total fixed assets 8,200

Current Assets
Bank Balance 1,400
Inventory 2,000
Accounts Receivable 2,500

\- - - - - - - - - - - - - -

Total 5,900

Accounts Payable 400

\- - - - - - - - - - - - - -

Net current assets 5,500

Long-Term Liabilities
Loans Repayable 2,200

Total Long Term Liabilities 2,200

Net Assets 11,500

Shareholders' Equity
Share Capital 10,000
Retained profits 1,500

Total Shareholders' Equity 11,500

Points to Note:

- Must be headed with the name of the reporting entity (e.g. Sunrise Ltd) and the date.
- The van has not been depreciated and there are no other trading expenses
- The terms 'Current Liability' and 'Long-Term Liability' are the traditional names possibly used by sole traders or partnerships. Limited companies may use the phrases 'Liabilities: Amounts falling due within 1 year' and 'Liabilities: Amounts falling due after 1 year'.
- The Total Equity may also be called the 'Net Worth'.
- The Net Worth is in principle what the company is worth, it shows the monetary amount that would effectively be left, if all assets were sold and all liabilities paid off.

Financial Ratio

Financial ratios are formed from two or more numbers taken from the financial statements of businesses. The numbers may be taken from the Balance sheet or the Income statement and combined in any number of combinations. Rarely are numbers taken from the Statement of Retained Earnings or Cash flow statement.

They are used by

- Debt issuers for analysing credit risk. They may be stipulated in the debt covenants for determining cause for default.
- Business insiders for evaluating performance of people (employee stock options) or projects, and by
- Stock pickers using fundamental analysis who use past performance to judge management and predict future performance.

The ratios quantify many aspects of the business, but they should not be used in isolation from the financials. Rather, they should be an integral part of financial statement analysis. The results of a ratio give rise to the question "why?". Further analysis is needed to answer. The ratios allow for comparisons

- Between companies,
- Between industries,
- Between different time periods of one company and
- Between a company and the industry average.

It is dangerous to compare the ratios of businesses in different industries, which face different risks, different fixed asset structures, and different competition.

INVESTMENT MANAGEMENT

Investment management, the professional management of various securities (shares, bonds etc) and other assets (e.g. real estate), to meet specified investment goals for the benefit of the investors. Investors may be institutions (insurance companies, pension funds, corporations etc.) or private investors (both directly via investment contracts and more commonly via collective investment schemes eg. mutual funds).

The term asset management is often used to refer to the investment management of collective investments, whilst the more generic fund management may refer to all forms of institutional investment as well as investment management for private investors. Investment managers who specialize in advisory or discretionary management on behalf of (normally wealthy) private investors may often refer to their services as wealth management or portfolio management often within the context of so-called "private banking".

The provision of 'investment management services' includes elements of financial analysis, asset selection, stock selection, plan implementation and ongoing monitoring of investments. Investment management is a large and important global industry in its own right responsible for caretaking of trillions of dollars, euros, pounds and yen. Coming under the remit of financial services many of the worlds largest companies are at least in part investment managers and employ millions of staff and create billions in revenue.

Fund manager (or investment advisor in the U.S.) refers to both a firm that provides investment management services and an individual(s) who directs 'fund management' decisions.

Industry Scope

The business of investment management has several facets, including the employment of professional fund managers, research (of individual assets and asset classes), dealing, settlement, marketing, internal auditing, and the preparation of reports for clients. The largest financial fund managers are firms that exhibit all the complexity their size demands. Apart from the people who bring in the money (marketers) and the people who direct investment (the fund managers), there are compliance staff (to ensure accord with legislative and regulatory constraints), internal auditors of various kinds (to examine internal systems and controls), financial controllers (to account for the institutions' own money and costs), computer experts, and "back office" employees (to track and record transactions and fund valuations for up to thousands of clients per institution).

Key Problems of Such Businesses

Key problems include:

- Revenue is directly linked to market valuations, so a major fall in asset prices causes a precipitous decline in revenues relative to costs;

- Above-average fund performance is difficult to sustain, and clients may not be patient during times of poor performance;
- Successful fund managers are expensive and may be headhunted by competitors;
- Above-average fund performance appears to be dependent on the unique skills of the fund manager; however, clients are loath to stake their investments on the ability of one or two men or women- they would rather see firm-wide success, attributable to a single philosophy and internal discipline;
- Evidence suggests that size of an investment firm correlates inversely with fund performance, i.e., the smaller the firm the better the chance of good performance.
- Analysts who can offer generate above-average returns often become sufficiently wealthy that they eschew corporate employment in favour of managing their personal portfolios.

The most successful investment firms in the world have probably been those that have been separated physically and psychologically from banks and insurance companies. That is, the best performance and also the most dynamic business strategies (in this field) have generally come from independent investment management firms.

Representing the Owners of Shares

Institutions often control huge shareholdings. In most cases they are acting as agents (intermediaries between owners of the shares and the companies owned) rather than principals (direct owners). The owners of shares theoretically have great power to alter the companies they own...via the voting rights the shares carry and the consequent ability to pressure managements, and if necessary out-vote them at annual and other meetings.

In practice, the ultimate owners of shares often do not exercise the power they collectively hold (because the owners are many, each with small holdings); financial institutions (as agents) sometimes do. There is a general belief that shareholders - in this case, the institutions acting as agents - could and should exercise more active influence over the companies in which they hold shares (e.g., to hold managers to account, to ensure Boards effective functioning). Such action would add a pressure group to those (the regulators and the Board) overseeing management.

Some institutions have been more vocal and active in pursuing such matters; for instance, some firms believe that there are investment advantages to accumulating substantial minority shareholdings (i.e, 10% or more) and putting pressure on management to implement significant changes in the business. In some cases, institutions with minority holdings work together to force management change. Perhaps more frequent is the sustained pressure that large institutions bring to bear on management teams through persuasive discourse and PR. On the other hand, some of the largest investment managers - such as Barclays Global Investors and Vanguard - advocate simply owning every company, reducing the incentive to influence management teams.

The national context in which shareholder representation considerations are set is variable and important. The USA is a litigious society and shareholders use the law as a lever to pressure management teams. In Japan it is traditional for shareholders to be low in the 'pecking order,' which often allows management and labour to ignore the rights of the ultimate owners. Whereas US firms generally cater to shareholders, Japanese businesses generally exhibit a *stakeholder* mentality, in which they seek consensus amongst all interested parties (against a background of strong unions and labour legislation).

Size of the Global Fund Management Industry

Assets of the global fund management industry increased for the second year running in 2004 to reach a record $45.9 trillion. This was up 6% on the previous year and 40% on 2002. Growth during the past two years has been due to an increase in capital inflows and strong performance of equity markets. Part of the increase in dollar terms was also a result of a 15% fall in the value of the dollar (USD index) during 2003 and a further 4% fall in its value in 2004. As shown in Chart 8, between 1999 and 2002 the value of assets under management fell as a result of declines in equity markets.

Pension assets accounted for $15.3 trillion of funds in 2004, with a further $16.2 trillion invested in mutual funds and $14.5 trillion in insurance funds. Merrill Lynch also estimates the value of private wealth at $30.8 trillion of which about a third was incorporated in other forms of conventional investment management. The US was by far the largest source of funds under management in 2004 with 43% of the world total. It was followed by Japan with 14% and the UK with 7%. The Asia-Pacific region has shown the strongest growth in recent years. Countries such as China and India offer huge potential and many companies are showing an increased focus in this region.

Philosophy, Process and People

The 3-P's (Philosophy, Process and People) are often used to describe the reasons why the manager is able to produce above average results.

- Philosophy refers to the over-arching beliefs of the investment organisation. For example, does the manager buy growth or value shares (and why), does he believe in market timing (and on what evidence), does he rely on external research or does he employ a team of researchers. It is helpful if any and all of such fundamental beliefs are supported by proof-statements.
- Process refers to the way in which the overall philosophy is implemented. For example, which universe of assets is explored before particular assets are chosen as suitable investments; how does the manager decide what to buy and when; how does the manager decide what to sell and when; who takes the decisions and are they taken by committee; what

controls are in place to ensure that a rogue fund (one very different from others and from what is intended) cannot arise;

- People refers to the staff, especially the fund managers. The question is who are they, how are they selected, how old are they, who reports to whom, how deep is the team (and do all the members understand the philosophy and process they are supposed to be using), and most important of all how long has the team been working together. This last question is vital because whatever performance record was presented at the outset of the relationship with the client may or may not relate to (have been produced by) a team that is still in place. If the team has changed greatly (high staff turnover), then arguably the performance record is completely unrelated to the existing team (of fund managers).

Investment Managers and Portfolio Structures

At the heart of the investment management industry are the managers who invest and divest client investments. A certified company investment advisor should conduct an assessment of each client's individual needs and risk profile. The advisor then recommends appropriate investments.

Asset Allocation

The different asset classes are stocks, bonds, real-estate, derivatives, and commodities. The exercise of allocating funds among these assets (and among individual securities within each asset class) is for what investment management firms are paid. Asset classes exhibit different market dynamics, and different interaction effects; thus, the allocation of monies among asset classes will have a significant effect on the performance of the fund. Some research suggests that allocation among asset classes has more predictive power than the choice of individual holdings in determining portfolio return. Arguably, the skill of a successful investment manager resides in constructing the asset allocation, and separately the individual holdings, so as to outperform certain benchmarks (e.g., the peer group of competing funds, bond and stock indices).

Long-term Returns

It is important to look at the evidence on the long-term returns to different assets, and to holding period returns (the returns that accrue on average over different lengths of investment). For example, over very long holding periods (eg. 10+ years) in most countries, equities have generated higher returns than bonds, and bonds have generated higher returns than cash. According to financial theory, this is because equities are riskier (more volatile) than bonds which are themselves more risky than cash.

Diversification

Against the background of the asset allocation, fund managers consider the degree of diversification that makes sense for a given client (given its risk preferences) and construct a list of planned holdings accordingly. The list will indicate what percentage of the fund should be invested in each particular stock or bond. The theory of portfolio diversification was originated by Markowitz and effective diversification requires management of the correlation between the asset returns and the liability returns, issues internal to the portfolio (individual holdings volatility), and cross-correlations between the returns.

Investment Styles

There are a range of different styles of fund management that the institution can implement. For example, growth, value, market neutral, small capitalisation, indexed, etc. Each of these approaches has its distinctive features, adherents and, in any particular financial environment, distinctive risk characteristics. For example, there is evidence that growth styles (buying rapidly growing earnings) are especially effective when the companies able to generate such growth are scarce; conversely, when such growth is plentiful, then there is evidence that value styles tend to outperform the indices particularly successfully.

Performance Measurement

Fund performance is the acid test of fund management, and in the institutional context accurate measurement is a necessity. For that purpose, institutions measure the performance of each fund (and usually for internal purposes components of each fund) under their management, and performance is also measured by external firms that specialise in performance measurement. The leading performance measurement firms (e.g. Frank Russell in the USA) compile aggregate industry data e.g showing how funds in general performed against given indices and peer groups over various time periods.

In a typical case (let us say an equity fund), then the calculation would be made (as far as the client is concerned) every quarter and would show a percentage change compared with the prior quarter (e.g. +4.6% total return in US dollars). This figure would be compared with other similar funds managed within the institution (for purposes of monitoring internal controls), with performance data for peer group funds, and with relevant indices (where available) or tailor-made performance benchmarks where appropriate. The specialist performance measurement firms calculate quartile and decile data and close attention would be paid to the (percentile) ranking of any fund.

Generally speaking it is probably appropriate for an investment firm to persuade its clients to assess performance over a longer periods (e.g. 3 to 5 years) to smooth out very short term fluctuations in performance and the influence of the business cycle. This can be difficult however and, industrywide, there is a serious pre-occupation with short-term numbers and the effect on the relationship with clients (and resultant business risks for the institutions).

Absolute Versus relative Performance

In the USA and the UK, two of the world's most sophisticated fund management markets, the tradition is for institutions to manage client money relative to benchmarks.

For example, an institution believes it has done well if it has generated a return of 5% when the average manager has achieved 4%. In other markets however, e.g. Switzerland, the mentality is different and clients and fund managers focus on absolute return management, i.e. returns relative to cash (e.g. Swiss franc or Yen cash) where (performance) fees are payable only if the return exceeds some absolute figure (e.g. 10% per annum).

Education or Certification

Increasingly, international business schools are incorporating the subject into their course outlines and some have formulated the title of 'Investment Management' conferred as specialist bachelors degrees. (i.e. Cass Business School, London). Due to global cross-recognition agreements with the 2 major accrediting agencies AACSB and ACBSP which accredit over 560 of the best business school programs, the Certification of MFP Master Financial Planner Professional from the American Academy of Financial Management is available to AACSB and ACBSP business school graduates with finance or financial services related concentrations.

LONG-TERM CAPITAL MANAGEMENT

Long-Term Capital Management (LTCM) was a hedge fund founded in 1994 by John Meriwether (the former vice-chairman and head of bond trading at Salomon Brothers). On its board of directors were Myron Scholes and Robert C. Merton, who shared the 1997 Nobel Memorial Prize in Economics. Initially successful, in 1998 it lost $4.6 billion in less than four months. The fund folded in early 2000.

Founding Members

In addition to Meriwether, Scholes, Chincarrini and Merton, also joining the company as principals were Eric Rosenfeld, Greg Hawkins, Larry Hilibrand, Dick Leahy, Victor Haghani and James McEntee. On 24 February 1994, LTCM began trading with $1,011,060,243 of investor capital.

Strategy

The company had developed complex mathematical models to take advantage of fixed income arbitrage deals (termed convergence trades) usually with U.S., Japanese, and European government bonds. The basic idea was that over time the value of long-dated bonds issued a short time apart would tend to become identical. However the rate at which these bonds approached this price would be different, and that more heavily traded bonds such as US Treasury bonds would approach the long term price more quickly than less heavily traded and less liquid bonds.

Thus by a series of financial transactions (essentially amounting to buying the cheaper 'off-the-run' bond and short selling the more expensive, but more liquid, 'on-the-run' bond) it would be possible to make a profit as the difference in the value of the bonds narrowed when a new bond came on the run.

As LTCM's capital base grew the need for additional returns on that expanded capital led it to undertake other trading strategies. Although these trading strategies were non-market directional, i.e. they were not dependent on overall interest rates or stock prices going up (or down), they were not convergence trades as such. By 1998 LTCM had extremely large positions in areas such as merger arbitrage and S&P 500 options (net short long-term S&P volatility). In fact some market participants believed that LTCM had been the primary supplier of S&P 500 gamma which had been in demand by US insurance companies selling equity indexed annuities products for the prior two years.

Because these differences in value were minute – especially for the convergence trades – the fund needed to take highly-leveraged positions in order to make a significant profit. At the beginning of 1998, the firm had equity of $4.72 billion and had borrowed over $124.5 billion with assets of around $129 billion. It had off-balance sheet derivative positions amounting to $1.25 trillion, most of which were in interest rate derivatives such as interest rate swaps. The fund also invested in other derivatives such as equity options.

1998 Downturn

The downfall of the fund started in May and June 1998 when net returns fell 6.42% and 10.14% respectively, reducing LTCM's capital by $461 million. This was further aggravated by the exit of Salomon Brothers from the arbitrage business in July 1998.

The scheme finally unraveled in August and September 1998 when the Russian government defaulted on their government bonds (GKOs). Panicked investors sold Japanese and European bonds to buy U.S. treasury bonds. The profits that were supposed to occur as the value of these bonds converged became huge losses as the value of the bonds diverged. By the end of August the fund had lost $1.85 billion in capital.

The company, which was providing annual returns of almost 40% up to this point, experienced a Flight-to-Liquidity. This prompted a bail-out of $3.625 bn by the banks, organized by the Federal Reserve Bank of New York, ostensibly in order to avoid a wider collapse in the financial markets. The fear was that there would be a chain reaction as the company liquidated its securities to cover its debt, leading to a drop in prices which would force other companies to liquidate their own debt creating a vicious cycle.

The total losses were found to be $4.6 billion. The losses in the major investment categories were (ordered by magnitude):

- $1.6 bn in swaps
- $1.3 bn in equity volatility
- $430 mn in Russian and other emerging markets
- $371 mn in directional trades in developed countries
- $215 mn in yield curve arbitrage
- $203 mn in S&P 500 stocks
- $100 mn in junk bond arbitrage
- No substantial losses in merger arbitrage

Long Term Capital was audited by Pricewaterhouse LLP. The lead partner on the engagement was John Reville (Pricewaterhouse LLP - Manhattan office).

A Deeper Understanding of the Risks Taken by LTCM

The profits from LTCM's trading strategies were generally not correlated with each other and thus normally LTCM's highly leveraged portfolio benefited from diversification. However, the general flight to liquidity in the late summer of 1998 led to a marketwide repricing of all risk leading these positions to all move in the same direction. As the correlation of LTCM's positions increased, the diversified aspect of LTCM's portfolio vanished and large losses to its equity value occurred. Thus the primary lesson of 1998 and the collapse of LTCM for Value at Risk (VaR) users is not a liquidity one, but more fundamentally that the underlying Covariance matrix used in VaR analysis is not static but changes over time.

In the end, LTCM's basic idea was correct, in that the values of government bonds did eventually converge, but only after the firm was wiped out. Nonetheless, the incident confirms an insight often (though perhaps apocryphally) attributed to the economist John Maynard Keynes, who is said to have warned investors that although markets do tend toward rational positions in the long run, "the market can stay irrational longer than you can stay solvent."

Many of LTCM's strategies had payouts similar to those from selling an out-of-the-money option; a likely small gain balanced against a small chance of a large loss. Their basic idea was "correct" in that these large losses would not, if the positions were held to maturity, have come to pass. However, the events of 1998 increased the perceived probability of large losses, to the point where LTCM's portfolio had negative value.

Incentive Structures: Alternatives to Direct Pay for Performance

Much of the discussion here has been in terms of individual pay-for-performance contracts; but many large firms use internal labour markets as a solution to some of the problems outlined. Here, there is "pay-for-performance" in looser sense over a longer time period. There is little variation in pay within grades, and pay increases come with changes in job or job title. The incentive effects of this structure are dealt with in what is known as "tournament theory", for multi-stage tournaments in hierarchies where it is explained why CEOs are paid many times more than other workers in the firm). Workers are motivated to supply effort by the wage increase they would earn if they win a promotion. Some of the extended tournament models predict that relatively weaker agents, be they competing in a sports tournaments or in the broiler chicken industry, would take risky actions instead of increasing their effort supply as a cheap way to improve the prospects of winning. These actions are inefficient as they increase risk taking without increasing the average effort supplied.

A major problem with tournaments is that individuals' are rewarded based on how well they do relative to others, co-workers might become reluctant to help out others and might even sabotage others' effort instead of increasing one's own eftort. This is supported empirically by Drago and Garvey. Why then are tournaments so popular?

Firstly, because - especially given compression rating problems - it is difficult to determine absolutely differences in worker performance. Tournaments merely require rank order evaluation.

Secondly, it reduces the danger of rent-seeking, because bonuses paid to favourite workers are tied to increased responsibilities in new jobs, and supervisors will suffer if they do not promote the most qualified person.

Thirdly, where prize structures are (relatively) fixed, it reduces the possibility of the firm reneging on paying wages. As Carmichael notes, a prize structure represents a degree of commitment, both to absolute and to relative wage levels. Lastly when the measurement of workers' productivity is difficult, e.g. say monitoring is costly, or when the tasks the workers have to perform for the job is varied in nature, making it hard to measure effort and/or performance, then running tournaments in a firm would encourage the workers to supply effort whereas workers would have shirked if there are no promotions.

Deferred Compensation

Tournaments represent one way of implementing the general principle of "deferred compensation", which is essentially an agreement between worker and firm to commit to each other. Under schemes of deferred compensation, workers are overpaid when old, at the cost of being underpaid when young. Salop and Salop argue that this derives from the need to attract workers more likely to stay at the firm for longer periods, since turnover is costly. Alternatively, delays in evaluating the performance of workers may lead to compensation being weighted to later periods, when better and poorer workers have to a greater extent been distinguished. (Workers may even prefer to have wages increasing over time, perhaps as a method of forced saving, or as an indicator of personal development. eg Loewenstein and Sicherman 1991, Frank and Hutchens 1993.)

For example Akerlof and Katz 1989: if older workers receive efficiency wages, younger workers may be prepared to work for less in order to receive those later. Overall, the evidence suggests the use of deferred compensation (eg Freeman and Medoff 1984, and Spilerman 1986 - seniority provisions are often included in pay, promotion and retention decisions, irrespective of productivity.)

The reason that employees are often paid according to hours of work rather than by direct measurement of results is that it is often more efficient to use indirect systems of controlling the quantity and quality of effort, due to a variety of informational and other issues (eg turnover costs, which determine the optimal minimum length of relationship between firm and employee). This means that methods such as deferred compensation and structures such as tournaments are often more suitable to create the incentives for employees to contribute what they can to output over longer periods (years rather than hours). These represent "pay-for-performance" systems in a looser, more extended sense, as workers who consistently work harder and better are more likely to be promoted (and usually paid more), compared to the narrow definition of "pay-for-performance", such as piece rates.

This discussion has been conducted almost entirely for self-interested rational individuals. In practice, however, the incentive mechanisms which successful firms use take account of the socio-cultural context they are embedded in, in order not to destroy the social capital they might more constructively mobilise towards building an organic, social organization, with the attendant benefits from such things as "worker loyalty and pride can be critical to a firm's success..."

BASEL II

Basel II, also called The New Accord (correct full name is the International Convergence of Capital Measurement and Capital Standards - A Revised Framework) is the second Basel Accord and represents recommendations by bank supervisors and central bankers from the 13 countries making up the Basel Committee on Banking Supervision (BCBS) to revise the international standards for measuring the adequacy of a bank's capital. It was created to promote greater consistency in the way banks and banking regulators approach risk management across national borders. The Bank for International Settlements (often confused with the BCBS) supplies the secretariat for the BCBS and is not itself the BCBS.

History

An earlier accord, Basel I, adopted in 1988, is now widely viewed as outmoded as it is risk insensitive and can easily be circumvented by regulatory arbitrage.

The Basel II deliberations began in January 2001, driven largely by concern about the arbitrage issues that develop when regulatory capital requirements diverge from accurate economic capital calculations.

With the first draft (called Consultative Paper 1) published in June 1999, further consultative papers followed together with a large quantity of other releases, Quantitative Impact Studies Nos. 2, 3 and 4, and papers. A final version was issued in June 2004, with a minor revision released in November 2005. In June 2006 a Comprehensive version was published including all Basel regulations up to this date. Implementation of the Accord is expected by 2008 in many of the over 100 countries currently using the Basel I accord.

The final version aims at:

1. Ensuring that capital allocation is more risk sensitive;
2. Separating operational risk from credit risk, and quantifying both;
3. Attempting to align economic and regulatory capital more closely to reduce the scope for regulatory arbitrage.

While the final accord has largely addressed the regulatory arbitrage issue, there are still areas where regulatory capital requirements will diverge from the economic.

Basel II has largely left unchanged the question of how to actually define bank capital, which diverges from accounting equity in important respects. The Basel I definition, as modified up to the present, remains in place.

The Accord In Operation

Basel II uses a "three pillars" concept - (1) minimum capital requirements, (2) supervisory review and (3) market discipline - to promote greater stability in the financial system. The Basel I accord only dealt with parts of each of these pillars. For example: of the key pillar one risk, credit risk, was dealt with in a simple manner and market risk was an afterthought. Operational risk was not dealt with at all.

The First Pillar

The first pillar provides improved risk sensitivity in the way that capital requirements are calculated for three major components of risk that a bank faces: credit risk, operational risk and market risk. In turn, each of these components can be calculated in two or three ways of varying sophistication. Other risks are not considered fully quantifiable at this stage.

Technical terms in the more sophisticated measures of market risk include VaR (Value at Risk), EL (Loss function) whose components are PD (Probability of Default), LGD (Loss Given Default), and EAD (Exposure At Default). Calculation of these components requires advanced data collection and sophisticated risk management techniques.

The Second Pillar

The second pillar deals with the regulatory response to the first pillar, giving regulators much improved 'tools' over those available to them under Basel I. It also provides a framework for dealing with all the other risks a bank may face, such as name risk, liquidity risk and legal risk, which the accord combines under the title of residual risk.

The Third Pillar

The third pillar greatly increases the disclosures that the bank must make. This is designed to allow the market to have a better picture of the overall risk position of the bank and to allow the counterparties of the bank to price and deal appropriately.

Criticisms

There are many criticisms that are made of Basel II. These include that the more sophisticated risk measures unfairly advantage the larger banks that are able to implement them and, from the same perspective, that the developing countries generally also do not have these banks and that Basel II will disadvantage the economically marginalized by restricting their access to credit or by making it more expensive.

The first of these is a valid point, but it is difficult to see how this can be overcome. More risk sensitive risk measures were required for the larger, more sophisticated banks and, while the less sophisticated measures are simpler to calculate, due to their lower risk sensitivity they need to be more conservative.

The second criticism has elements of truth; the better credit risks will be advantaged as banks move towards true pricing for risk. Experience with these systems in the United States and the United Kingdom, however, shows that the improved risk sensitivity means that banks are more willing to lend to higher risk borrowers, just with higher prices. Borrowers previously 'locked out' of the banking system have a chance to establish a good credit history.

A more serious criticism is that the operation of Basel II will lead to a more pronounced business cycle. This criticism arises because the credit models used for pillar 1 compliance typically use a one year time horizon. This would mean that, during a downturn in the business cycle, banks would need to reduce lending as their models forecast increased losses, increasing the magnitude of the downturn. Regulators should be aware of this risk and can be expected to include it in their assessment of the bank models used.

On September 30, 2005, the four US Federal banking agencies (the Office of the Comptroller of the Currency, the Board of Governors of the Federal Reserve System, the Federal Deposit Insurance Corporation, and the Office of Thrift Supervision) announced their revised plans for the U.S. implementation of the Basel II accord. This delays implementation of the accord for US banks by 12 months.

On November 15, 2005, the committee released a revised version of the Accord, incorporating changes to the calculations for market risk and the treatment of double default effects. These changes had been flagged well in advance, as part of a paper released in July 2005.

On July 4, 2006, the committee released a comprehensive version of the Accord, incorporating the June 2004 Basel II Framework, the elements of the 1988 Accord that were not revised during the Basel II process, the 1996 Amendment to the Capital Accord to Incorporate Market Risks, and the November 2005 paper on Basel II: International Convergence of Capital Measurement and Capital Standards: A Revised Framework. No new elements have been introduced in this compilation. This version is now the current version.

Basel II and the Regulators

One of the most difficult aspects of implementing an international agreement is the need to accommodate differing cultures, varying structural models, and the complexities of public policy and existing regulation. Banks' senior management will determine corporate strategy, as well as the country in which to base a particular type of business, based in part on how Basel II is ultimately interpreted by various countries' legislatures and regulators.

To assist banks operating with multiple reporting requirements for different regulators according to geographic location, there are several software applications available. These include capital calculation engines and extend to automated reporting solutions which include the reports required under COREP/FINREP.

Implementation Progress

Regulators in most jurisdictions around the world plan to implement the new Accord, but with widely varying timelines and use of the varying methodologies being restricted. The United States of America's various regulators are yet (October 2006) to agree on a final approach - see Basel IA for a discussion. In response to a questionaire released by the Financial Stability Institute (FSI), 95 national regulators indicated they were to implement Basel II, in some form or another, by 2015.

The future

Work is apparently already underway on Basel III, at least in a preliminary sense. The goals of this project are to refine the definition of bank capital, quantify further classes of risk and to further improve the sensitivity of the risk measures.

BUSINESS ETHICS

Business ethics is a form of applied ethics that examines ethical rules and principles within a commercial context, the various moral or ethical problems that can arise in a business setting, and any special duties or obligations that apply to persons who are engaged in commerce.

Business ethics can be both a normative and a descriptive discipline. As a corporate practice and a career specialisation, the field is primarily normative. In academia descriptive approaches are also taken. The range and quantity of business ethical issues reflects the degree to which business is perceived to be at odds with non-economic social values. Historically, interest in business ethics accelerated dramatically during the 1980's and 1990's, both within major corporations and within academia. For example, today most major corporate websites lay emphasis on commitment to promoting non-economic social values under a variety of headings (e.g. ethics codes, social responsibility charters). In some cases, corporations have redefined their core values in the light of business ethical considerations.

Overview of Issues in Business Ethics

General Business Ethics

- This part of business ethics overlaps with the philosophy of business, one of the aims of which is to determine the fundamental purposes of a company. If a company's main purpose is to maximize the returns to its shareholders, then it could be seen as unethical for a company to consider the interests and rights of anyone else.
- Corporate social responsibility or CSR: an umbrella term under which the ethical rights and duties existing between companies and society is debated.
- Issues regarding the moral rights and duties between a company and its shareholders: fiduciary responsibility, stakeholder concept v. shareholder concept.

- Ethical issues concerning relations between different companies: e.g. hostile take-overs, industrial espionage.
- Leadership issues: corporate governance.
- Political contributions made by corporations.
- Law reform, such as the ethical debate over introducing a crime of corporate manslaughter.
- The misuse of corporate ethics policies as marketing instruments.

PROFESSIONAL ETHICS

Professional ethics covers the myriad of practical ethical problems and phenomena which arise out of specific functional areas of companies or in relation to recognized business professions.

Ethics of Finance and Accounting

Enron logo

- Creative accounting, earnings management, misleading financial analysis.
- Insider trading, securities fraud, bucket shop, forex scams: concerns (criminal) manipulation of the financial markets.
- Executive compensation: concerns excessive payments made to corporate CEO's.
- Bribery, kickbacks, facilitation payments: while these may be in the (short-term) interests of the company and its shareholders, these practices may be anti-competitive or offend against the values of society.

Ethics of Human Resource Management

The ethics of human resource management (HRM) covers those ethical issues arising around the employer-employee relationship, such as the rights and duties owed between employer and employee.

- Discrimination issues include discrimination on the bases of age (ageism), gender, race, religion, disabilities, weight and attractiveness.

- Issues surrounding the representation of employees and the democratisation of the workplace: union busting, strike breaking.
- Issues affecting the privacy of the employee: workplace surveillance, drug testing.
- Issues affecting the privacy of the *employer*: whistle-blowing.
- Issues relating to the fairness of the employment contract and the balance of power between employer and employee: slavery, indentured servitude, employment law.
- Occupational safety and health.

Ethics of Sales and Marketing

Marketing which goes beyond the mere provision of information about (and access to) a product may seek to manipulate our values and behaviour. To some extent society regards this as acceptable, but where is the ethical line to be drawn? Marketing ethics overlaps strongly with media ethics, because marketing makes heavy use of media. However media ethics is a much larger topic and extends outside business ethics.

- Pricing: price fixing, price discrimination, price skimming.
- Anti-competitive practices: these include but go beyond pricing tactics to cover issues such as manipulation of loyalty and supply chains.
- Specific marketing strategies: greenwash, bait and switch, shill, viral marketing, spam (electronic), pyramid scheme, planned obsolescence.
- Content of advertisements: attack ads, subliminal messages, sex in advertising, products regarded as immoral or harmful
- Children and marketing: marketing in schools.
- Black markets, grey markets.

ETHICS OF PRODUCTION

This area of business ethics deals with the duties of a company to ensure that products and production processes do not cause harm. Some of the more acute dilemmas in this area arise out of the fact that there is usually a degree of danger in any product or production process and it is difficult to define a degree of permissibility, or the degree of permissibility may depend on the changing state of preventative technologies or changing social perceptions of acceptable risk.

- Defective, addictive and inherently dangerous products and services (e.g. tobacco, alcohol, weapons, motor vehicles, chemical manufacturing, bungee jumping).
- Ethical relations between the company and the environment: pollution, environmental ethics, carbon emissions trading
- Ethical problems arising out of new technologies: genetically modified food, mobile phone radiation and health.
- Product testing ethics: animal rights and animal testing, use of economically disadvantaged groups (such as students) as test objects.

Ethics of Intellectual Property, Knowledge and Skills

Knowledge and skills are valuable but not easily "ownable" objects. Nor is it obvious who has the greater rights to an idea: the company who trained the employee or the employee themselves? The country in which the plant grew, or the company which discovered and developed the plant's medicinal potential? As a result, attempts to assert ownership and ethical disputes over ownership arise.

- Patent infringement, copyright infringement, trademark infringement.
- Misuse of the intellectual property systems to stifle competition: patent misuse, copyright misuse, patent troll, submarine patent.

- Even the notion of intellectual property itself has been criticised on ethical grounds.
- Employee raiding: the practice of attracting key employees away from a competitor to take unfair advantage of the knowledge or skills they may possess.
- The practice of employing all the most talented people in a specific field, regardless of need, in order to prevent any competitors employing them.
- Bioprospecting (ethical) and biopiracy (unethical).
- Business intelligence and industrial espionage.

International Business Ethics and Ethics of Economic Systems

The issues here are grouped together because they involve a much wider, global view on business ethical matters.

International Business Ethics

While business ethics emerged as a field in the 1970's, international business ethics did not emerge until the late 1990's, looking back on the international developments of that decade. Many new practical issues arose out of the international context of business. Theoretical issues such as cultural relativity of ethical values receive more emphasis in this field. Other, older issues can be grouped here as well. Issues and subfields include:

- The search for universal values as a basis for international commercial behaviour.
- Comparison of business ethical traditions in different countries.
- Comparison of business ethical traditions from various religious perspectives.
- Ethical issues arising out of international business transactions; e.g. bioprospecting and biopiracy in the pharmaceutical industry; the fair trade movement; transfer pricing.

- Issues such as globalisation and cultural imperialism.
- Varying global standards - e.g. the use of child labour.
- The way in which multinationals take advantage of international differences, such as outsourcing production (e.g. clothes) and services (e.g. call centres) to low-wage countries.
- The permissibility of international commerce with pariah states.

Ethics of Economic Systems

This vaguely defined area, perhaps not part of but only related to business ethics, is where business ethicists venture into the fields of political economy and political philosophy, focussing on the rights and wrongs of various systems for the distribution of economic benefits. The work of John Rawls is a notable contribution.

Theoretical Issues in Business Ethics

Conflicting Interests

Business ethics can be examined from various perspectives, including the perspective of the employee, the commercial enterprise, and society as a whole. Very often, situations arise in which there is conflict between one or more of the parties, such that serving the interest of one party is a detriment to the other(s). For example, a particular outcome might be good for the employee, whereas, it would be bad for the company, society, or vice versa. Some ethicists (e.g., Henry Sidgwick) see the principal role of ethics as the harmonization and reconciliation of conflicting interests.

Ethical Issues and Approaches

Philosophers and others disagree about the purpose of a business in society. For example, some suggest that the principal purpose of a business is to maximize returns to its owners, or in the case of a publicly-traded concern, its shareholders. Thus, under this view, only those activities that increase profitability and shareholder value should be encouraged. Some believe that the only companies that are likely to survive in a competitive marketplace are those that place profit maximization above everything else. However, some point out that self interest would still require a business to obey the law and adhere to basic moral rules, because the consequences of failing to do so could be very costly in fines, loss of licensure, or company reputation. The economist Milton Friedman was a leading proponent of this view.

Other theorists contend that a business has moral duties that extend well beyond serving the interests of its owners or stockholders, and that these duties consist of more than simply obeying the law. They believe a business has moral responsibilities to so-called stakeholders, people who have an interest in the conduct of the business, which might include employees, customers, vendors, the local community, or even society as a whole. They would say that stakeholders have certain rights with regard to how the business operates, and some would even suggest that this even includes rights of governance.

Some theorists have adapted social contract theory to business, whereby companies become quasi-democratic associations, and employees and other stakeholders are given voice over a company's operations. This approach has become especially popular subsequent to the revival of contract theory in political philosophy, which is largely due to John Rawls' *A Theory of Justice*, and the advent of the consensus-oriented approach to solving business problems, an aspect of the "quality movement" that emerged in the 1980s.

Professors Thomas Donaldson and Thomas Dunfee proposed a version of contract theory for business, which they call Integrative Social Contracts Theory. They posit that conflicting interests are best resolved by formulating a "fair agreement" between the parties, using a combination of i) macro-principles that all rational people would agree upon as universal principles, and, ii) micro-principles formulated by actual agreements among the interested parties. Critics say the proponents of contract theories miss a central point, namely, that a business is someone's property and not a mini-state or a means of distributing social justice.

Ethical issues can arise when companies must comply with multiple and sometimes conflicting legal or cultural standards, as in the case of multinational companies that operate in countries with varying practices. The question arises, for example, ought a company to obey the laws of its home country, or should it follow the less stringent laws of the developing country in which it does business? To illustrate, United States law forbids companies from paying bribes either domestically or overseas; however, in other parts of the world, bribery is a customary, accepted way of doing business. Similar problems can occur with regard to child labour, employee safety, work hours, wages, discrimination, and environmental protection laws.

It is sometimes claimed that a Gresham's law of ethics applies in which bad ethical practices drive out good ethical practices. It is claimed that in a competitive business environment, those companies that survive are the ones that recognize that their only role is to maximize profits. On this view, the competitive system fosters a downward ethical spiral.

BUSINESS ETHICS IN THE FIELD

Many companies have formulated internal policies pertaining to the ethical conduct of employees. These policies can be simple exhortations in broad, highly-generalized language (typically called a corporate ethics statement), or they can be more detailed policies, containing specific behavioral requirements (typically called corporate ethics codes). They are generally meant to identify the company's expectations of workers and to offer guidance on handling some of the more common ethical problems that might arise in the course of doing business. It is hoped that having such a policy will lead to greater ethical awareness, consistency in application, and the avoidance of ethical disasters.

An increasing number of companies also requires employees to attend seminars regarding business conduct, which often include discussion of the company's policies, specific case studies, and legal requirements. Some companies even require their employees to sign agreements stating that they will abide by the company's rules of conduct. Many companies are assessing the environmental factors that can lead employees to engage in unethical conduct.

Not everyone supports corporate policies that govern ethical conduct. Some claim that ethical problems are better dealt with by depending upon employees to use their own judgment. Others believe that corporate ethics policies are primarily rooted in utilitarian concerns, and that they are mainly to limit the company's legal liability, or to curry public favour by giving the appearance of being a good corporate citizen. Ideally, the company will avoid a lawsuit because its employees will follow the rules. Should a lawsuit occur, the company can claim that the problem would not have arisen if the employee had only followed the code properly.

Sometimes there is disconnection between the company's code of ethics and the company's actual practices. Thus, whether or not such conduct is explicitly sanctioned by management, at worst, this makes the policy duplicitous, and, at best, it is merely a marketing tool.

To be successful, most ethicists would suggest that an ethics policy should be:

- Given the unequivocal support of top management, by both word and by example.
- Explained in writing and orally, with periodic reinforcement.
- Doable....something employees can both understand and perform.
- Monitored by top management, with routine inspections for compliance and improvement.
- Backed up by clearly stated consequences in the case of disobedience.
- Remain neutral and nonsexist.

Ethics officers

Ethics officers (sometimes called "compliance" or "business conduct officers") have been appointed formally by organizations since the mid-1980s. One of the catalysts for the creation of this new role was a series of fraud, corruption and abuse scandals that afflicted the U.S. defense industry at that time. This led to the creation of the Defense Industry Initiative (DII), a pan-industry initiative to promote and ensure ethical business practices. The DII set an early benchmark for ethics management in corporations. In 1991, the Ethics and Compliance Officer Association (ECOA) – originally the Ethics Officer Association (EOA)– was founded at the Center for Business Ethics(at Bentley College, Waltham, MA) as a professional association for those responsible for managing organizations' efforts to achieve ethical best practices. The membership grew rapidly (the ECOA now has over 1,100 members) and was soon established as an independent organization.

Another critical factor in the decisions of companies to appoint ethics/compliance officers was the passing of the Federal Sentencing Guidelines for Organizations in 1991, which set standards that organizations (large or small, commercial and non-commercial) had to follow to obtain a reduction in sentence if they should be convicted of a federal offense. Although intended to assist judges with sentencing, the influence in helping to establish best practices has been far-reaching.

In the wake of numerous corporate scandals between 2001-04 (affecting large corporations like Enron, WorldCom and Tyco), even small and medium-sized companies have begun to appoint ethics officers. They often report to the Chief Executive Officer and are responsible for assessing the ethical implications of the company's activities, making recommendations regarding the company's ethical policies, and disseminating information to employees. They are particularly interested in uncovering or preventing unethical and illegal actions. This trend is partly due to the Sarbanes-

Oxley Act in the United States, which was enacted in reaction to the above scandals. A related trend is the introduction of risk assessment officers that monitor how shareholders' investments might be affected by the company's decisions.

The effectiveness of ethics officers in the marketplace is not clear. If the appointment is made primarily as a reaction to legislative requirements, one might expect the efficacy to be minimal, at least, over the short term. In part, this is because ethical business practices result from a corporate culture that consistently places value on ethical behaviour, a culture and climate that usually emanates from the top of the organization. The mere establishment of a position to oversee ethics will most likely be insufficient to inculcate ethical behaviour: a more systemic programme with consistent support from general management will be necessary.

The foundation for ethical behaviour goes well beyond corporate culture and the policies of any given company, for it also depends greatly upon an individual's early moral training, the other institutions that affect an individual, the competitive business environment the company is in and, indeed, society as a whole.

Religious Views on Business Ethics

The historical and global importance of religious views on business ethics is sometimes underestimated in standard introductions to business ethics. Particularly in Asia and the Middle East, religious and cultural perspectives have a strong influence on the conduct of business and the creation of business values.

Examples include:

- Islamic banking, associated with the avoidance of charging interest on loans.
- Traditional Confucian disapproval of the profit-seeking motive.

Related Disciplines

Business ethics should be distinguished from the philosophy of business, the branch of philosophy that deals with the philosophical, political, and ethical underpinnings of business and economics. Business ethics operates on the premise, for example, that the ethical operation of a private business is possible — those who dispute that premise, such as libertarian socialists, (who contend that "business ethics" is an oxymoron) do so by definition outside of the domain of business ethics proper.

The philosophy of business also deals with questions such as what, if any, are the social responsibilities of a business; business management theory; theories of individualism vs. collectivism; free will among participants in the marketplace; the role of self interest; invisible hand theories; the requirements of social justice; and natural rights, especially property rights, in relation to the business enterprise.

Business ethics is also related to political economy, which is economic analysis from political and historical perspectives. Political economy deals with the distributive consequences of economic actions. It asks who gains and who loses from economic activity, and is the resultant distribution fair or just, which are central ethical issues.

Corporate Behaviour

Corporate Behaviour (or corporate behaviour) is the behaviour of a corporation or corporations (or company or companies). The corporate behaviour of for-profit (capitalist) corporations and not-for-profit (non-capitalist) corporations differ due to the fundamental drive for profit in for-profit corporations, compared to the non-monetary goals often held by not-for-profit corporations.

The Characteristics of for-profit (Capitalist) Corporate Behaviour

Corporate behaviour of for-profit corporations has characteristics. These characteristics are unlikely to remain fixed for various reasons, but key characteristics are discernable from the history of for-profit corporations. Some of the key characteristics may not apply to individual for-profit corporations at a point in time and space, though some key characteristics are probably present at all times. The best example is the drive for profit. The strength or importance of a key characteristic will also vary in time and space for many reasons. For instance a for-profit corporation may be able to grow at a faster rate if it has subsidiaries in other countries.

Reasons are numerous as to why key characteristics are absent or vary in strength or importance. Some reasons could be as follows:

- Economic decline
- Poor performance
- Size of for-profit corporation
- Management decisions
- Type of for-profit corporation
- Competition

Certain individuals and groups have proposed and described the characteristics of corporate behaviour. These attempts, whilst a useful contribution, are not objective and should be read with this in mind.

Key characteristics of for-profit Corporate Behaviour

The key characteristics of corporate behaviour are as follows:

- Profit: Profitability is the ultimate driver of corporate decisions. Corporations prefer higher profits to lower profits, at least in the long-run. Profitability is not necessarily the same as community well-being, though a profitable company is more likely to, for example, employ more people than an unprofitable company. Conflicts can exist, however, between what's good for a corporation and what's good for the environment, for example, or its employees or even the good of the state. A corporation is a complex organism and there has been much debate about what drives it. There is an argument that the divorce of ownership from decision-taking means that profitability isn't the main drive - senior managers may have other imperatives like keeping their jobs and avoiding being taken-over (which might run counter to the interests of shareholders). Corporations often like to grow, if only because they fear a bigger competitor having cost advantages. This is not always true, however: there have been cases where corporations have been broken up into constituent parts.

- Amorality: Not being human, corporations as such do not have morals or altruistic goals. Neither, though, does any other organisation. Corporations are, though, run by people who are subject to law and rules of morality.
- Hierarchy: Corporations are usually hierarchical, though the structure of the hierarchy varies. Some are relatively flat with a wide layer of middle managers answerable to a few individuals while others are like a pyramid. A very few corporations have a great degree of democracy to them. Ricardo Semmler owns corporations in Brazil but allows all his staff to pick managers and decide strategy. He puts himself up for election as a chief executive.

The Characteristics of not-for-profit (non-Capitalist) Corporate Behaviour

As non-capitalist corporations such as NGO's or charities are not driven by the fundamentals of profit and economic growth, these do not show many of the characteristics of capitalist corporations. The behaviour of non-capitalist corporations is however often influenced by these characteristics of capitalist corporations, in similar ways to the influence of corporate behaviour on individuals. Due to this influence non-capitalist corporations can sometimes be seen to exhibit the characteristics of hierarchy, competition and ephemerality.

The Influence of Corporate Behaviour on Individuals and Society

Due to the dominance of capitalist corporations in Western societies the behaviour of corporations can be seen to have significant impacts on individuals and society. A person or group of people can have links to a corporation or corporations that range from weak to strong, if a person or group of people exhibit corporate behaviour that does not mean the person or group of people is employed by a corporation or corporations. A person or group of people may show corporate behaviour for different lengths of time, for some people they exhibit this behaviour at their place of work; for others it is exhibited at work, home and outside the home. Many people display corporate behaviour but do not agree with actions and outcomes that result from it.

The fact that individuals may not agree with the outcomes of corporate behaviour is central to the concept in itself, the characteristics of capitalist corporations do not reflect the characteristics of any individual or group of individuals but are the characteristics required for the survival of capitalist corporations *due to the nature of the system within which corporations operate.*

Ethics

Under the law, corporations are treated in many ways as persons. However, in other ways, they are not. One example is as follows. The thought of being put in prison acts as a powerful deterrent for most people: it prevents people from committing many crimes. But this powerful deterrent to harming people or society has no effect on a corporation, for a corporation cannot be put in prison.

Corporate Benefit

Corporate benefit (sometimes referred to as commercial benefit) is the requirement under some legal systems that the directors of a company must exercise the powers of the company for the commercial benefit of the company and its members. At common law, transactions which were not ostensibly beneficial to the company were set aside as being void as against the company.

Perhaps the best illustration of this principle is to be found in Hutton v West Cork Railway Co (1883) 23 Ch D 654, where the English Court of Appeal held that the paying of a gratuity to employees prior to their dismissal was an improper exercise of the powers of the company, because the company was no longer a going concern, and thus stood to obtain no benefit (and no furtherance of its objects) through the payment of the gratuity; as Bowen L.J. memorably remarked: "there are to be no cakes and ale except such as are required for the benefit of the company."

Any transaction which the directors enter into which is outside the powers of the company (and thus outside the scope of their authority) may nonetheless be ratified by the shareholders of the company, and will thereby be binding upon the company, see Multinational Gas and Petrochemical Co v Multinational Gas and Petrochemical Services Ltd.

Modern Developments

The rule is generally seen to be particularly harsh towards both third parties and against directors, who are regarded as being in breach of their duty only be acting with what others might regard as common human decency. Where the company's property could not be recovered from the third party, the directors would be personally liable to recompense the company.

There were also concerns that running companies ruthless for the financial benefit of the shareholders had a countervailing cost, making directors unwilling to participate in programmes that were beneficial to the community generally, or to the environment. It also meant that companies became much less willing to make donations to political parties, which may have had more impetus in bringing about legislative change than concern for communities or the environment.

Most legal systems have now abrogated by statute the rule that as against third parties the transaction may be void if it has insufficient commercial benefit to the company. In some countries, statutes now expressly provide for the directors to consider interests other than the pure financial interests of the shareholders.

However, in some jurisdictions there are proposals to make the power to act otherwise than for the financial benefit of the company even wider. For example, in the United Kingdom, the Companies Act 2006, when brought into force, will require that directors have to consider the impact of their actions on a much wider range of stakeholders. That Act would require a director "to promote the success of the company for the benefit of its members as a whole", but sets out six factors to which a director must have regards in fulfilling the duty to promote success. These are:

- the likely consequences of any decision in the long term
- the interests of the company's employees
- the need to foster the company's business relationships with suppliers, customers and others
- the impact of the company's operations on the community and the environment
- the desirability of the company maintaining a reputation for high standards of business conduct, and
- the need to act fairly as between members of a company

The proposed new duties have been subject to some criticism, both from those who argue that the new duties do not have sufficient bite, and also from those who fear that it diverts directors' focus from what it is that they are meant to be doing (viz., generating profits), and there are fears of widespread litigation, and increase in director's insurance premiums. However, because the new duties are expressed in non-imperative terms, and there is no sanction, the likelihood is that although they will empower the board of directors to take decisions that do not appear to directly financially benefit the company, they are unlikely to ever be required to do so.

Distinction from Other Legal Concepts

Conceptually, it is important to distinguish failure of a transaction for want of corporate benefit from other related legal concepts. These include:

- *Failure of consideration*: Under contract law in most common law legal systems, to be enforceable a contract requires both parties to provide consideration (ie. something of value). However, the consideration does not need to be equal, and the gratuity given in *Hutton v West Cork Railway Co* would still have failed for want of corporate benefit if, for example, the company had allowed employees to purchase company property at a discount.
- *Transactions at an undervalue*: Although most examples of failure for want of corporate benefit involve transactions which were either a gift, or were made at a substantial undervalue, the concept is different in purpose and effect from provisions of insolvency law which prohibit undervalue transactions at a time when the company is insolvent.

Corporate Crime

In criminology, corporate crime refers to crimes either committed by a corporation, i.e. a business entity having a separate legal personality from the natural persons that manage its activities, or by individuals that may be identified with a corporation or other business entity. This type of crime therefore overlaps with:

- White-collar crime because the majority of individuals who may act as or represent the interests of the corporation will be employees or professionals of a higher social class;
- Organized crime because criminals can set up corporations either for the purposes of crime or as

vehicles for laundering the proceeds of crime. Organized crime has become a branch of big business and is simply the illegal sector of capital. It has been estimated that, by the middle of the 1990s, the "gross criminal product" of organised crime made it the twentieth richest organisation in the world and richer than 150 sovereign states. The world's gross criminal product has been estimated at 20 percent of world trade; and

- State-corporate crime because, in many contexts, the opportunity to commit crime emerges from the relationship between the corporation and the state.

Definitional Issues

Legal Person

The Fourteenth Amendment to the U.S. Constitution stipulates that,

> "No State shall make or enforce any law which shall abridge the privileges or immunities of citizens of the United States; nor shall any State deprive any person of life, liberty, or property, without due process of law; nor deny to any person within its jurisdiction the equal protection of the laws."

In Santa Clara County v. Southern Pacific Railroad, 118 U.S. 394 (1886) the United States Supreme Court declared that a corporation was a "person" as interpreted by the Fourteenth Amendment. In a preface to the Court's argument, Chief Justice Morrison R. Waite stated the unanimous opinion that the Fourteenth Amendment applied equally to persons and "applied to these corporations." In English law, this was matched the decision in Salomon v Salomon & Co.

Function of Law

History shows that laws have sometimes been used as instruments of repression, exclusion, and marginalisation; and that certain criminal justice policies may sometimes be intended to serve the interests of particular groups or to undermine other groups. Thus, the definition of crime and the nature of criminal justice policies in society usually reflect the structures of power in that society. Also, while mainstream criminologists tend to focus mostly on street crimes and crimes of marginalised groups, the less obvious crimes of states, corporate organisations, and powerful groups are often ignored or under-emphasised. Lea (2001) argues that whereas crime used to be the exceptional event, disrupting the otherwise normal socio-economic processes, as crime becomes more frequent it lost its status as an exceptional event and became "a standard, background feature of our lives—a taken for granted element of late modernity."

Policy to Enforce the Law Against Corporations

Corporate crime has become politically sensitive in some countries. For example, in the United Kingdom following a number of fatal disasters on the rail network and at sea, the term is used to refer to corporate manslaughter and to involve a more general discussion about the technological hazards posed by business enterprises and consider incidents such as the 1985 Union Carbide accident in Bhopal, India and the behaviour of the pharmaceutical industry.

The Law Reform Commission of New South Wales puts it thus:

> Corporate crime poses a significant threat to the welfare of the community. Given the pervasive presence of corporations in a wide range of activities in our society, and the impact of their actions on a much wider group of people than are affected by individual action, the potential for both economic and physical harm caused by a corporation is great.

Similarly, Mokhiber and Weismann (1999) assert:

At one level, corporations develop new technologies and economies of scale. These may serve the economic interests of mass consumers by introducing new products and more efficient methods of mass production. On another level, given the absence of political control today, corporations serve to destroy the foundations of the civic community and the lives of people who reside in them.

Discussion

What Behaviour to Criminalize

Behaviour can be regulated by the civil law (including administrative law) or the criminal law. In deciding to criminalise particular behaviour, the legislature is making the political judgment that this behaviour is sufficiently culpable to deserve the stigma of being labelled as a crime. In law, corporations can commit the same offences as natural persons. Simpson avers that this process should be straightforward because a state should simply engage in victimology to identify which behaviour causes the most loss and damage to its citizens, and then represent the majority view that justice requires the intervention of the criminal law. But states depend on the business sector to deliver a stable economy, so the politics of regulating the individuals and corporations that supply that stability become more complex. For the views of Marxist criminology, see Snider and Snider & Pearce, for Left realism, see Pearce & Tombs and Schulte-Bockholt, and for Right Realism, see Reed & Yeager. More specifically, the historical tradition of sovereign state control of prisons is ending through the process of privatisation. Corporate profitability in these areas therefore depends on building more prison facilities, managing their operations, and selling inmate labour. In turn, this requires a steady stream of prisoners able to work.

The majority of crimes are committed because the offender has the "right" opportunity, i.e. where the offender simply sees the chance and thinks that he or she will be able to commit the crime and not be detected. For the most part, greed, rather than conceit, is the motive, and the rationalisation for choosing to break the law usually arises out of a form of contempt for the victim, namely that he, she or it will be powerless to prevent it, and has it coming for some reason. For these purposes, the corporation is the vehicle for the crime. This may be a short-term crime, i.e. the corporation is set up as a shell to open credit trading accounts with manufacturers and wholesalers, trades for a short period of time and then disappears with the revenue and without paying for the inventory. Alternatively and most commonly, the primary purpose of the corporation is as a legitimate business, but criminal activity is secretly intermixed with legal activity to escape detection. To achieve a suitable level of secrecy, senior managers will usually be involved. The explanations and exculpations may therefore centre around rogue individuals who acted outside the organisational structures, or there may be a serious examination of the occupational and organisational structures that facilitated the crime. and around the socio-economic system, gender, racism and age.

While bribery and corruption are problems in the developed world, the corruption of public officials is one of the main causes of crime in developing societies because it is a precondition for much of the state, corporate, and organised crime which occurs. Peear discussing the implications for poiicing in Eastern Europe as it seeks to adapt its laws to match a capitalist model, pointing to the difficulty of distinguishing between lack of morality and criminality in economic crimes that tend to emerge from the structural relationships in modern commerce.

What Penalties to Impose

In part, this will be a function of the public perception of the degree of culpability involved. Weissman and Mokhiber (1999) catalogue the silence and indifference of the major media in the face of the widespread corporate corruption. Only in part is this justifiable. The news media find it difficult to respond to corporate crime both because reporting may compromise the trial by tainting the jury's perceptions, or because of the danger of defamation proceedings. Further, major corporate crime is often complicated and more difficult to explain to the lay public, as against street crime which may provide visuals of victims injured or of property damaged in spectacular fashion. But, more significantly, the news media are owned by large corporations which may also own prisons.

Thus, the political decisions on the resources to allocate to investigate and prosecute will tend to match the electorate's understanding of the dangers posed by "crime". In sentencing, the fact that the convicted individuals may have had an impeccable character as presidents, CEOs, chairmen, directors and managers is likely to be a mitigating factor.

Examples of criminal behaviour in most jurisdictions include: insider trading, antitrust violations, fraud (usually involving the consumers), damage to the environment, exploitation of labour in violation of labour and health and safety laws, and the failure to maintain a fiduciary responsibility towards shareholders.

Corporate Law Economic Reform Programme Act 2004

Corporate Law Economic Reform Programme (Audit Reform & Corporate Disclosure) Act 2004, commonly called CLERP 9, is the most recent reform to the Corporations Act 2001 (Commonwealth) which governs corporations law in Australia. It was enacted in July 2004.

It is based on the reform proposals contained in the CLERP 9 discussion paper, Corporation disclosure - strengthening the financial reporting framework, which was released by the Australian government in September 2002. The CLERP Act also contains a number of reforms flowing from the recommendations contained in the report of the HIH Insurance Royal Commission released in April 2003.

The CLERP Act proposes three bodies to represent a range of interests:

1. The Financial Reporting Council to oversee standard setting for audit and accounting;
2. The Australian Stock Exchange's Corporate Governance Council to oversee the development of best practice guidelines for corporate governance within listed companies;
3. And the Shareholders and Investors Advisory Council to provide a forum for the consideration of retail investors' concerns.

CPA Australia suggested that the legislation should build a framework that also identifies the conduct and practices of boards of directors, staff who prepare financial reports and internal and external audit functions. It also suggested including the roles of institutional investors, credit rating agencies, financial analysts and investment banks.

Corporate Social Responsibility

Corporate social responsibility (CSR) is a concept that suggests that commercial corporations have a duty of care to all of their stakeholders in all aspects of their business operations. A company's stakeholders are all those who are influenced by, or can influence, a business's decisions and actions. These can include (but are not limited to): employees, customers, suppliers, community organizations, subsidiaries and affiliates, joint venture partners, local neighborhoods, investors, and shareholders.

CSR requires that businesses account for and measure the actual or potential economic, social and environmental impacts of their decisions. In some cases the application of a strong CSR policy by a business can involve actions being taken which exceed the mere compliance with minimum legal requirements. This can sometimes give a company a competitive/reputational advantage by demonstrating that they have the interests of society at large as an integral part of their policy making. CSR goes beyond simple philanthropy and is more about corporate behaviour than it is about a company's charitable donation budget.

CSR is closely linked with the principles of Sustainable Development which argue that enterprises should be obliged to make decisions based not only on financial/economic factors (e.g. Profits, Return on Investment, dividend payments etc.) but also on the social, environmental and other consequences of their activities.

Development and Analysis

Today's heightened interest in the role of businesses in society has been promoted by increased sensitivity to, and awareness of environmental and ethical issues. Issues like environmental damage, improper treatment of workers, and faulty production leading to customers inconvenience or danger, are highlighted in the media. In some countries government regulation regarding environmental and social issues has increased, and standards and laws are also often set at a supranational level (e.g., by the European Union). Some investors and investment fund managers have begun to take account of a corporation's CSR policy in making investment decisions (so called "ethical investing"). Some consumers have become increasingly sensitive to the CSR performance of the companies from which they buy their goods and services. These trends have contributed to the pressure on companies to operate in an economically, socially and environmentally sustainable way.

It is important to distinguish CSR from charitable donations and "good works" (i.e., philanthropy, e.g., Habitat for Humanity or Ronald McDonald House). Corporations have often, in the past, spent money on community projects, the endowment of scholarships, and the establishment of foundations. They have also often encouraged their employees to volunteer to take part in community work and thereby create goodwill in the community which will directly enhance the reputation of the company and strengthen its brand. CSR goes beyond charity and requires that a responsible company take into full account their impact on all stakeholders and on the environment when making decisions. This requires them to balance the needs of all stakeholders with their need to make a profit and reward their shareholders adequately.

A widely quoted definition by the World Business Council for Sustainable Development states that "Corporate social responsibility is the continuing commitment by business to behave ethically and contribute to economic development while improving the quality of life of the workforce and their families as well as of the local community and society at large." This holistic approach to business regards organizations as (for example) being full partners in their communities, rather than seeing them more narrowly as being primarily in business to make profits and serve the needs of their shareholders.

Auditing and Reporting

To demonstrate good business citizenship, firms can report compliance with a number of CSR standards, including:

- AccountAbility's AA1000 standard, based on John Elkington's triple bottom line (3BL) reporting
- Global Reporting Initiative's Sustainability Reporting Guidelines
- Social Accountability International's SA8000 standard
- The ISO 14000 environmental management standard

Some nations require CSR reporting, though agreement on meaningful measurements of social and environmental performance is difficult. Many companies now produce externally audited annual reports that cover Sustainable Development and CSR issues, but the reports vary widely in format, style, and evaluation methodology (even within the same industry). Critics dismiss these reports as lip service, a charge that carries some weight given notable examples: Enron's yearly "Corporate Responsibility Annual Report" and tobacco corporations' social reports. CSR reporting draws much inspiration from its much older cousin, environmental and sustainability reporting.

The Business Case for CSR

The benefits of CSR to businesses vary depending on the nature of the enterprise, and are difficult to quantify, though there is a large body of literature exhorting business to adopt measures beyond financial ones (e.g., Deming's Fourteen Points, balanced scorecards). Orlizty, Schmidt, and Rynes found a correlation between social/environmental performance and financial performance. However, businesses may not be looking at short-run financial returns when developing their CSR strategy.

The definition of CSR used within business can vary from the strict "stakeholder impacts" definition used in this article and will often include charitable efforts and volunteering. CSR may be based within the human resources, business development or PR departments of a company, or may be given a separate unit reporting to the CEO or in some cases directly to the board. Progressive companies do not have a CSR department or function at all – the concept is so ingrained in the company itself that employees implement the company's values directly. The business case for CSR within a company will likely rest on one or more of these arguments:

Human Resources

Corporate Social Responsibility can be an important aid to recruitment and retention, particularly within the competitive graduate student market. Potential recruits are increasingly likely to ask about a firm's CSR policy during an interview and having a comprehensive policy can give an advantage. CSR can also help to build a "feel good" atmosphere among existing staff, particularly when they can become involved through payroll giving, fundraising activities or community volunteering.

Managing risk is a central part of many corporate strategies. Reputations that take decades to build up can be ruined in hours through incidents such as corruption scandals or environmental accidents. These events can also draw unwanted attention from regulators, courts, governments and media. Building a genuine culture of 'doing the right thing' within a corporation can offset these risks.

Brand Differentiation

In crowded marketplaces companies strive for 'X Factors' which can separate them from the competition in the minds of consumers. Several major brands, such as The Co-operative Group and The Body Shop are built on ethical values. Business service organisations can benefit too from building a reputation for integrity and best practice.

License to Operate

Corporations are keen to avoid interference in their business through taxation or regulations. By taking substantive voluntary steps they can persuade governments and the wider public that they are taking current issues like health and safety, diversity or the environment seriously and so avoid intervention. This also applies to firms seeking to justify eye-catching profits and high levels of boardroom pay. Those operating away from their home country can make sure they stay welcome by being good corporate citizens with respect to labour standards and impacts on the environment.

Critics of CSR will attribute other business motives, which the companies would dispute. For example, some believe that CSR programmes are often undertaken in an effort to distract the public from the ethical questions posed by their core operations. Some that have been accused of this motivation include British American Tobacco (BAT) which produces major CSR reports and the petroleum giant BP which is well known for its high profile advertising campaigns on environmental aspects of their operations. For a comprehensive survey of attitudes of business leaders in the U.S. towards CSR, there are biannual reports at

Another view

Some critics of CSR, such as the economist Milton Friedman, argue that a corporation's principal purpose is to maximize returns to its shareholders, while obeying the laws of the countries within which it works. Others argue that the only reason corporations put in place social projects is utilitarian; that they see a commercial benefit in raising their reputation with the public or with government. Proponents of CSR, however, would suggest a number of reasons why self-interested corporations, solely seeking to maximise profits are unable to advance the interests of society as a whole.

Key challenges to the idea of CSR include:

- The rule of corporate law that a corporation's directors are prohibited from any activity that would reduce profits
- Other mechanisms established to manage the principal-agent problem, such as accounting oversight,

stock options, performance evaluations, deferred compensation and other mechanisms to increase accountability to shareholders.

Because of this, it has been suggested that CSR activity is most effective in achieving social or environmental outcomes when there is a direct link to profits: hence the CSR slogan "Doing Well by Doing Good". Note that this requires that the resources applied to CSR activities must have at least as good a return as that that these resources could generate if applied anywhere else, e.g. capital or productivity investment, lobbying for tax relief, outsourcing, offshoring, fighting against unionization, taking regulatory risks, or taking market risks—all of which are frequently-pursued strategies. This means that the possible scope of CSR activities is drastically narrowed. And corporations, with their constant incentive to maximize profits, often have identified all areas where profits could be increased, including those that have positive external social and environmental outcomes. The scope for CSR is thus narrowed to situations in which:

- Resources are available for investment
- The CSR activity will yield higher profits than any other potential investment or activity
- The corporation has been remiss in identifying this profit opportunity

A conflict can arise when a corporation espouses CSR and its commitment to Sustainable Development on the one hand, whilst damaging revelations about its business practices emerge on the other. For example the McDonald's Corporation has been criticised by CSR campaigners for unethical business practices, and was the subject of a decision by Justice Roger Bell in the McLibel case (which upheld some of these claims, regarding mistreatment of workers, misleading advertising, and unnecessary cruelty to animals). Similarly Shell has a much publicised CSR policy and was a pioneer in triple bottom line reporting, but was involved in 2004 in a scandal over the misreporting of its oil reserves which seriously damaged its reputation and led to charges of hypocrisy.

Universities and business schools, many of them with keen advocates of CSR amongst their teaching staffs, have themselves come in for criticism concerning their dealings with corporations (note the different stances taken by ESADE and Wheeling Jesuit University with regard to Aramark).

Critics of the role of business in society argue that:

- Corporations care little for the welfare of workers, and given the opportunity will move production to sweatshops in less well regulated countries.
- Unchecked, companies will squander scarce resources.
- Companies do not pay the full costs of their impact. For example the costs of cleaning pollution often fall on society in general. As a result profits of corporations are enhanced at the expense of social or ecological welfare.
- Regulation is the best way to ensure that companies remain socially responsible.

Supporters of a more market based approach argue that:

- By and large, free markets and capitalism have been at the centre of economic and social development over the past two hundred years and that improvements in health, longevity or infant mortality (for example) have only been possible because economies - driven by free enterprise - have progressed.
- In order to attract quality workers, it is necessary for companies to offer better pay and conditions which leads to an overall rise in standards and to wealth creation.
- Investment in less developed countries contributes to the welfare of those societies, notwithstanding that these countries have fewer protections in place for workers. Failure to invest in these countries decreases the opportunity to increase social welfare.
- Free markets contribute to the effective management of scarce resources. The prices of many commodities

have fallen in recent years. This contradicts the notion of scarcity, and may be attributed to improvements in technology leading to the more efficient use of resources.

- There are indeed occasions when externalities, such as the costs of pollution are not built into normal market prices in a free market. In these circumstances, regulatory intervention is important to redress the balance, to ensure that costs and benefits are correctly aligned.
- Whilst regulation is necessary in certain circumstances, over regulation creates barriers to entry into a market. These barriers increase the opportunities for excess profits, to the delight of the market participants, but do little to serve the interests of society as a whole.

Other Perspectives

Some would argue that it is self-evidently "good" that businesses should seek to minimize any negative social and environmental impact resulting from their economic activity. It can also be beneficial for a company's reputation to publicise (for example) any environmentally beneficial business activities. A company which develops new engine technology to reduce fuel consumption will be able (if it chooses) to promote its CSR credentials as well as increase profits.

Some commentators are cynical about the true level of commitment of corporations to ideas like CSR and Sustainable Development, and their actual motivations for responsible behaviour. (Corporations that create the appearance of acting responsibly just for its public relations value are said to be "greenwashing.")

Such commentators also say, citing Friedman's dictum, that the idea of an "ethical company" is an oxymoron, since the corporation is by its nature compelled to maximize its own interest, whatever the external price. Corporate executives and employees in turn have strong incentives to internalize the corporation's statutory obligations to maximize profits, sometimes to the extent that they abdicate their individual moral and ethical obligations as human beings. This tendency is, of course, encouraged by the desire to keep one's job, and by a system that judges and rewards performance strictly by bottom-line returns. The results of this tendency were clearly seen in the many corporate scandals of the late twentieth and early twenty-first centuries.

So the CSR movement may perhaps be understood as an attempt not so much to regulate the activities of corporations per se, as to remind the people who constitute these corporations that they nonetheless have other responsibilities beyond the corporate ones.

INTANGIBLE ASSET

Intangible assets are defined as assets that are not physical in nature. The most common types of intangible assets are trade secrets (e.g., customer lists and know-how), copyrights, patents, trademarks, and goodwill. The Uniform Commercial Code (Section 9-102(a)(42)) defines "general intangibles" as "any personal property other than accounts, chattel paper, commercial tort claims, deposit accounts, documents, goods, instruments, investment property, letter of credit rights, letters of credit, money, and oil, gas, or other minerals before extraction. The term includes payment intangibles and software."

Research and Development

Millions are spent each year by corporations to research and develop new intangible assets. To protect their research and development (R&D) efforts, corporations generally rely on intellectual property laws and unfair competition laws.

General Standards

The Financial Accounting Standards Board (FASB) offers some guidance as to how intangible assets should be accounted for in financial statements. In general, intangibles that are developed internally are not recognized and intangibles that are purchased from third-parties are recognized.

Expense Recognition

Intangible assets are typically expensed according to their respective life expectancy. Intangible assets have either an identifiable or indefinite useful life. Intangible assets with identifiable useful lives are amortized on a straight-line basis over their economic or legal life, whichever is shorter. Examples of intangible assets with identifiable useful lives include copyrights and patents. Intangible assets with indefinite useful lives are reassessed each year for impairment. If an impairment has occurred, then a loss must be recognized. An impairment loss is determined by subtracting the asset's fair value from the asset's book/carrying value. This impairment loss may only be reversed under certain circumstances. Trademarks and goodwill are examples of intangible assets with indefinite useful lives.

COST OF CAPITAL

The cost of capital for a firm is a weighted sum of the cost of equity and the cost of debt. Firms finance their operations by three mechanisms: issuing stock (equity), issuing debt (borrowing from a bank is equivalent for this purpose) (those two are external financing), and reinvesting prior earnings (internal financing). Capital (money) used to fund a business should earn returns for the capital owner who risked their saved money. For an investment to be worthwhile the estimated return on capital must be greater than the cost of capital. Otherwise stated, the risk-adjusted return on capital (incorporating not just the projected returns, but the probabilities of those projections) must be higher than the cost of capital.

The cost of debt is relatively simple to calculate, as it is composed of the interest paid (interest rate), including the cost of risk (the risk of default on the debt). In practice, the interest paid by the company will include the risk-free rate plus a risk component, which itself incorporates a probable rate of default (and amount of recovery given default). For companies with similar risk or credit ratings, the interest rate is largely exogenous.

Cost of equity is more challenging to calculate as equity does not pay a set return to its investors. Similarly to the cost of debt, the cost of equity is broadly defined as the risk-weighted projected return required by investors, where the return is largely unknown. The cost of equity is therefore inferred by comparing the investment to other investments with similar risk profiles to determine the "market" cost of equity. The cost of equity is also known as the discount rate, the rate at which projected earnings will be discounted to give a present value.

Cost of Debt

The cost of debt is computed by taking the rate on a non-defaulting bond whose duration matches the term structure of the corporate debt, then adding a default premium. This default premium will rise as the amount of debt increases (since the risk rises as the amount of debt rises). Since in most cases debt expenses is a deductible expense, the cost of debt is computed as an after tax cost to make it comparable with the cost of equity (earnings are after-tax as well). Thus, for profitable firms, debt is discounted by the tax rate. This is used for large corporations only.

Cost of Equity

The cost of equity is calculated as the "expected" return on equity during a past or future period (usually a year or annualized) based on interest rate levels and historical average equity market return. It can be calculated for an individual company's equity, or for a whole portfolio of companies. For a diversified portfolio, the equity risk is close to the average market risk.

Expected Return

The expected return can be calculated as the "dividend capitalization model" which is (dividend per share / price per share) + growth rate of dividends. Which is the dividend yield + growth rate of dividends.

Capital Asset Pricing Model

The capital asset pricing model (CAPM) is used in finance to determine a theoretically appropriate price of an asset such as a security. The expected return on equity according to the capital asset pricing model. The market risk is normally characterized by the â parameter. Thus, the investors would expect (or demand) to receive:

$$E_s = R_f + \beta_s(R_m - R_f)$$

Where:

E_s

The expected return for a security

R_f

The expected risk-free return in that market (government bond yield)

β_s

The sensitivity to market risk for the security

R_M

The historical return of the equity market

$(R_M\text{-}R_f)$

The risk premium of market assets over risk free assets.

In writing:

- The expected return (%) = risk-free return (%) + sensitivity to market risk * (historical return (%) - risk-free return (%))
- Put another way the expected rate of return (%) = the yield on the treasury note closest to the term of your project + the beta of your project or security * (the market risk premium)
- the market risk premium has historically been between 3-5%

The models states that investors will expect a return that is the risk-free return plus the security's sensitivity to market risk times the market risk premium. The risk free rate is taken from the lowest yielding bonds in the particular market, such as government bonds.

The risk premium varies over time and place, but in some developed countries during the twentieth century it has averaged around 5%. The equity market real capital gain return has been about the same as annual real GDP growth. The capital gains on the Dow Industrials have been 1.6% 1910-2005. The dividends have increased the total "real" return on average equity to the double, about 3.2%.

The sensitivity to market risk (â) is unique for each firm and depends on everything from management to its business and capital structure. This value cannot be known "ex ante" (beforehand), but can be estimated from "ex post" (past) returns and past experience with similar firms. Note that retained earnings are a component of equity, and therefore the cost of retained earnings is equal to the cost of equity. Dividends (earnings that are paid to investors and not retained) are a component of the return on capital to equity holders, and influence the cost of capital through that mechanism.

Cost of capital

The total capital for a firm is the value of its equity (for a firm without outstanding warrants and options, this is the same as the company's market capitalization) plus the cost of its debt (the cost of debt should be continually updated as the cost of debt changes as a result of interest rate changes). Notice that the "equity" in the debt to equity ratio is the market value of all equity, not the shareholders' equity on the balance sheet.

Formula

The cost of capital is then given as:

$K_c = (1\text{-}ä)K_e + äK_d$

Where:

K_c

The weighted cost of capital for the firm

δ

The debt to capital ratio, $D / (D + E)$

K_e

The cost of equity

K_d

The after tax cost of debt

D

The market value of the firm's debt, including bank loans and leases

E

The market value of all equity (including warrants, options, and the equity portion of convertible securities)

In writing:

WACC = (1 - debt to capital ratio) * cost of equity + debt to capital ratio * cost of debt

Capital Structure

Because of tax advantages on debt issuance, it will be cheaper to issue debt rather than new equity (this is only true for profitable firms, tax breaks are available only to profitable firms). At some point, however, the cost of issuing new debt will be greater than the cost of issuing new equity. This is because adding debt increases the default risk - and thus the interest rate that the company must pay in order to borrow money. By utilizing too much debt in its capital structure, this increased default risk can also drive up the costs for other sources (such as retained earnings and preferred stock) as well. Management must identify the "optimal mix" of financing – the capital structure where the cost of capital is minimized so that the firms value can be maximized. The Thomson Financial league tables show that global debt issuance exceeds equity issuance with a 90 to 10 margin.

Capital Cost

Capital costs are costs incurred on the purchase of land, buildings, construction and equipment to be used in the production of goods or the rendering of services. In other words, the total cost needed to bring a project to a commercially operable status. However, capital costs are not limited to the initial construction of a factory or other business. For example, the purchase of a new machine that will increase production and last for years is a capital cost. Capital costs do not include labour costs except for the labour used for construction. Unlike operating costs, capital costs are one-time expenses, although payment may be spread out over many years. Capital costs are fixed and are therefore independent of the level of output.

A fossil fuel power plant's capital costs include the purchase of the land the plant is built on, the equipment needed to run the plant, and the cost of the plant's construction. They do not include the cost of the natural gas, fuel oil or coal used to fire the plant or any taxes on the electricity that is produced. They also do not include the labour used to run the plant or the labour and supplies needed for maintenance.

CAPITAL EXPENDITURE

Capital expenditures ("CAPEX") are expenditures used by a company to acquire or upgrade physical assets such as equipment, property, industrial buildings. In accounting, a capital expenditure is added to an asset account (*i.e.* capitalized), thus increasing the asset's basis (i.e. the cost or value of an asset as adjusted for tax purposes). Funds used by a company to acquire or upgrade physical assets such as property, industrial buildings or equipment. This type of outlay is made by companies to maintain or increase the scope of their operation. These expenditures can include everything from repairing a roof to building a brand new factory. Investopedia Says: The amount of capital expenditures a company is likely to have depends on the industry it occupies. Some of the most capital intensive industries include oil, telecom and utilities.

In terms of accounting, an expense is considered to be a capital expenditure when the asset is a newly purchased capital asset or an investment that improves the useful life of an existing capital asset. If an expense is a capital expenditure, it needs to be capitalized; this requires the company to spread the cost of the expenditure over the useful life of the asset. If, however, the expense is one that maintains the asset at its current condition, the cost is deducted fully in the year of the expense.

An ongoing question of the accounting of any company is whether certain expenses should be capitalized or expensed. Costs that are expensed in a particular month simply appear on the financial statement as a cost that was incurred that month. Costs that are capitalized, however, are amortized over multiple years. Most ordinary business expenses are clearly either expensable or capitalizable, but some expenses could be treated either way, according to the preference of the company.

Chapter 3

Managing Working Capital

WORKING CAPITAL CYCLE

Cash flows in a cycle into, around and out of a business. It is the business's life blood and every manager's primary task is to help keep it flowing and to use the cashflow to generate profits. If a business is operating profitably, then it should, in theory, generate cash surpluses. If it doesn't generate surpluses, the business will eventually run out of cash and expire. The faster a business expands, the more cash it will need for working capital and investment. The cheapest and best sources of cash exist as working capital right within business. Good management of working capital will generate cash will help improve profits and reduce risks. Bear in mind that the cost of providing credit to customers and holding stocks can represent a substantial proportion of a firm's total profits.

There are two elements in the business cycle that absorb cash - Inventory (stocks and work-in-progress) and Receivables (debtors owing you money). The main sources of cash are Payables (your creditors) and Equity and Loans. Each component of working capital (namely inventory, receivables and payables) has two dimensions time and money. When it comes to managing working capital - time is money. If you can get money to move faster around the cycle (e.g. collect monies due from debtors more quickly) or reduce the amount of money tied up (e.g. reduce inventory levels relative to sales), the business will generate more cash or it will need to borrow less money to fund working capital. As a consequence, you could reduce the cost of bank interest or you'll have additional *free* money available to support additional sales growth or investment. Similarly, if you can negotiate improved terms with suppliers e.g. get longer credit or an increased credit limit, you effectively create *free* finance to help fund future sales.

- Collect receivables (debtors) faster
- You release cash from the cycle
- Collect receivables (debtors) slower
- Your receivables soak up cash
- Get better credit (in terms of duration or amount) from suppliers
- You increase your cash resources
- Shift inventory (stocks) faster
- You free up cash
- Move inventory (stocks) slower
- You consume more cash

It can be tempting to pay cash, if available, for fixed assets e.g. computers, plant, vehicles etc. If you do pay cash, remember that this is now longer available for working capital. Therefore, if cash is tight, consider other ways of financing capital investment - loans, equity, leasing etc. Similarly, if you pay dividends or increase drawings, these are cash outflows and, like water flowing down a plug hole, they remove liquidity from the business. More businesses fail for lack of cash than for want of profit.

Sources of Additional Working Capital

Sources of additional working capital include the following:

- Existing cash reserves
- Profits (when you secure it as cash !)
- Payables (credit from suppliers)
- New equity or loans from shareholders

- Bank overdrafts or lines of credit
- Long-term loans

If you have insufficient working capital and try to increase sales, you can easily over-stretch the financial resources of the business. This is called overtrading.

Early warning signs include:

- Pressure on existing cash
- Exceptional cash generating activities e.g. offering high discounts for early cash payment
- Bank overdraft exceeds authorized limit
- Seeking greater overdrafts or lines of credit
- Part-paying suppliers or other creditors
- Paying bills in cash to secure additional supplies
- Management pre-occupation with *surviving* rather than managing
- Frequent short-term emergency requests to the bank (to help pay wages, pending receipt of a cheque).

HANDLING RECEIVABLES (DEBTORS)

Cashflow can be significantly enhanced if the amounts owing to a business are collected faster. Every business needs to know who owes them money how much is owed how long it is owing for what it is owed.

Late Payments Erode Profits and can Lead to Bad Debts

Slow payment has a crippling effect on business, in particular on small businesses who can least afford it. If you don't manage debtors, they will begin to manage your business as you will gradually lose control due to reduced cashflow and, of course, you could experience an increased incidence of bad debt. The following measures will help manage your debtors:

1. Have the right mental attitude to the control of credit and make sure that it gets the priority it deserves.
2. Establish clear credit practices as a matter of company policy.

3. Make sure that these practices are clearly understood by staff, suppliers and customers.
4. Be professional when accepting new accounts, and especially larger ones.
5. Check out each customer thoroughly before you offer credit. Use credit agencies, bank references, industry sources etc.
6. Establish credit limits for each customer... and stick to them.
7. Continuously review these limits when you suspect tough times are coming or if operating in a volatile sector.
8. Keep very close to your larger customers.
9. Invoice promptly and clearly.
10. Consider charging penalties on overdue accounts.
11. Consider accepting credit /debit cards as a payment option.
12. Monitor your debtor balances and ageing schedules, and don't let any debts get too large or too old.

Recognize that the longer someone owes you, the greater the chance you will never get paid. If the average age of your debtors is getting longer, or is already very long, you may need to look for the following possible defects:

- Weak credit judgement
- Poor collection procedures
- Lax enforcement of credit terms
- Slow issue of invoices or statements
- Errors in invoices or statements
- Customer dissatisfaction.

Debtors due over 90 days (unless within agreed credit terms) should generally demand immediate attention. Look for the warning signs of a future bad debt. For example.........

– Longer credit terms taken with approval, particularly for smaller orders

- Use of post-dated checks by debtors who normally settle within agreed terms
- Evidence of customers switching to additional suppliers for the same goods
- New customers who are reluctant to give credit references
- Receiving part payments from debtors.

Profits only Come from Paid Sales

The act of collecting money is one which most people dislike for many reasons and therefore put on the long finger because they convince themselves there is something more urgent or important that demand their attention now. There is nothing more important than getting paid for your product or service. A customer who does not pay is not a customer. Here are a few ideas that may help you in collecting money from debtors:

- Develop appropriate procedures for handling late payments.
- Track and pursue late payers.
- Get external help if your own efforts fail.
- Don't feel guilty asking for money.... its yours and you are entitled to it.
- Make that call now. And keep asking until you get some satisfaction.
- In difficult circumstances, take what you can now and agree terms for the remainder. It lessens the problem.
- When asking for your money, be hard on the issue - but soft on the person. Don't give the debtor any excuses for not paying.
- Make it your objective is to get the money - not to score points or get even.

MANAGING PAYABLES (CREDITORS)

Creditors are a vital part of effective cash management and should be managed carefully to enhance the cash position.

Purchasing initiates cash outflows and an over-zealous purchasing function can create liquidity problems.

Consider the following:

- Who authorizes purchasing in your company - is it tightly managed or spread among a number of (junior) people?
- Are purchase quantities geared to demand forecasts?
- Do you use order quantities which take account of stock-holding and purchasing costs?
- Do you know the cost to the company of carrying stock ?
- Do you have alternative sources of supply ? If not, get quotes from major suppliers and shop around for the best discounts, credit terms, and reduce dependence on a single supplier.
- How many of your suppliers have a returns policy ?
- Are you in a position to pass on cost increases quickly through price increases to your customers ?
- If a supplier of goods or services lets you down can you charge back the cost of the delay ?
- Can you arrange (with confidence !) to have delivery of supplies staggered or on a just-in-time basis ?

There is an old adage in business that if you can buy well then you can sell well. Management of your creditors and suppliers is just as important as the management of your debtors. It is important to look after your creditors - slow payment by you may create ill-feeling and can signal that your company is inefficient (or in trouble).

Remember, a good supplier is someone who will work with you to enhance the future viability and profitability of your company.

INVENTORY MANAGEMENT

Managing inventory is a juggling act. Excessive stocks can place a heavy burden on the cash resources of a business.

Insufficient stocks can result in lost sales, delays for customers etc. The key is to know how quickly your overall stock is moving or, put another way, how long each item of stock sit on shelves before being sold. Obviously, average stock-holding periods will be influenced by the nature of the business. For example, a fresh vegetable shop might turn over its entire stock every few days while a motor factor would be much slower as it may carry a wide range of rarely-used spare parts in case somebody needs them.

Nowadays, many large manufacturers operate on a *just-in-time* (JIT) basis whereby all the components to be assembled on a particular today, arrive at the factory early that morning, no earlier - no later. This helps to minimize manufacturing costs as JIT stocks take up little space, minimize stock-holding and virtually eliminate the risks of obsolete or damaged stock. Because JIT manufacturers hold stock for a very short time, they are able to conserve substantial cash. JIT is a good model to strive for as it embraces all the principles of prudent stock management.

The key issue for a business is to identify the fast and slow stock movers with the objectives of establishing optimum stock levels for each category and, thereby, minimize the cash tied up in stocks. Factors to be considered when determining optimum stock levels include:

- What are the projected sales of each product?
- How widely available are raw materials, components etc.?
- How long does it take for delivery by suppliers?
- Can you remove slow movers from your product range without compromising best sellers?

Remember that stock sitting on shelves for long periods of time ties up money which is not working for you. For better stock control, try the following:

- Review the effectiveness of existing purchasing and inventory systems.

- Know the stock turn for all major items of inventory.
- Apply tight controls to the *significant few* items and simplify controls for the *trivial many.*
- Sell off outdated or slow moving merchandise - it gets more difficult to sell the longer you keep it.
- Consider having part of your product outsourced to another manufacturer rather than make it yourself.
- Review your security procedures to ensure that no stock "is going out the back door !"

Higher than necessary stock levels tie up cash and cost more in insurance, accommodation costs and interest charges.

Key Working Capital Ratios

The following, easily calculated, ratios are important measures of working capital utilization.

Stock Turnover (in days)

Average Stock * 365/Cost of Goods Sold = x days

On average, you turn over the value of your entire stock every x days. You may need to break this down into product groups for effective stock management.

Obsolete stock, slow moving lines will extend overall stock turnover days. Faster production, fewer product lines, just in time ordering will reduce average days.

Receivables Ratio (in days)

Debtors * 365/Sales
= x days

It take you on average x days to collect monies due to you. If your official credit terms are 45 day and it takes you 65 days... why ?

One or more large or slow debts can drag out the average days. Effective debtor management will minimize the days.

Payables Ratio (in days)

Creditors * 365/Cost of Sales (or Purchases)
= x days

On average, you pay your suppliers every x days. If you negotiate better credit terms this will increase. If you pay earlier, say, to get a discount this will decline. If you simply defer paying your suppliers (without agreement) this will also increase - but your reputation, the quality of service and any flexibility provided by your suppliers may suffer.

Current Ratio

Total Current Assets/Total Current Liabilities
= x times

Current Assets are assets that you can readily turn in to cash or will do so within 12 months in the course of business. Current Liabilities are amount you are due to pay within the coming 12 months. For example, 1.5 times means that you should be able to lay your hands on $1.50 for every $1.00 you owe. Less than 1 times e.g. 0.75 means that you could have liquidity problems and be under pressure to generate sufficient cash to meet oncoming demands.

Quick Ratio

(Total Current Assets - Inventory)/Total Current Liabilities
= x times

Similar to the Current Ratio but takes account of the fact that it may take time to convert inventory into cash.

Working Capital Ratio

(Inventory + Receivables - Payables)/Sales
As % Sales

A high percentage means that working capital needs are high relative to your sales.

Other working capital measures include the following:

- Bad debts expressed as a percentage of sales.
- Cost of bank loans, lines of credit, invoice discounting etc.
- Debtor concentration - degree of dependency on a limited number of customers.

Once ratios have been established for your business, it is important to track them over time and to compare them with ratios for other comparable businesses or industry sectors.

When planning the development of a business, it is critical that the impact of working capital be fully assessed when making cashflow forecasts. Our financial planning software packages - Exl-Plan and Cashflow Plan - can facilitate this task as they provide for the setting of targets for receivables, payables and inventory.

Financial Planning

- Recognize the benefits of financial planning.
- Identify the contents of an effective financial plan in a given scenario.
- Determine how much additional financing a company will require, using the percentage of sales forecasting method.
- Apply the cash budgeting model for a given scenario.
- Determine how much additional financing a company will require, using the pro forma Statement of Cash Flows.
- Choose an appropriate planning model for a business that is using financial forecasting.

Short-term Financing and Managing Working Capital

- Recognize the benefits of understanding short-term financing and managing working capital.
- Differentiate between unsecured and secured sources, given a list of short-term credit sources.
- Make working capital management and investment decisions for a company.
- Perform an analysis of the financial risk/return tradeoffs of debt financing.

Cash and Marketable Securities Management

- Recognize the importance o: managing cash and marketable securities.
- Match motives for holding cash with appropriate cash management decisions.

- Determine criteria for selecting marketable securities.
- Choose the proper method of managing cash inflows and outflows, given a scenario.

Accounts Receivable and Inventories Management

- Recognize the importance of accounts receivable and inventories management.
- Calculate the results of a proposed change in accounts receivable policy, given a scenario.
- Choose appropriate inventory management decisions for a firm, given a scenario.

MANAGING DEBTORS

Many debts in the day today business of hotel that are left in 'limbo' there is a genuine need to deal with your creditors before the situation gets beyond your control. This is especially so if you have worthwhile assets. In such circumstances, you either need to deal with your creditors yourself, or get someone to do it for you. The 'art' of negotiating with your creditors is one that does not come easy. Debt Management companies deal with many debtor/creditor scenarios every day, and are experienced and knowledgeable to deal with any mixture of debts:

1. Credit Cards
2. Bank Loans
3. Car Finance
4. Mortgage/Rent Arrears
5. Home Shopping
6. Hire Purchase
7. and any number of debts where creditors exist

Debt Management is a fair and growing service within the UK. It is understandable that banks and finance companies are less than happy to see this service, but even they would find it hard to deny that Debt Management has not only succeeded in getting payments re-started, albeit reduced ones, but that it has also enabled many ex-debtors to come back into the credit scene (love it or hate it, credit is here to stay and IS the second oldest service known to mankind).

If you want to talk to someone about how your debts could be restructured into one affordable payment (without further loans) so that you no longer have to deal directly with your hotel's debts.

Keep track of who owes your business money and minimise the time between when you sell or give away the goods, services or work effort to your customer or client and when they pay you. This process is easier when you have a system to record who owes you money and how long they have owed it to you. These reports will help you to:

- Know how long it has been since the invoice was sent out
- Use facts to remind or negotiate with customers
- List totals of any money outstanding to the business.
- It helps to have a routine to check for outstanding money and a procedure for following up with the clients or customers. This can be a sensitive or delicate process and some people are better suited to doing this than are others.

Some tactics your business may choose:

- Get them to pay as soon as possible
- Maintain constant contact with your customers
- Send invoices out promptly
- Check reports each month and identify overdue accounts
- Follow up overdue accounts promptly
- Use the Debtors day calculation to check how quickly you are collecting cash – Set rules to limit customers who can become debtors
- Agree collection terms with your customers
- Identify doubtful debts
- Monitor bad or doubtful debts very closely

DEBT

Debt is that which is owed; usually referencing assets owed, but the term can cover other obligations. In the case of assets, debt is a means of using future purchasing power in the present before a summation has been earned. Some companies and corporations use debt as a part of their overall corporate finance strategy. A debt is created when a creditor agrees to loan a sum of assets to a debtor. In modern society, debt is usually granted with expected repayment; in many cases, plus interest. Historically, debt was responsible for the creation of indentured servants.

Payment

Before a debt can be had, both the debtor and the creditor must agree on the manner in which the debt will be repaid, known as the standard of deferred payment. This payment is usually denominated as a sum of money in units of currency, but can sometimes be denominated in terms of goods. Payment can be made in increments over a period of time, or all at once at the end of the loan agreement.

Types of debt

There are numerous types of debt, including basic loans, syndicated loans, bonds, and promissory notes. Debt, especially large sums of debt, can also be secured through a mortgage or other security interest over some of the debtor's property, in which case the creditor will have some rights over that property in the event that the debtor becomes unable to repay the debt and defaults on the loan.

A basic loan is the simplest form of debt. It consists of an agreement to lend a principal sum for a fixed period of time, to be repaid by a certain date. In commercial loans interest, calculated as a percentage of the principal sum per annum, will also have to be paid by that date. A syndicated loan is a loan that is granted to companies that wish to borrow more money than any single lender is prepared to risk in a single loan, usually many millions of dollars. In such a case, a syndicate of banks can each agree to put forward a portion of the principal sum.

A bond is a debt security issued by certain institutions such as companies and governments. A bond entitles the holder to repayment of the principal sum, plus interest. Bonds are issued to investors in a marketplace when an institution wishes to borrow money. Bonds have a fixed lifetime, usually a number of years; with long-term bonds, lasting over 30 years, being less common. At the end of the bond's life the money should be repaid in full. Interest may be added to the end payment, or can be paid in regular instalments (known as coupons) during the life of the bond. Bonds may be traded in the bond markets, and are widely used as relatively safe investments in comparison to stocks.

Accounting Debt

In national accounting debts are added according to those who are indebted. Household debt is the debt held by households. "National" or Public debt is the debt held by the various governmental institutions (federal government, states, cities...). Business debt is the debt held by businesses. Financial debt is the debt held by the financial sector (from one financial institution to another). Total debt is the sum of all those debts, excluding financial debt to prevent double accounting. These various types of debt can be computed in debt/GDP ratios. Those ratios help to assess the speed of variations in the indebtness and the size of the debt due. For example the USA has a high consumer debt and a low public debt, while in European countries the opposite tends to be true.

There are differences in the accounting of debt for private and public agents. If a private agent promises to pay something later, it has a debt, and this debt is enforceable by public agents. If a public body passes a law stating that it'll pay something later (a kind of promise), it keeps the right to change the law later (and not to pay). This is why for instance the money governments promised to pay for retirements does not show up in the public debt assessment, whereas the money private companies promised to pay for retirements do.

Securitization

Securitization occurs when a company groups together assets or receivables and sells them in units to the market through a trust. Any asset with a cashflow can be securitized. The cash flows from these receivables are used to pay the holders of these units. Companies often do this in order to remove these assets from their balance sheets and monetize an asset. Although these assets are "removed" from the balance sheet and are supposed to be the responsibility of the trust, that does not end the company's involvement. Often the company maintains a special interest in the trust which is called an "interest only strip" or "first loss piece". Any payments from the trust must be made to regular investors in precedence to this interest. This protects investors from a degree of risk, making the securitization more attractive. The aforementioned brings into question whether the assets are truly off balance sheet given the company's exposure to losses on this interest.

Debt, Inflation and the Exchange Rate

As noted above, debt is normally denominated in a particular monetary currency, and so changes in the valuation of that currency can change the effective size of the debt. This can happen due to inflation or deflation, so it can happen even though the borrower and the lender are using the same currency. Thus it is important to agree on standards of deferred payment in advance, so that a degree of fluctuation will also be agreed as acceptable. It is for instance common to agree to "US dollar denominated" debt.

The form of debt involved in banking accounts for a large proportion of the money in most industrialised nations. There is therefore a complex relationship between inflation, deflation, the money supply, and debt. The store of value represented by the entire economy of the industrialized nation itself, and the state's ability to levy tax on it, acts to the foreign holder of debt as a guarantee of repayment, since industrial goods are in high demand in many places worldwide.

Inflation Indexed Debt

Borrowing and repayment arrangements linked to inflation-indexed units of account are possible and are used in some countries. For example, the US government issues two types of inflation-indexed bonds, Treasury Inflation-Protected Securities (TIPS) and I-bonds. These are one of the safest forms of investment available, since the only major source of risk – that of inflation – is eliminated. A number of other governments issue similar bonds, and some did so for many years before the US government. In countries with consistently high inflation, ordinary borrowings at banks may also be inflation indexed.

Debt Ratings, Risk and Cancellation

Lendings to stable financial entities such as large companies or governments are often termed "risk free" or "low risk" and made at a so-called "risk-free interest rate". This is because the debt and interest are highly unlikely to be defaulted. A good example of such risk-free interest is a US Treasury security - it yields the minimum return available in economics, but investors have the comfort of the (almost) certain expectation that the US Treasury will not default on its debt instruments. A risk-free rate is also commonly used in setting floating interest rates, which are usually calculated as the risk-free interest rate plus a bonus to the creditor based on the creditworthiness of the debtor (in other words, the risk of him defaulting and the creditor losing the debt). In reality, no lending is truly risk free, but borrowers at the "risk free" rate are considered the least likely to default.

However, if the real value of a currency changes during the term of the debt, the purchasing power of the money repaid may vary considerably from that which was expected at the commencement of the loan. So from a practical investment point of view, there is still considerable risk attached to "risk free" or "low risk" lendings. The real value of the money may have changed due to inflation, or, in the case of a foreign investment, due to exchange rate fluctuations.

Ratings and Creditworthiness

Specific bond debts owed by both governments and private corporations is rated by rating agencies, such as Moody's, A.M. Best and Standard and Poor's. The government or company itself will also be given its own separate rating. These agencies assess the ability of the debtor to honor his obligations and accordingly give him a credit rating.

A change in ratings can strongly affect a company, since its cost of refinancing depends on its creditworthiness. Bonds below Baa/BBB (Moody's/S&P) are considered junk- or high risk bonds. Their high risk of default (approximately 1.6% for Ba) is compensated by higher interest payments. Bad Debt is a loan that can not (partially or fully) be repaid by the debtor. The debtor is said to default on his debt. These types of debt are frequently repackaged and sold below face value. Buying junk bonds is seen as a risky but potentially profitable form of investment.

Cancellation

Short of bankruptcy, very often debts are wholly or partially forgiven. Traditions in some cultures demand that this be done on a regular (often annual) basis, in order to prevent systemic inequities between groups in society, or anyone becoming a specialist in holding debt and coercing repayment. Under English law, when the creditor is deceived into forgoing payment, this is a crime. International Third World debt has reached the scale that many economists are convinced that debt cancellation is the only way to restore global equity in relations with the developing nations.

Effects of debt

Debt allows people and organizations to do things that they otherwise wouldn't be able or allowed to. Commonly, people in industrialised nations use it to purchase houses, cars and many other things too expensive to buy with cash on hand. Companies also use debt in many ways to leverage the investment made in their private equity. This leverage, the proportion of debt to equity, is considered important in determining the riskiness of an investment; the more debt per equity, the riskier.

Debt as a whole is a sign that a society is optimistic, that it believes in its future earnings capacity, arguably that it lacks a strong work ethic (though the money must be repaid), and perhaps that it is postponing the solution to present problems (for example, it may compensate a fall in revenues that is perceived as short term by an increase in debt).

Excesses in debt accumulation have been blamed for exacerbating economic problems. For example, prior to the beginning of the Great Depression debt/GDP ratio was very high. Economic agents were heavily indebted. This excess in debt, equivalent to excessive expectations on future returns, accompanied asset bubbles on the stock markets. When expectations corrected, deflation and credit crunch followed. Deflation effectively made debt more expansive and, as Fisher explained, this reinforced deflation again, because, in order to reduce their debt level, economic agents reduced their consumption and investment. The reduction in demand reduced business activity and caused further unemployment. In a more direct sense, more bankruptcies also occurred due both to increased debt cost caused by deflation and to the reduced demand.

It is possible for some organizations to enter into alternative types of borrowing and repayment arrangements which will not result in bankruptcy. For example, companies can sometimes convert debt that they owe into equity in themselves. In this case, the creditor hopes to regain something equivalent to the debt and interest in the form of dividends and capital gains of the borrower. The "repayments" are therefore proportional to what the borrower earns and so can not in themselves cause bankruptcy. Once debt is converted in this way, it is no longer known as debt.

Arguments Against Debt

Some argue against debt as an instrument and institution, on a personal, family, social, corporate and governmental level.

Economics criticism focuses on debt fostering inequality. Islam forbids lending with interest, as the Catholic church long did, and the Torah states that all debts should be erased every 7 years and every 50 years. Debt from a religious view point is condemned because, by tying past and future, it cuts from the present where God is to be found.

Feminism concentrates on the perceived coercive nature of debt contracts. Environmental critics point out the disparity between the material use of resources from economic growth and the limited resources of natural production. Examples would be the low ecological yield of natural resources and the limited usable energy from the sun. Debt will increase through time if it is not repaid faster than it grows through interest. In some systems of economics this effect is termed usury, in others, the term "usury" refers only to an excessive rate of interest, in excess of a reasonable profit for the risk accepted.

CREDITOR

A creditor is a party (e.g. person, organization, company, or government) that claims that a second party owes the first party some properties or services. The first party, in general, has provided some property or service to the second party under the assumption (usually enforced by contract) that the second party will return an equivalent property or service. The first party is frequently called a lender, and the second party is frequently called a debtor or borrower.

In other words, your creditors are people to whom you owe money. The term creditor is frequently used in the financial world, especially in reference to short term loans, long term bonds, and mortgages. The term creditor derives from the notion of credit. In modern America, credit refers to a rating which indicates the ability of a borrower and likelihood to pay back his or her loan. In earlier times, credit also referred to reputation or trustworthiness.

Credit as a financial term, used in such terms as credit card, refers to the granting of a loan and the creation of debt. Any movement of financial capital is normally quite dependent on credit, which in turn is dependent on the reputation or creditworthiness of the entity which takes responsibility for the funds. A similar usage is in commercial trade, where *credit* is used to refer to the approval for delayed payments for goods purchased. Sometimes if a person has financial instability or difficulty, credit is not granted. Companies frequently offer credit to their customers as part of the terms of a purchase agreement. Organizations that offer credit to their customers frequently employ a credit manager.

Credit is denominated by a unit of account. Unlike money (by a strict definition), credit itself cannot act as a unit of account. However, many forms of credit can readily act as a medium of exchange. As such, various forms of credit are frequently referred to as *money* and are included in estimates of the money supply.

Credit is also traded in the market. The purest form is the "Credit Default Swap" market, which is essentially a traded market in credit insurance. A credit default swap represents the price at which two counterparties will exchange this risk – the protection "seller" takes the risk of default of the credit in return for a payment, commonly denoted in basis points (one basis point being 1/100 of a percent) of the notional amount to be referenced, while the protection "buyer" pays this premium and in the case of default of the underlying (a loan, bond or other receivable), delivers this receivable to the protection seller and receives from the seller the par amount.

Managing Creditors

You rely on good relations with creditors for the smooth operation of your business. Suppliers (trade creditors), the bank, and statutory bodies such as Inland Revenue all have a major effect on the cashflow of most businesses. When your cashflow is tight, you may not be able to pay your bills on time. If you manage the situation well, your creditors will have more trust and confidence in you than before. But managed badly, the situation can quickly develop into a major crisis. There are simple steps you can take to help you manage your creditors, and these need to be part of the day-to-day running of your business.

"Put a comprehensive credit policy in place," advises Kate Beddington-Brown, assistant director general at the Institute of Credit Management. "The main thing is to agree everything up front with suppliers, and set out terms in writing. "If you want to negotiate longer payment terms, you may have to pay a little more for the goods. Negotiation can help, but remember - business relationships are most beneficial when both parties are happy."

Make sure you know what will happen at times when you are unable to pay. Is your creditor likely to extend your credit or will they put you 'on stop'? Identify your key creditors: those which have the biggest impact on your business (eg your bank or main supplier); those which might be inflexible (eg HM Revenue & Customs); and those whose services are not immediately available elsewhere (perhaps your IT-support supplier). Then work out the best tactics for dealing with each.

"Form a good relationship with suppliers by being clear in your dealings with them," adds Beddington-Brown. "Find out what their requirements are and then keep to the agreement that you've made. Paying on time helps a lot!"

If you know you cannot pay all your creditors at a given time, prioritise those which are most important to your business and then talk to the others. Communication is key. Explain your exact circumstances and reassure them that it is a temporary problem. This is the best hope you have of suppliers helping you in the short term to keep your long-term business. Avoid delaying payments when it isn't necessary - however tempting this might be. Although, in practice, business credit tends to be interest-free, suppliers have a right to charge interest on late payments.

Beddington-Brown warns against other tactics. "Common mistakes include hoping that unpaid bills will 'go away'; not having a good system in place to clear disputes quickly; not agreeing payment terms at the outset; and simply not engaging with the creditor. Friendly, efficient, open business relationships benefit both parties."

If you are regularly unable to pay your suppliers, it is likely to be because you are managing your cashflow badly. If you are in severe financial difficulties, Beddington-Brown advises seeking advice from your accountant immediately. "They know your company, will understand how bad things are and will know whether anything can be done to improve the situation. Do not put things off. If you do, matters will only get worse," she concludes.

STOCK

In financial markets, stock is the capital raised by a corporation through the issuance and distribution of shares. A person or organisation which holds at least a partial share of stocks is called a shareholder. The aggregate value of a corporation's issued shares is its market capitalization. In the United Kingdom and Australia, the term *share* is used the same way, but *stocks* there refer to either a completely different financial instrument, the bond, or more widely to all kinds of marketable securities.

Type of Stock

There are several types of stock.

Common Stock

Common stock, also referred to as common shares or ordinary shares, are, as the name implies, the most usual and commonly held form of stock in a corporation. Shareholders of common stock have voting rights in corporate decision matters. It is the residual corporate interest that bears the ultimate risks of loss and receives the benefits of success.

Preferred Stock

Preferred stock, sometimes called preference shares, have priority over common stock in the distribution of dividends and assets. Most preferred shares provide no voting rights in corporate decision matters. However, some preferred shares have special voting rights to approve certain extraordinary events (such as the issuance of new shares, or the approval of the acquisition of the company), or to elect directors.

Dual Class Stock

Dual class stock is shares issued for a single company with varying classes indicating different rights on voting and dividend payments. Each kind of shares has its own class of shareholders entitling different rights.

Treasury Stock

Treasury stock is shares that have been bought back from the public. Treasury Stock is considered issued, but not outstanding.

STOCK DERIVATIVES

A stock derivative is any financial claim which has a value that is dependent on the price of the underlying stock. Futures and options are the main types of derivatives on stocks. The underlying security may be a stock index or an individual firm's stock, e.g. single-stock futures. Stock futures are contracts where the buyer, or long, takes on the obligation to buy on the contract maturity date, and the seller, or short takes on the obligation to sell. Stock index futures are generally not delivered in the usual manner, but by cash settlement.

A stock option is a class of option. Specifically, a call option is the right (*not* obligation) to buy stock in the future at a fixed price and a put option is the right (*not* obligation) to sell stock in the future at a fixed price. Thus, the value of a stock option changes in reaction to the underlying stock of which it is a derivative. The most popular method of valuing stock options is the Black Scholes model.

Apart from call options granted to employees, most stock options are transferable. The first company to issue shares of stock was the Dutch East India Company, in 1602. The innovation of joint ownership made a great deal of Europe's economic growth possible following the Middle Ages. The technique of pooling capital to finance the building of ships, for example, made the Netherlands a maritime superpower. Before adoption of the joint-stock corporation, an expensive venture such as the building of a merchant ship could be undertaken only by governments or by very wealthy individuals or families.

SHAREHOLDER

A shareholder or *stockholder* is an individual or company (including a corporation) that legally owns one or more shares of stock in a joint stock company. Companies listed at the stock market strive to enhance shareholder value. Stockholders are granted special privileges depending on the class of stock, including the right to vote (usually one vote per share owned) on matters such as elections to the board of directors, the right to share in distributions of the company's income, the right to purchase new shares issued by the company, and the right to a company's assets during a liquidation of the company. However, stockholder's rights to a company's assets are subordinate to the rights of the company's creditors. This means that stockholders typically receive nothing if a company is liquidated after bankruptcy (if the company had had enough to pay its creditors, it would not have entered bankruptcy), although a stock may have value after a bankruptcy if there is the possibility that the debts of the company will be restructured.

Stockholders or shareholders are considered by some to be a partial subset of stakeholders, which may include anyone who has a direct or indirect equity interest in the business entity or someone with even a non-pecuniary interest in a non-profit organization. Thus it might be common to call volunteer contributors to an association stakeholders, even though they are not shareholders.

Although directors and officers of a company are bound by fiduciary duties to act in the best interest of the shareholders, the shareholders themselves normally do not have such duties towards each other. However, in a few unusual cases, some courts have been willing to imply such a duty between shareholders. For example, in California, majority shareholders of closely held corporations have a duty to not destroy the value of the shares held by minority shareholders. The largest shareholders (in terms of percentages of companies owned) are often mutual funds, and especially passively managed exchange-traded funds.

Application

The owners of a company may want additional capital to invest in new projects within the company. They may also simply wish to reduce their holding, freeing up capital for their own private use. By selling shares they can sell part or all of the company to many part-owners. The purchase of one share entitles the owner of that share to literally share in the ownership of the company a fraction of the decision-making power, and potentially a fraction of the profits, which the company may issue as dividends.

In the common case of a publicly traded corporation, where there may be thousands of shareholders, it is impractical to have all of them making the daily decisions required to run a company. Thus, the shareholders will use their shares as votes in the election of members of the board of directors of the company.

In a typical case, each share constitutes one vote (except in a co-operative society where every member gets one vote regardless of the number of shares he holds). Corporations may, however, issue different classes of shares, which may have different voting rights. Owning the majority of the shares allows other shareholders to be out-voted - effective control rests with the majority shareholder (or shareholders acting in concert). In this way the original owners of the company often still have control of the company.

Shareholder Rights

Although ownership of 51% of shares does result in 51% ownership of a company, it does not give the shareholder the right to use a company's building, equipment, materials, or other property. This is because the company is considered a legal person, thus it owns all its assets itself. This is important in areas such as insurance, which must be in the name of the company and not the main shareholder.

In most countries, including the United States, boards of directors and company managers have a fiduciary responsibility to run the company in the interests of its stockholders. Nonetheless, as Martin Whitman writes:

"it can safely be stated that there does not exist any publicly traded company where management works exclusively in the best interests of OPMI [Outside Passive Minority Investor] stockholders. Instead, there are both "communities of interest" and "conflicts of interest" between stockholders (principal) and management (agent). This conflict is referred to as the principal/agent problem. It would be naive to think that any management would forego management compensation, and management entrenchment, just because some of these management privileges might be perceived as giving rise to a conflict of interest with OPMIs."

Even though the board of directors runs the company, the shareholder has some impact on the company's policy, as the shareholders elect the board of directors. Each shareholder typically has a percentage of votes equal to the percentage of shares he or she owns. So as long as the shareholders agree that the management (agent) are performing poorly they can elect a new board of directors which can then hire a new management team. In practice, however, genuinely contested board elections are rare. Board candidates are usually nominated by insiders or by the board of the directors themselves, and a considerable amount of stock is held and voted by insiders.

Owning shares does not mean responsibility for liabilities. If a company goes broke and has to default on loans, the shareholders are not liable in any way. However, all money obtained by converting assets into cash will be used to repay loans and other debts first, so that shareholders cannot receive any money unless and until creditors have been paid (most often the shareholders end up with nothing).

Means of Financing

Financing a company through the sale of stock in a company is known as equity financing. Alternatively, debt financing (for example issuing bonds) can be done to avoid giving up shares of ownership of the company. Unofficial financing known as trade financing usually provides the major part of a company's working capital (day-to-day operational needs). Trade financing is provided by vendors and suppliers who sell their products to the company at short-term, unsecured credit terms, usually 30 days. Equity and debt financing are usually used for longer-term investment projects such as investments in a new factory or a new foreign market. Customer provided financing exists when a customer pays for services before they are delivered, e.g. subscriptions and insurance.

TRADING

A stock exchange is an organization that provides a marketplace (either physical or virtual) for trading shares, where investors (represented by stock brokers) may buy and sell shares in a wide range of companies. A given company will usually list its shares by meeting and maintaining the listing requirements of a particular stock exchange. In the United States, through the inter-market quotation system, stocks listed on one exchange can also be bought or sold on several other exchanges, including relatively new internet-only exchanges. Stocks are broadly grouped into NYSE-listed and NASDAQ-listed stocks. Exchanges where NYSE-listed stocks may be bought are generally not the same group as the exchanges where NASDAQ-listed stocks may be bought. Many large foreign companies choose to list on a U.S. exchange as well as an exchange in their home country in order to broaden their investor base. These shares are called American Depository Receipts (ADRs) – or, in the case of companies such as UBS and Daimler Chrysler – "foreign ordinary shares."

The most common way to trade stock options is trading standardized options contracts that are listed by various futures and options exchanges – there are currently six exchanges in the United States that list standardized options contracts based on underlying stocks – The Philadelphia Stock Exchange (PHLX), American Stock Exchange (AMEX) and NYSE Arca in New York City, and the Chicago Board Options Exchange (CBOE) which are all open-outcry marketplaces, and the International Securities Exchange (ISE) and Boston Options Exchange (BOX) are electronic marketplaces. However, even for the non-electronic exchanges, competition and the introduction of automated execution (AutoEx) has led, by late 2006, to hybridization where all but the largest trades are executed electronically. In Europe the main exchanges where stock options are traded are Euronext.liffe and Eurex.

There are also over-the-counter options contracts that are traded not on exchanges, but between two independent parties. At least one of those parties is usually a large financial institution with a balance sheet big enough to underwrite such a contract. Large U.S. companies also list in foreign exchanges for the same reason. Although it makes sense for some companies to raise capital by offering stock on more than one exchange, in today's era of electronic trading, there is limited opportunity for private investors to make profit on pricing discrepancies between one stock exchange and another. As such, arbitrage opportunities disappear quickly due to the efficient nature of the market.

Buying

There are various methods of buying and financing stocks. The most common means is through a stock broker. Whether they are a full service or discount broker, they arrange the transfer of stock from a seller to a buyer. Most trades are actually done through brokers listed with a stock exchange, such as the New York Stock Exchange.

There are many different stock brokers from which to choose, such as full service brokers or discount brokers. The full service brokers usually charge more per trade, but give investment advice or more personal service; the discount brokers offer little or no investment advice but charge less for trades. Another type of broker would be a bank or credit union that may have a deal set up with either a full service or discount broker.

There are other ways of buying stock besides through a broker. One way is directly from the company itself. If at least one share is owned, most companies will allow the purchase of shares directly from the company through their investor relations departments. However, the initial share of stock in the company will have to be obtained through a regular stock broker. Another way to buy stock in companies is through Direct Public Offerings which are usually sold by the company itself. A direct public offering is an initial public offering in which the stock is purchased directiy from the company, usually without the aid of brokers.

When it comes to financing a purchase of stocks there are two ways: purchasing stock with money that is currently in the buyers ownership, or by buying stock on margin. Buying stock on margin means buying stock with money borrowed against the stocks in the same account. These stocks, or collateral, guarantee that the buyer can repay the loan; otherwise, the stockbroker has the right to sell the stock (collateral) to repay the borrowed money. He can sell if the share price drops below the margin requirement, at least 50% of the value of the stocks in the account. Buying on margin works the same way as borrowing money to buy a car or a house, using the car or house as collateral. Moreover, borrowing is not free; the broker usually charges 8-10% interest.

Selling

Selling stock is procedurally similar to buying stock. Generally, the investor wants to buy low and sell high, if not in that order (short selling); although a number of reasons may induce an investor to sell at a loss.

As with buying a stock, there is a transaction fee for the broker's efforts in arranging the transfer of stock from a seller to a buyer. This fee can be high or low depending on which type of brokerage, discount or full service, handles the transaction.

After the transaction has been made, the seller is then entitled to all of the money. An important part of selling is keeping track of the earnings. Importantly, on selling the stock, in jurisdictions that have them, capital gains taxes will have to be paid on the additional proceeds, if any, that are in excess of the cost basis.

Stock Price Fluctuation

The price of a stock fluctuates fundamentally due to the theory of supply and demand. Like all commodities in the market, the price of a stock is directly proportional to the demand. However, there are many factors on basis of which the demand for a particular stock may increase or decrease. These factors are studied using methods of fundamental analysis and technical analysis to predict the changes in the stock price.

Technology's Influence on Trading

Stock trading has evolved tremendously. Since the very first Initial Public Offering (IPO) in the 13th century owning shares of a company has been a very attractive incentive. Even though the origins of stock trading go back to the 13th century, the market as we know it today did not catch on strongly until the late 1800s.

Co-production between technology and society has led the push for effective and efficient ways of trading. Technology has allowed the stock market to grow tremendously, and society has encouraged the growth. Within seconds of an order for a stock, the transaction can now take place. Most recent advancements with trading have been due to the Internet. The Internet has allowed online trading. In contrast to the past where only those who could afford expensive stockbrokers, anyone who wishes to be active in the stock market can now do so at a very low cost per transaction. Trading can even be done through Computer-Mediated Communication (CMC) use of mobile devices such as handheld computers and cellular phones. These advances in technology have made day trading possible.

Option Naming Conventions

Stock option names are written in the following format: Symbol+Months+Strike

Symbol = Option Root Symbol

Month = Month the option expires

Strike = Strike price

The basic Trades or Traded Stock Options

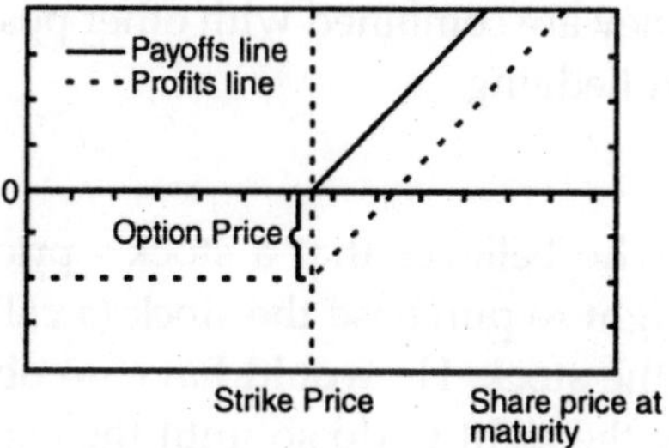

Payoffs and profits from a long call.

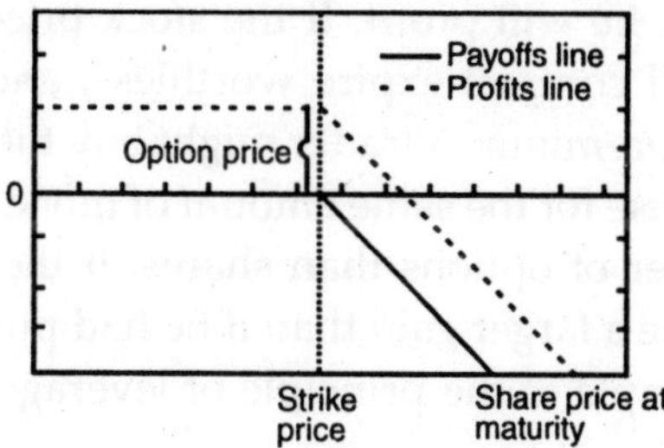

Payoffs and profits from a short call.

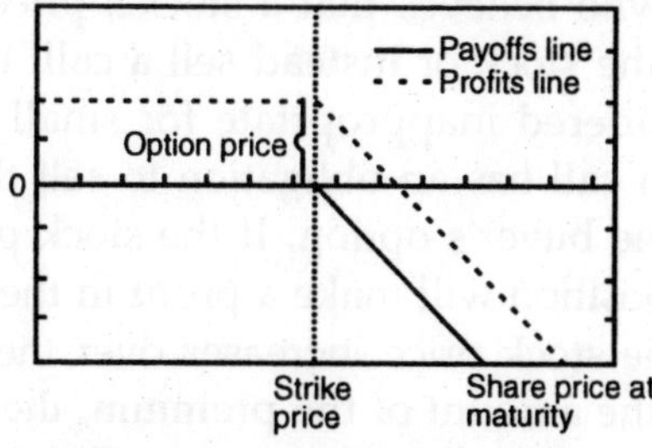

Payoffs and profits from a long put.

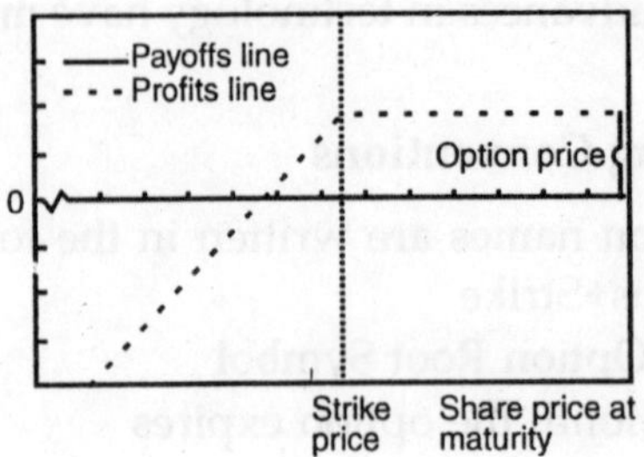

Payoffs and profits from a short put.

These trades are described from the point of view of a speculator. If they are combined with other positions, they can also be used in hedging.

Long Call

A trader who believes that a stock's price will increase may buy the right to purchase the stock (a call option) rather than just buy the stock. He would have no obligation to buy the stock, only the right to do so until the expiry date. If the stock price increases over the exercise price by more than the premium paid, he will profit. If the stock price decreases, he will let the call contract expire worthless, and only lose the amount of the premium. A trader might buy the option instead of shares, because for the same amount of money, he can obtain a larger number of options than shares. If the stock rises, he will thus realize a larger gain than if he had purchased shares. This is an example of the principle of leverage.

Short Call (Naked short call)

A trader who believes that a stock's price will decrease can short sell the stock or instead sell a call. Both tactics are generally considered inappropriate for small investors. The trader selling a call has an obligation to sell the stock to the call buyer at the buyer's option. If the stock price decreases, the short call position will make a profit in the amount of the premium. If the stock price increases over the exercise price by more than the amount of the premium, the short will lose money. Unless a trader already owns the shares which he may be required to provide, the potential loss is unlimited. However, such a trader who sells a call option for those shares he already owns has sold a covered call.

Long Put

A trader who believes that a stock's price will decrease can buy the right to sell the stock at a fixed price. He will be under no obligation to sell the stock, but has the right to do so until the expiry date. If the stock price decreases below the exercise price by more than the premium paid, he will profit. If the stock price increases, he will just let the put contract expire worthless and only lose his premium paid.

Short Put (Naked put)

A trader who believes that a stock's price will increase can sell the right to sell the stock at a fixed price. The trader now has the obligation to purchase the stock at a fixed price. The trader has sold insurance to the buyer of the put requiring the trader to insure the stockholder below the fixed price. This trade is generally considered inappropriate for a small investor. If the stock price increases, the short put position will make a profit in the amount of the premium. If the stock price decreases below the exercise price by more than the premium, the short position will lose money.

Introduction to Option Strategies

Combining any of the four basic kinds of option trades (possibly with different exercise prices) and the two basic kinds of stock trades (long and short) allows a variety of options strategies. Simple strategies usually combine only a few trades, while more complicated strategies can combine several.

Covered call – Long the stock, short a call. This has essentially the same payoff as a short put.

Straddle – Long a call and long a put with the same exercise prices (a long straddle), or short a call and short a put with the same exercise prices (a short straddle).

Strangle – Long a call and long a put with different exercise prices (a long strangle), or short a call and short a put with different exercise prices (a short strangle).

Bull spread – Long a call with a low exercise price and short a call with a higher exercise price, or long a put with a low exercise price and short a put with a higher exercise price.

Bear spread – Short a call with a low exercise price and long a call with a higher exercise price, or short a put with a low exercise price and long a put with a higher exercise price.

Butterfly – Butterflies require trading options with 3 different exercise prices. Assume exercise prices X1 < X2 < X3 and that (X1 + X3) /2 = X2

Long butterfly – long 1 call with exercise price X1, short 2 calls with exercise price X2, and long 1 call with exercise price X3. Alternatively, long 1 put with exercise price X1, short 2 puts with exercise price X2, and long 1 put with exercise price X3.

Short butterfly – short 1 call with exercise price X1, long 2 calls with exercise price X2, and short 1 call with exercise price X3. Alternatively, short 1 put with exercise price X1, long 2 puts with exercise price X2, and short 1 put with exercise price X3.

Box spreads – Any combination of options that has a constant payoff at expiration. For example combining a long butterfly made with calls, with a short butterfly made with puts will have a constant payoff of zero, and in equilibrium will cost zero. In practice any profit from these spreads will be eaten up by commissions (hence the name "alligator spreads").

Uses of Options

Contracts similar to options are believed to have been used since ancient times. In the real estate market, call options have long been used to assemble large parcels of land from separate owners, *e.g.* a developer pays for the right to buy several adjacent plots, but is not obligated to buy these plots and might not unless he can buy all the plots in the entire parcel. Film or theatrical producers often buy the right – but not the obligation – to dramatize a specific book or script.

Lines of credit give the potential borrower the right – but not the obligation – to borrow within a specified time period.

Many choices, or embedded options, have traditionally been included in bond contracts. For example many bonds are convertible into common stock at the buyer's option, or may be called (bought back) at specified prices at the issuer's option. Mortgage borrowers have long had the option to repay the loan early.

Privileges were options sold over the counter in nineteenth century America, with both puts and calls on shares offered by specialized dealers. Their exercise price was fixed at a rounded-off market price on the day or week that the option was bought, and the expiry date was generally three months after purchase. They were not traded in secondary markets.

TREASURY STOCK

In the United Kingdom, treasury stocks refer to government bonds or gilts. The British equivalent of *treasury stock* as used in the United States is treasury share. In the United States, a treasury stock or reacquired stock is stock which is bought back by the issuing hotel. It reduces the number of outstanding stocks on the open market ("open market" including insiders' holdings). On the balance sheet, treasury stock is listed under shareholder equity as a negative number. Stock repurchases are often used as a tax-efficient method to put cash into shareholders' hands, rather than pay dividends. Sometimes, companies do this when they feel that their stock is undervalued on the open market. Other times, companies do this to provide a "bonus" or incentive compensation plan for employees. Rather than receive cash, recipients receive an asset that might appreciate in value faster than cash saved in a bank account.

Limitations of treasury stock include:

Treasury stock does not pay a dividend

Treasury stock has no voting rights

Total treasury stock can not exceed the maximum proportion of total capitalization specified by law in the relevant country

After buyback, the hotel can either retire the shares (however, retired shares are not listed as treasury stock on the hotel's financial statements) or hold the shares for later resale. Buying back stocks reduces the number of outstanding shares. However, the smaller number of shares outstanding is not the reason why stock prices usually increase after announcements of buybacks. To see this, note that achoteling the decrease in the number of shares outstanding is a reduction in hotel assets, in particular, cash assets, which are used to buy back shares. The correct reason for the price jump is that by buying back its own shares, the hotel, who supposedly knows more about the true value of its stock than investors, sends a signal to investors that the stock is currently undervalued. The stock price increases as a response to this positive signal.

One way of accounting for treasury stock is with the cost method. In this method, the paid-in capital account is reduced in the balance sheet when the treasury stock is bought. When the treasury stock is sold back on the open market, the paid-in capital is either debited or credited if it is sold for more or less than the initial cost respectively. Another common way for accounting for treasury stock is the par value method. In the par value method, when the stock is purchased back from the market the books will reflect the action as a retirement of the shares. Therefore, common stock is debited and treasury stock is credited. However, when the treasury stock is resold back to the market the entry in the books will be the same as the cost method.

In either method, any transaction involving treasury stock cannot increase the amount of retained earnings. If the treasury stock is sold for more than cost, then the paid-in capital treasury stock is the account that is increased not retained earnings. In auditing financial statements, there is a common practice to check for this error to detect possible attempts to "cook the books".

If you believe in efficient market theory, a hotel buying back its stock should have no effect at all on its stock price. If the market fairly prices a hotel's shares at $50/share, if a hotel buys back 100 shares for $5000, it now has $5000 less cash but there are 100 fewer shares outstanding; the net effect should be that the value per share is unchanged. However, buying back shares does improve certain per-share ratios, such as price/earnings (earnings per share is increased due to fewer shares outstanding), but that is only because valuing a hotel's shares according to those ratios is not accurate when a hotel is holding a lot of cash. If a hotel's shares are underpriced, then a hotel can benefit its other shareholders by buying back shares. If a hotel's shares are overpriced, then a hotel is actually hurting its remaining shareholders by buying back stock.

One other reason for a hotel to buy back its own stock is to reward holders of stock options. Option holders are not rewarded by dividends, if issued, since holders of options have not invested any capital into the hotel. Option holders are often employees and executives of the hotel that benefit from the rise in stock. If you believe that share buyback programs increase the share value, at least temporarily, the option holder is the benficiary if she/he sells the options.

MANAGING STOCKS

Stock portfolio management is often left to professionals to handle because of the complexities that exist, but for those who want to manage their own investments, there is software available that will help with that task. For those persons who are at ease with numbers and stocks, there are programs that help to evaluate various stocks, educate a person on tracking the history of stocks before investing, and some even make recommendations based on personal information. The investor who wants to take care of his own stock portfolio can do so, but it takes constant monitoring.

Some of the programs available through online merchants even do analysis of stocks for the investor for a monthly fee. There is at least one that can be set to automatically buy and sell certain stocks, according to preset conditions, i.e., they reach certain levels on the stock market. For knowledgeable investors, this could be a time saver in managing stock portfolios. Along with the software for an individual to manage his own stock holdings, there are contacts online for having an expert manage an individual's stock shares.

For the vast majority of individual stockholders, the portfolio is managed by a company with experts in the field who will make the decisions that will protect that person's initial investment and make it grow for future withdrawal. Often this begins at the work place with an employer-sponsored IRA account. The stock portfolio management company handling the IRA accounts for an employer will give each employee options as to how much to invest, and what percentage to invest in certain kinds of stocks. The employee who owns the account can make changes to it at any time by letting the investment firm know through written communication. The investment firm will make recommendations from time to time, if warranted, to keep the investor from suffering large losses. Loss isn't always avoidable when managing stock portfolios, but professionals can at least keep losses from being too large some of the time.

Companies owned by stockholders are part of the free enterprise system, and benefits a great many people. Not only do stockholders get to vote on company policy decisions, they share in its successes. Of course, they share in the losses as well, which is sometimes not so good. It isn't only the rich who invest and need to know about stock portfolio management these days. Anyone can invest money in stocks, and enjoy the profits of a company by receiving dividends on the investment. This practice has become more common in the last twenty or thirty years. Companies often offer stock shares to their employees as part of their savings for retirement. When the company is solid and run by people who are honest, this works well. Of course, there are some rather notable exceptions to that rule.

One thing everyone can learn from events like a company collapsing or declaring bankruptcy is that when investing, it is better not to put all of one's eggs in one basket. The professionals in stock portfolio management always choose a wide variety of stocks for their clients to hedge against large losses. There is always risk with investing because outside events sometimes affect the stock market and will cause serious losses. All investors need to be aware of that when choosing what will be included in their stock portfolios. However, it is also established that there are some companies that have stood the test of time, are solid, and can be trusted to regain those losses and move forward to gains again. As long as those kinds of companies are the subject of most of one's investment funds, there will be gains rather than losses most of the time, so that in the end the amount of money a person has invested will earn a profit. Being careful in the decisions for stock portfolios are as important as taking care in making life decisions. "This is a faithful saying, and these things I will that thou affirm constantly, that they which have believed in God might be careful to maintain good works. These things are good and profitable unto men."

The Patriot Act, which Congress passed as part of the nation's security measures, has added questions that banks and investment firms must ask of potential investors. Picture Ids are now required, and if there are different physical and mail addresses for a client, both must be included in the file. Generally speaking, though, it isn't difficult to participate in this segment of the free enterprise system we enjoy. In summary, stock portfolio management can be something the stockholder learns to do himself, or he can turn that task over to professionals to handle for him. Either way, if one undertakes a strategy of prudent investing losses will be few and gains many.

Chapter 4

Relative Price Changes and Financial Decision

INFLATION, BALANCE OF PAYMENTS

This report describes, reviews and illustrates the underlying relationships between inflation and a country's balance of payments and currency exchange rates. The relationships are illustrated by clear diagrams. Ways of balancing income and expenditure are described.

There is a discussion of the way in which changes in the centrally-determined general interest rate determine share prices, with examples. Also discussed are the effects of multinational operations such as devaluation pricing and profits maximisation, transfer pricing, importing from low-wage countries, transferring work to low-wage countries.

There are worked examples illustrating the effects of changes in the currency exchange rate on competitiveness, pricing and profits. The effect of a weakening currency is discussed in detail, taking into account differing rates of inflation in different countries. The calculations are simple, straightforward and illuminating. They show, for example, how devaluation (weakening of a country's currency exchange rate) is used to drive up profits instead of resulting in increasing competitiveness and exports.

As share values increased, corporations (companies) have withdrawn corresponding 'surpluses' from their company pension funds and added them, or a substantial part of them, to shareholders' profits. But as share prices fall, pension funds can become underfunded. Companies may then be obliged to make up the underfunding to some extent. The likelihood of this happening may be a factor when companies change, or advocate changing, established company (corporation) pension schemes.

Causes of inflation are described and discussed. Particular attention is given to inflation in relation to pay, with worked examples. The calculations are simple and straightforward, with particular reference to how the burden is shared out between different sections of the community.

As costs increase, bitter confrontation and struggle can develop between those who own and employ, and those who are employed, about how to share out the burden. The report point to the large cost of this way of sharing-out the burden among the different sections of the population. Also discussed are criteria for judging the quality of government in relation to a country's balance of payments, inflation and the quality of life and living of its inhabitants. As well as objective ways of comparing different countries worldwide.

1. And this report is one of a series of seven reports which cover, and underlie, the field of General Management, for middle, senior and top management.

BALANCING INCOME AND EXPENDITURE

We all have to balance what we are spending against what we are earning. If we consistently overspend then we either have to earn more or else reduce our spending. Until we make the necessary adjustments, we can increase our spending money by drawing on savings, by selling jewellery, by short-term borrowing from the bank or friends and perhaps by long-term borrowing such as taking out a mortgage.

For a little while our friends or the bank manager will help us by lending money but the loan has to be repaid and we may have to pay interest. The same applies to a mortgage. The interest we have to pay makes our position worse. As a result of having to pay interest we now have less to spend and overspend more heavily. If we consistently overspend and cannot increase our income then we are forced to reduce our spending and thus are forced to reduce our standard of living. Hence we aim to increase our income until it more than balances what we are spending and in this way aim to increase our standard of living.

The same considerations apply to countries, 'Making Ends Meet' which illustrates what is being said here, which illustrates the balance-of-payments interrelationships. Take the case where the total cost of a country's imports is more than the value of its exports. This means that more is being spent on imports than is being earned from exports. We see a payments deficit which needs to be made good as imports have to be paid for, and we pay using our money, that is we pay from our foreign currency reserves.

The value of our currency depends on the assets backing it and on the amount of money in circulation. Included in our assets are our foreign currency reserves. When these reserves drop then the value of our assets drops accordingly, and so does the value of our currency as each currency unit is then backed by fewer assets. Our currency becomes weaker compared with other currencies.

We have reserves which we hold in the form of foreign currency and also in the form of gold. The deficit is made up from the foreign currency reserve. If the deficit persists and we are using up too much of our foreign currency reserve, we can:

1. Increase the value of exports or reduce the value of imports, or do both. And here we need to consider our multinational operations.
2. Increase the amount of foreign currency deposited with us by increasing the interest paid by us to depositors. This is a form of short-term borrowing.
3. Obtain considerable sums for long periods against terms which depend to some extent on our credit

worthiness. Interest charges have to be paid regularly and the loan repaid in due course.

4. Sell some of our stock of gold to obtain foreign currency.
5. Sell assets such as land, hotels, factories and business interests to foreign buyers.There are considerable dangers inherent in allowing such investments to take place on any scale, in allowing control of important assets to pass into foreign hands.

In practice any combination of these may be used, dependent on the circumstances the country finds itself in and on its credit worthiness. Each one affects the country's progress and prospects differently, particularly as regards inflation, as follows.

Attracting Short-term Foreign Currency Deposits

Currency is deposited in another country so as to earn interest. The depositor chooses the country to obtain the highest rate of interest, taking into account the effect of likely changes in the currency exchange rate on the purchasing power of the currency, taking into account also the security of the deposited moneys. Dependent on the general demand for money at the time, which means on the general level of interest rates, one may have to offer a relatively high rate of interest to attract this kind of investment when competing with other countries for whatever money is available.

What attracts deposits is the relative interest rate, and how the currency exchange rate is expected to change. If another country offers more, that is where the deposits are likely to go. So what we are doing is to attract more deposits by increasing our interest rate in relation to that of others. And we adjust our interest rate when other countries change theirs. As long as the money is needed, interest rates are kept high but when the country's earnings pay, and more than pay, for what it spends and reserves increase, then interest rates can be lowered.

To attract foreign currencies so as to keep one's reserves above a certain level, one has to offer higher rates of interest. Other rates of interest increase accordingly within the country and this increases both the cost of borrowing and the profit from lending. So increasing interest rates increase prices, increase the cost of living and increase profit from lending. We hear about the effect of changes in the bank rate, in the general interest rate, on unemployment and inflation. I consider that such relationships are at best indirect and theoretical, have not been proved conclusively either way. As regards such matters, however, what I am doing here is to discuss only selected aspects. Inflation and unemployment are discussed later.

An increase in general interest rates increases profits for lenders (within a country and internationally). It also increases costs for borrowers and thus inflation, but only to the extent to which loan interest plays a part in the costs. So inflation increases profits in greater measure than costs.

General Interest Rates, Share Prices and Pensions

Money moves towards a better investment. If interest-paying investments give a better return than dividend-paying shares, people will buy interest-paying investments and sell their shares. Interest-paying investments are then in demand and their prices increase, shares are not in demand and their prices drop. Share prices may then continue to drop until the amount of the dividend payment (in currency units such as USD) represents a return from the share which is the same as the interest paid by interest-paying investments.

So increasing the general interest rate reduces share prices, and reducing the general interest rate increases share prices. The return from shares (dividend payment as a percentage of share price) tends to move towards the new interest rates. This sample calculation illustrates the mechanism. However, share prices also depend on other factors such as the risk associated with the investment, and the country's creditworthiness as reflected in currency exchange rates. Profits tend to increase in measure with inflation and profitability also determines share prices. So share values may increase steeply, and may be kept up artificially, by reducing interest rates and by keeping interest rates low.

As interest rates were reduced and as share values increased, corporations (companies) have withdrawn corresponding 'surpluses' from their company pension funds and added them, or a substantial part of them, to shareholders' profits. As share prices fall, pension funds can become underfunded. Companies may then be obliged to make up the underfunding to some extent. It appears that the likelihood of this happening may be a factor when companies change, or advocate changing, established pension schemes.

Long-term Borrowing

One can borrow the money but interest has to be paid regularly and the loan repaid in due course. This is an additional strain on an already stretched economy. Britain, for example, had to borrow vast sums annually so as to pay for imported oil until North Sea oil became available. Combined with a considerable increase in borrowing requirements by local government, this materially contributed to the annual deficit. It soon became apparent that it is not easy to reduce one's standard of living, and different sections of the population were confronting each other, struggling to maintain their own level, their own standard of living, struggling for a bigger share of what was available.

Many underdeveloped countries find themselves working to an increasing extent for those who lent them money in the past, or for those who provided essential goods such as oil at high prices, working very hard to export more and more merely to pay interest and repay loans granted in the past instead of bettering their economic capability and the standard of living of the people.

Printing More Money

Instead of increasing the interest rate we can pay our debts by printing more money. This increases the amount of money in circulation. As our assets have remained unchanged, each currency unit is now backed by fewer assets. The value of each currency unit decreases accordingly and our currency weakens relative to other currencies. In other words, as the assets of the country remain unchanged this means that each note is backed by less, is worth less. The resources and the assets and reserves have not changed, each money unit is now worth less than before and buys less and it seems that prices rise accordingly.

The disastrous German inflation which followed the first world war is an example of what happens when one attempts to pay one's way by increasing the amount of money which is circulating.

Selling Gold

Countries sell gold to raise money and this is much like people selling their jewellery. The result is that one has a certain amount of money to spend. But one's assets, and thus in the end one's credit worthiness, are correspondingly reduced. America, for example, at one time was selling very considerable quantities of gold from its reserves in an attempt to get somewhere near to making ends meet, to approach a balance of payments, to prevent its reserves from being depleted.

Selling Assets

Another way of making ends meet is to bring in foreign currency by selling not just gold but also one's assets, to foreigners. Assets here are land, factories, enterprises, human resources. Japanese trade surpluses have been used extensively for buying American assets and those of other countries. Another example is that money earned by the sale of oil at kept-high prices is being used to buy assets of countries which allow this.

Selling one's assets in addition amounts to a loss of earnings as profits may be taken out of the country by the new owner, and also represents a loss of control over one's own destiny. Further, countries like India and Turkey earn much from the amount of money their citizens send back to their countries, to their families, from employment abroad.

Investing Abroad and Invisible Earnings

One may invest one's money abroad and can indeed borrow the necessary money either at home or abroad. The resulting earnings are part of one's income. Income from abroad also includes so-called 'invisible' earnings from selling abroad services such as banking and insurance. A balance-of-payments deficit can be changed from a deficit to a surplus by high invisible earnings. On the other hand one can invest more than the payments surplus by investing abroad, by buying foreign assets. Spare cash enables one to repay loans, to buy gold, to invest abroad so as to increase one's income, and so on. Also, when considering payments balances, one needs to include profitable oil exports and include oil trade balances when comparing international trade figures.

Balance of Payments and Currency Exchange Rates

When we do not make ends meet we become less creditworthy, our currency weakens and so does its purchasing power. It buys less and prices increase. As our currency weakens (devalues) so our exports become cheaper abroad but we have to pay more for imports. This reduces our standard of living relative to others abroad as they find our produce cheaper while we find theirs more expensive. We now have to produce and sell a greater volume of exports so as to earn as much foreign currency as we did before and have to sell even more if we are to improve our position, if we are to benefit from a devaluating currency.

RISING PRICES (INFLATION)

Causes of Inflation

We saw in the last chapter that when we spend more than we earn that the country's payments deficit can be paid for by combining a number of different methods such as increasing the interest rate for money deposited from abroad or by long term borrowing, or by printing more money. 'Causes of Inflation' shows that each of these methods increases prices and thus causes inflation. It seems that printing more money and thus increasing the amount of money in circulation drives up prices to a greater extent than the other two, dependent on how much additional money is being printed.

Effect of Inflation on Currency Exchange Rates

'Inflation and Currency Exchange Rates' gives some other causes of inflation and illustrates what happens as a result of inflation when there is a balance-of-payments deficit. Prices increase also in other countries from which we buy, because their inflation increases their prices and thus the cost of our imports. At the same time prices are likely to increase also because our government may be printing more money to cover its own deficit, to cover the amount by which its spending exceeds its income.

As prices increase so do percentage markups such as profits and dividends which in this way increase automatically in line with increasing prices.

The higher prices are felt by wage and salary earners who demand increases in line with increasing prices, in line with the increasing cost of living. Prices increase as a result, the increase depending both on the extent to which wage and salary demands are satisfied and on how much of the price consists of labour costs.

Our prices have increased, our exports have become more expensive, we sell less abroad, our payments deficit gets even worse. When this condition persists and gets worse then we can devalue our currency, the extent of the devaluation depending on whether we are devaluing

(1) To stay competitive or

(2) To become more competitive.

As a result of the devaluation our exports become cheaper abroad but we have to pay more for imports. The increased cost of imports in turn increases our own prices but only to the extent to which imports figure in the price. However, this has already been allowed for when deciding the extent to which we devalue.

The devaluation reduces our standard of living relative to others abroad as they find our produce cheaper while we find theirs more expensive. We now have to produce and sell a greater volume of exports so as to earn as much foreign currency as we did before and have to sell even more if we are to improve our position, if we are to benefit from the devaluation.

Sharing-out the Burden

It is easier to increase one's spending than to reduce it and one is reluctant to reduce one's standard of living. So one tries to avoid increasing the price of imports and tries to avoid devaluation. Hence one attempts to hold down those price increases which result from incomes rising in line with inflation. In other words, one attempts to absorb rising prices internally by reducing the standard of living. The individual's income does not increase in proportion to increasing prices and this means that the individual sees his own standard of living falling as a result of inflation.

The question which then arises is how the burden is shared among different sections of the population. It is more likely to be wages and salaries which suffer as the amount represented by percentage markups, such as profits and dividends, increases automatically. Even when not paid out, profits and dividends can easily be retained in the enterprise and paid out later. Hence an often bitter confrontation and struggle can develop between those who own and employ, and those who are employed.

Common Myths about Inflation

'Price Inflation' and 'Wage Inflation'

When prices of imported goods increase or wages go up, costs increase. Profit is commonly marked-up at a fixed percentage of cost. As costs increase, profits increase automatically. These profits are paid to shareholders by way of dividends and as capital gains. Part of the profits are paid out as dividends which are annual cash payments. The remaining profits are retained in the enterprise and increase the value of its shares. The shareholder realises this capital gain when selling his shares.

Inflation is an increase in prices, in the cost-of-living. Inflation increases costs. Profits increase correspondingly and automatically. All the profits are given to shareholders by way of dividends and capital gains. The higher prices are felt by wage and salary earners who demand pay increases in line with increasing prices, in line with the increasing cost of living. Prices increase as a result, the increase depending both on the extent to which wage and salary demands are satisfied and on how much of the price consists of labour costs.

So costs increase, profits increase automatically, prices increase, employees struggle to keep up, wages increase, so costs increase, profits increase automatically, prices increase, employees struggle to keep up, wages increase, so costs increase.

It does not really matter where you enter the upward spiral to tell the story. Start with wages going up and 'wage inflation' looks like the cause. Start with profits going up and increasing prices ('price inflation') looks like the cause.

So as prices increase, profits increase correspondingly and automatically and are given to shareholders. Wages and salaries increase only after employees struggle to maintain the purchasing power of their take-home pay and then only to the extent to which their demands are satisfied. The reality is that profits are inflation-proofed and that cost-of-living pay increases are achieved only as a result of struggle.

Inflation and Unemployment

Correlations relating unemployment with inflation appear to be inconsistent, apparently depending on how unemployment and inflation are defined, on time and place. Consider this argument. Say unemployment is low and labour is in demand. 'Free enterprise' competition for labour causes wage rates to increase. Increasing wage rates cause inflation.

The argument then goes that one is fighting against inflation, that low (or falling) unemployment causes inflation so that to keep inflation down one has to increase unemployment or at least keep it above a certain level.

In other words, one is supposed to keep unemployment up, or increase it, so as to prevent free-market competition for labour pushing wages up, as this would reduce profits. This piece of logical-seeming misleading argument is based on the untrue assumption that inflation is caused only, or mainly, by wage increases.

Conveniently ignored by those putting forward such misleading arguments are all the other causes and relevant considerations mentioned in different places in this report including the effect of a country's balance of payments and consequent economic policies on the exchange rate and the purchasing power of its currency.

MULTINATIONAL OPERATIONS

Devaluation Pricing

The effect of a weakening currency on prices, competitiveness and profits is discussed in detail in the Appendix. The calculations are simple, straightforward and illuminating. They show, for example, how devaluation (weakening of a country's currency exchange rate) is used to drive up profits instead of resulting in increasing competitiveness and output.

As a country's currency weakens, the country's exports need to be increased both in volume and in value by reducing prices abroad and in this way increasing sales. However, there is a strong temptation for manufacturers and exporters not to reduce prices below those being charged by their competitors abroad, but to be more than satisfied with the vast increase in profits which results from sitting back and doing nothing other than increase prices abroad in line with prices charged by one's competitors abroad. When this occurs then the benefits of the devaluation are lost to the country as a whole and the few gain enormously at the expense of all the rest. In the case, profits increased by about 90 percent.

The value of assets held abroad, and income from abroad, similarly increase in line with devaluation. Foreign held capital and foreign income appreciate as one's currency depreciates and there is then the tendency for capital to find its way abroad, when such capital should be invested within the country so as to improve its economic potential and for economic growth.

Maximising Profits

Imports are priced at what the market will bear, or just under. The enormous profit margins then cause production to move from high-wage to low-wage countries. The consequence is a lowering of standard of living in high-wage countries to that in low-wage countries, instead of a raising of standard of living in low-wage countries to that in high wage countries.

Effect of Importing from Low-wage to High-wage Country, and of Transferring Work from High-wage to Low-wage Country

Corporations (Companies)

1. Import goods and services which originate in low-wage countries, into a high-wage home country.
2. Transfer manufacturing and service work from a high-wage home country to low wage countries.

The mark-up between buying or producing in a low-wage country, and then selling in a high-wage country, is often enormous. Large additional profits result. Unemployment increases in the home country. There are many costs associated with unemployment such as social security payments to the newly unemployed.

It is accepted as a principle of economics that social costs have to be paid by those causing them, so that the social costs of unemployment have to be paid by the enterprise which caused the unemployment in the first place. The different costs to individuals and community which result from unemployment are listed in the section on 'Social Cost of

Unemployment'. The total cost to the community is the sum of all the items listed there.

Companies, however, are not made to pay the resulting costs of unemployment, are allowed to pass these operating costs to the community and are thus making large profits at the expense of the community. In the UK, an individual was in 1998 reported to have been jailed for seven years for only threatening to contaminate a food if the producer did not pay him GBP 30,000. If he had carried out his threat the social costs would have been considerable and so he was jailed, presumably both as a punishment and to deter others from similar activities.

On the other hand, companies and corporations threaten to make people unemployed, and carry out these threats actually making hundreds and thousands of people unemployed with massive consequential social costs. They also do so for the sake of private profit but no action is taken to prevent them from doing so by recovering the social costs from them, or to punish and deter by punitive sentencing. All for the sake of profit, for personal gain of wealth, power, influence and control over others, for 'empire building'.

Transfer Pricing

A multinational company can minimise its liability for corporation tax by transfer pricing, that is by making book entries which transfer profits to the country with the lowest corporation tax. This tax avoidance is legal and governments have not legislated to prevent this practice. Say a multinational has increased its profits by tax avoidance. The government's income from taxation has decreased accordingly. As the government's expenses have not changed it must make up this shortfall elsewhere. Usually from its other taxpayers, say from its citizens. So its citizens pay more tax, the government can now spend the same amount as before, the multinational's profits have increased.

In other words, the multinational's increased profits arise from money which is in effect collected by the government by taxation from its taxpayers. The multinational, and this means the owners and directors of the multinational, are thus in effect taxing the people and in this way increasing the multinational's profits and thus their own incomes and wealth.

THE STRUGGLE FOR A BIGGER SHARE

Gainers and Losers

Cutting back one's standard of living is not easy and here also the question arises how the burden should be shared. There are those who will attempt not only to maintain but improve their own standard of living while expecting others to bear the economies which have to be made and a harder life, and so conflict develops about how the burden should be shared. Those who are well paid who gain a percentage increase gain far more in purchasing power than those who are badly paid who receive the same percentage increase and who in any case have to spend any increase on necessities.

This applies equally to percentage markups such as profits and dividends. We need to look at the amounts rather than at percentages. Inflation is used to concentrate purchasing power into the hands of those who are already well paid, into the hands of those who are already at or near the top, is used to concentrate wealth and power into the hands of a few. In other words, inflation is used to redistribute income from the bottom to the top, concentrating purchasing power at the top and thus increasing differentials.

The country is in difficulties, fighting first for survival and then for economic success and strength. The standard of living is dropping so that attention concentrates on how to share out what is available, between those who run things and those who work. Conflict results. This attack on the living standards of the working population is misleadingly called a 'fight (or battle) against inflation' to persuade the working population to tighten its belts, to reduce its standard of living.

The arguments by which owners blame the employees' wage and salary demands for inflation while in turn the employees blame the owners' price increases are too often no more than propaganda aimed at increasing one's own slice of the national cake at the expense of the other 'side', at the expense of the rest of the community. The so-called 'fight against inflation' appears to be an economic deception designed to exploit the working population even further. Just how one-sided this is can be judged by the fight supposedly being against 'wage inflation'. Left out of consideration are excessive price increases, profits, dividends or capital gains. Also more or less ignored is the large top-level remuneration which has been increasing yearly for some years at up to four or five times the rate of inflation, increasing each year by amounts many times exceeding the average income of the working population. In such circumstances people work against each other instead of working with each other and we see conflict instead of cooperation.

While profits, dividends and 'capital gains' increase automatically in measure with inflation, a bitter struggle develops as owners and employers attempt to use inflation as an excuse for reducing labour costs, that is wage rates, wages and salaries of the working population, so as to increase profits still further. Employees are then not compensated for increased skill, experience and responsibility (increased merit), nor do they receive their share of the increasing national income and wealth (the betterment), do not receive merit increases and betterment increases. Pensioners also stand to lose betterment increases, do not receive their share of the increasing national income and wealth (the betterment) which is being achieved on the basis of their past labours.

Here is an example. UK pensions had been linked to the index of average earnings but from 1980 they were linked to the cost-of-living index. Hence since 1980 the UK government has, for no apparent good reason, withheld from pensioners their share of the increasing national income and wealth, amounting to something like 2 percent of their pension every year. As a result their present pensions are a fraction of what they ought to be, and would now have to be increased by 34 percent just to reach the level at which they should be now.

And pensioners would still have to be compensated for the moneys withheld from them without good reason by the government since 1980.

This needs to be compared with the closely knit family which not only weathers the storm but finishes in an even stronger position than before. The way in which difficulties are overcome is very much a question of good household management which shows itself in the way in which people work together. People cooperate with each other for the common good in the knowledge that good and ill are shared fairly among them, it being appreciated that the family exists to meet the needs of all its members and that it does so to the best of its ability. The family weathers the storm and gains strength because its members pull together jointly under the leadership of those most able to deal with the particular problems being encountered. It is seen that overcoming tough, difficult and challenging problems depends on good leadership and on all cooperating for the common good, depends on sharing not just that which is bad but also that which is good, depends on reward in measure with an individual's contribution towards the common good.

Profits and Pricing

So profits are apparently being maximised regardless of the cost to others, to the community. Without care or concern for the condition, standard of living or quality of life of the working population. Without being concerned about the in sum-total enormous human suffering which results. Overall, what we see are consequences of decisions made at the top, and the results of putting them into effect. Results and consequences which at times make the decisions seem so brutal that they appear inhuman.

One of the most effective restraints has been found to be the fear of bad publicity, of public awareness of socially irresponsible company behaviour, with its effect on company image, consumer trust and market share, and thus on profits. Particularly so when publicity names those responsible for making antisocial decisions within the company or for condoning and omitting to restrain the company's antisocial activities. In the end, it is prices (that is profits) which need to be controlled, as well as unjustifiable items which are charges as costs when calculating profits.

Quality of Management

Local Government Spending

It is the job of local government to make ends meet and provide the services required by the community including an efficient and effective police force, medical and educational services and amenities. They need to provide a first class service at an economic cost from income provided by local residents and enterprises as well as central government. Local government cannot print its own money and hence finances overspending by borrowing. The increasing cost of debt servicing (interest and loan repayments), which depends on how much has been borrowed, is a danger sign which cannot be ignored.

What stands out is that local government has to borrow and often borrows increasing amounts. If local government is not making ends meet this ought to be clearly appreciated by those living and working in the area and local government's income and expenditure scrutinised in detail. New York's closeness to bankruptcy accompanied by cuts in essential services is a warning of an increasing threat to the quality of life elsewhere.

Local government is responsible for looking after the short and long term interests of its citizens, backed by central government aid for those with inadequate, less than average, resources and for those which otherwise would be unable to provide average services and amenities as judged by results. Local government has to make ends meet, has to be effective and this means profitable, where by 'profitable' I mean that it needs to offer a rising standard of secure living and social security, an increasing quality of life, to its citizens.

Government Income and Spending

We can see from 'Making Ends Meet' that governments which spend more than they receive, attempt to reduce or to make up the difference by borrowing internally and by borrowing abroad. The remaining difference between what is coming in and the amount they want to spend is then made up by printing more money. The illustration shows how printing more money increases the amount of money which is circulating and we saw that this causes inflation and how it does so. In such circumstances there is usually much talk about reducing inflation by balancing income and expenditure.

In other words, we are told that to reduce inflation we have to reduce the deficit and that the way to do so is to reduce government spending, that less has to be spent on essential services to the community such as on education, health services, unemployment benefits, social security payments and social care.

The government spends for the community the money it receives from the community, collecting it through taxation. If it spends more than it collects, then it has to make good the shortage by borrowing and/or by printing more money. Debts have to be serviced and repaid so that borrowing increases future spending, absorbs income, increases the difficulties. But look in more detail at government income and spending. It is clear that to reduce and eliminate the deficit we need to increase income or reduce spending, or both.

We could increase income by increasing taxation but this may be counter-productive. Hence questions which need to be answered are:

1. 'Who contributes how much?', to see how the tax burden is shared among different sections of the population.
2. Who should have contributed but does not?
3. Who ought to contribute more?
4. 'Who benefits at whose cost?' from this system of distributing the tax burden.

5. What is the cost to the community of the deficit which results from this way of distributing the load among the different sections of the population?

'Appropriate Pay' discusses such questions at some length, illustrating them by changes which took place in the United Kingdom over a period of ten years.

It is clear that to reduce government expenditure by cutting social services is one-sided. Why should community services be cut in preference to cutting the vast sums which are collected from the people, that is from the community, and handed over annually to a select few, to owners, shareholders and to those who control financial institutions? These astronomical sums, which are handed over annually, increase the wealth and power of a very small number of people without any corresponding return to the community. They are generally given without obligation to repay, without a corresponding transfer of ownership and control to those who provided the money. No banker, no financial institution, no shareholder would dream of giving away their capital without making sure of retaining ownership and control over this money, through the transfer of corresponding securities and ownership rights, and of direct and indirect participation in the resulting profits.

Very large sums are involved. The array of investment grants, depreciation allowances, grants in aid, tax allowances, tax-free benefits, tax reductions, loans at favourable terms and other ways of financial support to various enterprises in industry, agriculture and services, speaks for itself. How come that the people's money is distributed in such a fashion? How come that corresponding ownership rights are not transferred to those who work in the enterprise, on behalf of the community?

Hence there are further questions which need to be considered:

1. Can we afford to give away such large sums to enlarge the wealth, power and patronage of a very small section of the population at the expense of the whole population?
2. Can we continue to afford to do so at a time of crisis?

The crisis is likely to have been caused or aggravated by inadequate management and administration, so resources including capital are being used ineffectively and are often wasted. In such circumstances one looks closely at the quality of the leadership, of those who direct, of those who manage, one looks at the way resources are being used. Reducing wages (cutting essential community services) merely makes the workforce pay the bill for inadequate management, allows the management to carry on just as wastefully as before at the expense of the standard of living of the workforce.

Demanding a fair return for one's investment (shareholders' investment, bank loans, money provided by the community in various ways) wakens up management to its responsibilities, encourages and rewards good management. Hence while on the one hand one can consider cutting essential community services, on the other hand one can also cut the flow of capital from the community to the select few and in any case can expect a fair commercial and social return to the community for the enormous sums which are annually handed over in this way.

Quality of Management

Just like any enterprise or local government, so national government has to make ends meet, has to bring about a rising standard of secure living and social security, an increasing quality of life to its citizens.

Failure to do so is just as directly and surely the result of bad leadership and management as it is in any commercial enterprise. It is a severe criticism not only of those who lead and manage but also of the kind of experts and consultants they use. Leadership and the quality of one's experts and whether and how their expertise is used and applied, are of determining importance and this applies to central as well as to local government.

Differentials Between Countries

At this point in time the inequalities between countries are of course appalling, as can be appreciated from the following which compares the developed countries looked at in some detail in the report on 'Style of Management and Leadership', but also includes Switzerland which is the country with the highest national product per person, and a few of those at the bottom end who are underdeveloped, poor and in great need.

How income and production are distributed among them? It shows how big a part of the world's population lives within the country's borders and what part of the world's goods and services they produce for themselves and for others. At one end of the scale 0.18 percent of the world's population who live in Switzerland generated and benefited in 1978 from about 1 percent of the world's production, while at the other end of the scale about 18 percent of the world's population who live in India generated and benefited from roughly the same amount. About the same output is derived from and shared by 106 times more people in India, the Indian's share being roughly a hundredth part of that of a Swiss person.

It is the democracies which assist those who are underdeveloped and who do not as a rule attempt to use aid and assistance as a lever or as stepping stones towards control and take-over. But there needs to be control of the way aid and assistance is applied and of who benefits, and one would expect some sort of return, namely some sort of lasting commitment to democracy and to the application of democratic principles. There needs to be some sort of indication that the people are interested in making the effort, that they wish to work their way up and struggle for democracy and freedom, both internally and by international cooperation and commitment to democratic principles.

Devaluation (Weakening Currency Exchange Rates)

Considering competitiveness abroad, we have seen that our export prices can rise to the extent that increasing prices are not absorbed internally by a lowering of the standard of living of some or all of the population. Hence we become less competitive and may then have to devalue or allow the exchange rate to adjust itself so as to stay competitive in the short term and to become more competitive in the long term.

In this way we reduce our prices abroad and become more competitive but as we now get paid less for each item sold we must now sell more items so as to earn as much as we did before. Not only is it essential that we sell more so as to make ends meet but it is also essential that we fully utilise the opportunity presented by being more competitive so as to sell much more. We need to do this so as to end up with a balance-of-payments surplus in order to regain economic strength and power so that we in due course once again increase our standard of living compared with others.

We have seen that currency devaluations adjust the rate of exchange so as to reduce the prices of our exports so that they remain competitive and perhaps become even cheaper. This helps us to sell much more. We have also seen that the price paid for this is a lowering of the standard of living of the population as a whole, so that it is important to do all one can to make full use of the opportunity presented by a devaluation so as to regain one's strength through selling far more than before. This means that we need to lower the foreign currency prices of our exports accordingly.

Only too often do producers and exporters charge abroad what the market will bear, charging the highest price their goods will fetch, without reducing prices when their currency is devalued. The result is that the producer's and exporter's profits increase enormously but at the expense of a general lowering of the standard of living of the country as a whole, because they sell the same volume as before but make a far greater profit on each sale. In this way they use devaluation to increase their profits but from the point of view of the country as a whole production does not increase as the number of items sold does not increase. Prices have not been lowered, there is no corresponding gain in the volume of production, that is in economic growth.

We saw that as our currency weakens (devalues) so our standard of living is reduced relative to others abroad. So these greater profits are made at the expense of a general lowering of the standard of living of the country as a whole. And as prices have not been lowered, there is no corresponding gain in the volume of production, that is in economic growth. And the greatly increased profit redistributes income and wealth from the general population whose standard of living is falling, distributing it to those at the top who benefit from such profit increases. The calculations are simple and straightforward, as can be seen from the following examples.

Inflation and Pricing, Currency Devaluation and Competitiveness

An article contains imported items and column 1 shows that 25 percent of the price is for imported items, that internally produced items amount to 65 percent of the price, the remainder being a clear profit of 10 percent. Assuming that the price of the article is GBP 100 at the beginning of the year, column 2 shows how the price is made up.

Assuming an internal rate of inflation of 25 percent and an external rate of inflation in other countries of 5 percent, then the price after one year is that shown in column 4. The imported price component is increased by 5 percent, while internal price component and clear profit have each increased by 25 percent. As inflation abroad is much less than the internal rise in prices, 25 percent of the price of the article being for imported items, the overall increase in price (20 percent) is considerably less than the internal rate of inflation (25 percent).

Assuming that the same article is being exported to and sold in Germany and that the currency exchange rate is 4 DEM/GBP, then the article which sold for DEM 400 at the beginning of the year would have to be sold for DEM 480 at the end of the year. But, during this same period, prices increased by only 5 percent in Germany and the cost of the equivalent German article increased as a result of their inflation from DEM 400 to DEM 420.

It is seen that we have become less competitive abroad as the article we previously sold at DEM 400 in competition with an equivalent German article also selling at DEM 400, is now being sold by us at DEM 480 while the competing German article now sells for only DEM 420.

Devaluing to Remain Competitive

Similarly we can follow what happens when we devalue so as to remain competitive. Here we continue the previous example by devaluing to remain competitive, that is by adjusting the currency exchange rate from 4 DEM/GBP to 3.36 DEM/GBP, which has the effect of reducing the price abroad of our own article from DEM 480 to DEM 420. As a result of this devaluation we now have to pay more for our imports. The imported items cost DEM 105 which at the old exchange rate of 4 DEM/GBP amounted to GBP 26.30. At the new exchange rate we have to pay GBP 31.30 for the same imported items. The new exchange rate of DEM 3.36/GBP already allows for this. The overall effect is that our price has increased internally from GBP 120 up to GBP 125 as a result of the higher cost of imports and that we have reduced the price of the article abroad from DEM 480 to DEM 420.

Devaluing to Become More Competitive Abroad

If we devalue further so as to become more competitive by lowering our price abroad below that being charged by our competitors, then our internal price again increases a little because of the higher cost of imported items. Continuing with the same example, it is seen (column 2) that if we devalue our currency so that the exchange rate becomes 3 DEM/GBP then the internal price increases to roughly GBP 129 which at the new exchange rate amounts to about DEM 386.

This devaluation thus reduced our price abroad to DEM 386, this being about 8 percent below our foreign competitor's price of DEM 420. Our price is 8 percent below our competitor's, a very useful competitive advantage. However, this competitive advantage has been gained at a very considerable drop in the standard of living of the population, compared with others abroad, as we devalued by about 30 percent.

At the new exchange rate of 3 DEM/GBP, they now receive GBP 140 for each article. As internal costs and the cost of imported items remain unchanged, all the extra money collected is clear profit.

The country's exports need to be increased both in volume and in value by reducing prices abroad and in this way increasing sales. However, there is a strong temptation for manufacturers and exporters not to reduce prices below those being charged by their competitors abroad, but to be more than satisfied with the vast increase in profits which results from sitting back and doing nothing other than increase prices abroad in line with prices charged by one's competitors abroad. When this occurs then the benefits of the devaluation are lost to the country as a whole and the few gain enormously at the expense of all the rest.

Chapter 5

Computers and Financial Decision Making

INTELLIGENT TASK

Costs are either one-off, or may be ongoing. Benefits are most often received over time. We build this effect of time into our analysis by calculating a payback period. This is the time it takes for the benefits of a change to repay its costs. Many companies look for payback over a specified period of time e.g. three years.

How to Use Tool

In its simple form, cost-benefit analysis is carried out using only financial costs and financial benefits. For example, a simple cost benefit ration for a road scheme would measure the cost of building the road, and subtract this from the economic benefit of improving transport links. It would not measure either the cost of environmental damage or the benefit of quicker and easier travel to work.

A more sophisticated approach to building a cost benefit models is to try to put a financial value on intangible costs and benefits. This can be highly subjective - is, for example, a historic water meadow worth $25,000, or is it worth $500,000 because if its environmental importance? What is the value of stress-free travel to work in the morning? These are all questions that people have to answer, and answers that people have to defend.

The version of the cost benefit approach we explain here is necessarily simple. Where large sums of money are involved (for example, in financial market transactions), project evaluation can become an extremely complex and sophisticated art. The fundamentals of this are explained in Principles of Corporate Finance by Richard Brealey and Stewart Myers - this is something of a 'bible' on the subject. The book is reviewed at the top of our right hand side bar.

Example

A sales director is deciding whether to implement a new computer-based contact management and sales processing system. His department has only a few computers, and his salespeople are not computer literate. He is aware that computerized sales forces are able to contact more customers and give a higher quality of reliability and service to those customers. They are more able to meet commitments, and can work more efficiently with fulfilment and delivery staff.

Inevitably the estimates of the benefit given by the new system are quite subjective. Despite this, the Sales Director is very likely to introduce it, given the short payback time.

Key Points

Cost/Benefit Analysis is a powerful, widely used and relatively easy tool for deciding whether to make a change. To use the tool, firstly work out how much the change will cost to make. Then calculate the benefit you will from it. Where costs or benefits are paid or received over time, work out the time it will take for the benefits to repay the costs. Cost/Benefit Analysis can be carried out using only financial costs and financial benefits. You may, however, decide to include intangible items within the analysis. As you must estimate a value for these, this inevitably brings an element of subjectivity into the process.

SPREADSHEET

A spreadsheet is a rectangular table (or grid) of information, often financial information. The word came from "spread" in its sense of a newspaper or magazine item (text and/or graphics) that covers two facing pages, extending across the center fold and treating the two pages as one large one. The compound word "spread-sheet" came to mean the format used to present bookkeeping ledgers—with columns for categories of expenditures across the top, invoices listed down the left margin, and the amount of each payment in the cell where its row and column intersect—which were traditionally a "spread" across facing pages of a bound ledger (book for keeping accounting records) or on oversized sheets of paper ruled into rows and columns in that format and approximately twice as wide as ordinary paper.

Batch Spreadsheets

One of the first commercial uses of computers was in processing payroll and other financial records, so the programs (and, indeed, the programming languages themselves) were designed to generate reports in the standard "spreadsheet" format bookkeepers and accountants used. As computers became more available and affordable in the last quarter of the 20th century, more software became available for them, and programs to keep financial records and generate spreadsheet reports were always in demand. Those spreadsheet programs can be used to tabulate many kinds of information, not just financial records, so the term "spreadsheet" has developed a more general meaning as information presented in a rectangular table, usually generated by a computer.

The concept of an electronic spreadsheet was outlined in the 1961 paper "Budgeting Models and System Simulation" by Richard Mattessich. Some credit for the computerized spreadsheet perhaps belongs to Rene K. Pardo and Remy Landau, who filed U.S. Patent 4,398,249 on some of the related algorithms in 1970. While the patent was initially rejected by the patent office as being a purely mathematical invention, Pardo and Landau won a court case in 1983 establishing that "something does not cease to become patentable merely because the point of novelty is in an algorithm." This case helped establish the viability of software patents.

Interactive Spreadsheets

It was not until the ready availability of visual display units ("VDU's") that fully interactive spreadsheets became possible. Earlier implementations were mainly designed around batch programs. In the early 1970's text based VDU's began to be used as input/output devices for interactive transaction processes. It was several years later before full function graphic user interfaces were available for spreadsheets.

The generally recognized inventor of the spreadsheet as a commercial product for the personal computer is Dan Bricklin although a fully interactive implementation produced in the United Kingdom at Imperial Chemical Industries, running on an IBM mainframe platform using CICS pre-dated Bricklin's version by several years even featuring shared public spreadsheets from the outset.

Works Records System

The system, known as "The Works Records System", was designed by Robert Mais then an employee of ICI Mond Division in the UK and was implemented in 1974 by a team which included Ken Dakin, author of several successful CICS debugging products which were used extensively during its development to ensure the highest possible performance by detecting "hot spots" (high execution locations) during code execution.

All operations were performed using "double precision" floating point arithmetic and formulae (which performed calculations and linked cells, either in the same spreadsheet or in completely separate spreadsheets) could be entered on multiple lines to aid comprehension. Formulae were converted (compiled) to "machine" language "on the fly" on first use and stored for subsequent executions.This technique is now known as Just-in-time compilation (JIT) or, more specifically, "incremental compilation" - but given no label at the time.

Data including "aged" values was stored using an Adabas database (described as a "Relational Like" database in the Wikipedia article about Adabas, although it was not fundamental to the operation of the system).

The IBM 3270 workstation chosen for its implementation at the time was a new "breed" of not so dumb terminals which had some basic built-in hardware validity checking such as 'numeric only' input fields.

Despite the limitations of the device, the input screens could nevetheless be designed interactively by non programmers by using simple "<" and ">" as "field" (cell) delimiters during "the design phase" (building the spreadsheet). As with modern day word processors, these "tab characters" would not normally be visible during normal usage. The same technique was used to define "on screen" the layouts of printed reports that were not limited to the 80 column screen width of the 3270.

It is interesting to note that the system was capable of detecting some illogical operations because of a "units" attribute (such as "kilograms", "ounces", "feet" or "inches") for numeric values (analogous to currency symbol attributes in today's spreadsheets). It was impossible therefore to multiply kilograms by ounces or commit similar logic errors.

By contrast, today's commercial spreadsheets will willingly allow a column of mixed currencies (say pounds and dollars) for example, to be summed or multiplied with not even a warning. The Works records system represents the first known use of a shared public spreadsheet since it allowed multiple users to access the linked spreadsheets across a private online network covering many remote locations.

Apldot

Another example of an "industrial weight" spreadsheet produced two years later in 1976 at the United States Railway Association on an IBM 360/91 running at The John Hopkins University Applied Physics Laboratory in Laurel MD. The application, named APLDOT, was used successfully for many years in developing such applications as financial and costing models for the US Congress and for Conrail.All software development was in the public domain. The software system underwent a court challenge in US Government vs PennCentral Et al. in 1978, 1979. It was dubbed a "spreadsheet" because that was what the financial analysts and strategic planners called those green pads they used to do their planning on in 1976.

Visicalc

Dan Bricklin has spoken of watching his university professor create a table of calculation results on a blackboard. When the professor found an error, he had to tediously erase and rewrite a number of sequential entries in the table, triggering Bricklin to think that he could replicate the process on a computer, using the blackboard as the model to view results of underlying formulas. His idea became VisiCalc, the first application that turned the personal computer from a hobby for computer enthusiasts into a business tool.

VisiCalc went on to become the first "killer app", an application that was so compelling, people would buy a particular computer just to own it. In this case the computer was the Apple II, and VisiCalc was no small part in that machine's success. The Programme was later ported to a number of other early computers, notably CP/M machines, the Atari 8-bit family and various Commodore platforms. Nevertheless, VisiCalc remains best known as "an Apple II Programme".

The acceptance of the IBM PC following its introduction in August, 1981, began slowly, because most of the programs available for it were ports from other 8-bit platforms. Things changed dramatically with the introduction of Lotus 1-2-3 in November, 1982, and release for sale in January, 1983. It became that platform's killer app, and drove sales of the PC due to the improvements in speed and graphics compared to VisiCalc. VisiCorp was unable to respond competitively, and disappeared within a few years.

Lotus 1-2-3 underwent an almost identical cycle with the introduction of Windows 3.x in the late 1980s. Microsoft had been developing Excel on the Macintosh platform for several years at this point, and it had developed into a fairly powerful system. A port to Windows 3.1 resulted in a fully functional Windows spreadsheet which quickly took over from Lotus in the early 1990s. By the time Lotus responded with a usable Windows version of their own, Microsoft had started compiling their Office suite, which still dominates the industry.

A number of companies have attempted to break into the spreadsheet market with programs based on very different paradigms. Lotus introduced what is likely the most successul example, Lotus Improv, which saw some commercial success, notably in the financial world where its powerful data mining capabilities remain well respected to this day. Spreadsheet 2000 attempted to dramatically simplify formula construction, but was generally not successful. Stories attempted to make it easier to deal with 3-D blocks of data (as opposed to the 2-D nature of most spreadsheets), but appears to have seen little or no use.

Programming Issues

Just as the early programming languages were designed to generate spreadsheet printouts, programming techniques themselves have evolved to process tables (also known as spreadsheets or matrices) of data more efficiently in the computer itself. Spreadsheets have evolved into powerful programming languages; specifically, they are functional, visual, and multiparadigm languages.

Many people find it easier to perform calculations in spreadsheets than by writing the equivalent sequential Programme. This is due to two traits of spreadsheets. They use spatial relationships to define Programme relationships. Like all animals, humans have highly developed intuitions about spaces, and of dependencies between items. Sequential programming usually requires typing line after line of text, which must be read slowly and carefully to be understood and changed.

They are forgiving, allowing partial results and functions to work. One or more parts of a Programme can work correctly, even if other parts are unfinished or broken. This makes writing and debugging programs much easier, and faster. Sequential programming usually needs every Programme line and character to be correct for a Programme to run. One error usually stops the whole Programme and prevents any result. A spreadsheet Programme is designed to perform general computation tasks using spatial relationships rather than time as the primary organizing principle. Many programs designed to perform general computation use timing, the ordering of computational steps, as their primary way to organize a Programme. A well defined entry point is used to determine the first instructions, and all other instructions must be reachable from that point.

In a spreadsheet, however, a set of cells is defined, with a spatial relation to one another. In the earliest spreadsheets, these arrangements were a simple two-dimensional grid. Over time, the model has been expanded to include a third dimension, and in some cases a series of named grids. The most advanced examples allow inversion and rotation operations which can slice and project the data set in various ways.

The cells are functionally equivalent to variables in a sequential programming model. Cells often have a formula, a set of instructions which can be used to compute the value of a cell. Formulas can use the contents of other cells or external variables such as the current date and time. It is often convenient to think of a spreadsheet as a mathematical graph, where the nodes are spreadsheet cells, and the edges are references to other cells specified in formulas. This is often called the dependency graph of the spreadsheet. References between cells can take advantage of spatial concepts such as relative position and absolute position, as well as named locations, to make the spreadsheet formulas easier to understand and manage.

Spreadsheets usually attempt to automatically update cells when the cells on which they depend have been changed.

The earliest spreadsheets used simple tactics like evaluating cells in a particular order, but modern spreadsheets compute a minimal recomputation order from the dependency graph. Later spreadsheets also include a limited ability to propagate values in reverse, altering source values so that a particular answer is reached in a certain cell. Since spreadsheet cells formulas are not generally invertable, though, this technique is of somewhat limited value.

A cell may contain a value or a formula, or be empty. In addition it can contain information about the data type of the data it holds, or expects when a value is entered. This may determine the format in which a value is displayed, and the allowed operations on it. A formula often contains references to other cells. Such a cell reference is a kind of variable. Its value is the value of the referenced cell. If that cell in turn references other cells, the value depends on the values of those. Note that in general the cell content should be distinguished from the cell value.

A typical cell reference consists of one or two case-insensitive letters to identify the column (if there are up to 256 columns: A-Z and AA-IV) followed by a row number (e.g. in the range 1-65536). Either part can be relative (it changes when the formula it is in is moved or copied), or absolute (indicated with $ in front of the part concerned of the cell reference).

Many of the concepts common to sequential programming models have analogues in the spreadsheet world. For example, the sequential model of the indexed loop is usually represented as a table of cells, with similar formulas.

Shortcomings

While extremely popular, spreadsheets are not without their downsides. Some of the problems associated with spreadsheets include:

Lack of auditing and revision control. This makes it difficult to determine who changed what and when. This can cause problems with regulatory compliance, among other things.

Lack of security. Generally, if one has permission to open a spreadsheet, one has permission to modify any part of it. This, combined with the lack of auditing above, can make it easy for someone to commit fraud.

Lack of concurrency. Unlike databases, spreadsheets typically allow only one user to be making changes at any given time.

Because they are loosely structured, it is easy for someone to introduce an error, either accidentally or intentionally, by entering information in the wrong place or expressing dependencies among cells (such as in a formula) incorrectly.

The results of a Formula (example "=A1*B1") applies only to a single cell (that is, the cell the formula is actually located in - in this case perhaps C1), even though it can "extract" data from many other cells, and even real time dates and actual times. This means that to cause a similar calculation on an array of cells, an almost identical formula (but residing in its own "output" cell) must be repeated for each row of the "input" array.This differs from a "formula" in a conventional computer Programme which would typically have one calculation which would then apply to all of the input in turn. With current spreadsheets, this forced repetition of near identical formulae can have detrimental consequences from a quality assurance standpoint and is often the cause of many spreadsheet errors.This last problem could be solved conceptually, simply by permitting the specification of a new category of "spatially independent" formula, allowing the "left hand" (target) of the formula to be entered combined with use of "indexed cell addressing" of the generic form:-

This theoretical category of formula could reside anywhere within the spreadsheet since its target cell(s) are specified independently of their location in the spreadsheet. (However, for clarity, the "cloned" formula could optionally be shown in each target cell, any change to one affecting all its clones automatically, thereby reducing errors) or, to conform more to current "spreadsheet like" syntax perhaps:-

To be applied to each occurence - but entered only in the first cell, the rest of them displaying the cloned formula.

With the recent advent of remote data update of cells, the need to specify conditional formula of this type will assume a new urgency since the precise contents and extents of external spreadsheets may not be fully discernable before execution.

While there are built-in and third-party tools for desktop spreadsheet applications that address some of these shortcomings, awareness of these is generally low, and usage lower still. However, many of these earlier shortcomings can be handled by online spreadsheets such as EditGrid and Google Docs & Spreadsheets.

THE CASE PROJECTS

The Dynamic Strategic Planning workbook is accompanied by a number of spreadsheet-based tools for data analysis. We have supplied these tools so that the users of this workbook can concentrate upon the use and implementation of decision analysis and strategic planning, rather than focusing upon the mechanics of the mathematics underlying their use. The current form of the spreadsheets is a consequence of a combination of factors: academic research, pedagogical design, and in-class experiences. Based upon new developments, they are being routinely improved.

However, no amount of care in tool design can substitute for expertise on the part of the user. The case projects have been designed assuming that these tools will be used effectively. The purpose of this document is to assure that you, the user of these tools, are prepared to exploit them to their fullest - specifically, that you are able to make use of spreadsheet sensitivity analysis tools.

Spreadsheet Basics

Electronic spreadsheets (as opposed to the paper kind!) have revolutionized business analysis. This should be no surprise, given that one of the developers of the original tool, Visicalc, was a Harvard Business School dropout who recognized that a computer-based tool to facilitate business analysis would have made his life a little simpler at the HBS, and might even help managers when they got out into the real world. However, it took the happy historical coincidence of the personal computer, and the concomitant dispersion of computer power to every modern manager's desk, to assure the success of the concept. Conceptually, the spreadsheet is simply a representation of the original accountant's paper spreadsheet, composed of finely lined pages of labeled columns of numbers. The original concept was to provide the user with a way not only to present these numbers, but also to embed the mathematical relationship *between* those numbers, so that the implications of different assumptions could be easily and consistently prepared.

Given the prevalence of the spreadsheet, we assume that the reader is conversant with the basics of their use. In particular, we assume that you can easily accomplish the following tasks:

1. Start the spreadsheet Programme running;
2. Load and save your spreadsheet work;
3. Print the contents of your spreadsheet; and
4. Construct simple mathematical relationships between spreadsheet cells.

If these tasks are daunting to you, we hope that you can use the "F1" Help functions that accompany these programs. Furthermore, we assume that you are aware that spreadsheets can be used to perform the following functions, even though you may not be fully conversant with all aspects of them:

1. The ability to embed functions more complex than the basic arithmetic operations, including financial calculations like net present value, internal rates of return, etc.; and
2. The ability to construct graphical representations of numerical values in the spreadsheet.

The "Help" functions of the spreadsheet programs are reasonably good guides, and can be an effective aid to accomplishing these tasks.

"What if?" Analysis - Data Tables

Although spreadsheets embed an overwhelming number of advanced capabilities, these are largely beyond the scope of most users. However, one important function, sensitivity analysis, is a feature of spreadsheets that has been available in spreadsheets since the development of the first truly integrated spreadsheet/graphing product, Lotus 123. This useful feature is the automating of 'What-if' analyses. This bit of spreadsheet functionality is sadly neglected by most instructors in the use of spreadsheets, in spite of its immense value in business analysis. You simply will not be able to do the case projects in this workbook if you cannot use the spreadsheet to do automated sensitivity analysis. "What if?" analysis is an important notion at the core of any application of decision tools. Since we cannot assume that you know how much about spreadsheet sensitivity analysis, the remainder of this document will introduce you to its mysteries, and teach you how it's done.

Concept

Consider the following part of an example spreadsheet (not a part of one of the workbook spreadsheets). There are a couple of process parameters (Part weight, Production volume, and Material cost), and a resulting Total Cost. The cost is dependent upon the other three parameters through a series of interrelationships embedded in the spreadsheet nothing fancy; just enough to serve as a useful demonstration.

Now, while the parameters shown here suggest that Total Cost is $21.36, we know that there is no guarantee that the actual production volume will be 250,000 units. It may be more; it may be less. In order to hedge against variations in sales, you may wish to determine the impact of changes in production volume upon the cost of making the part before you attempt to set a price. How might you go about establishing the relationship between production volume and part cost? The classical approaches come in two forms. You might either (1) attempt to establish analytically the relationship between the two by tracing the calculations through the spreadsheet; or (2) you might try changing the production volume (in cell B2) and making note of the changes in total cost. Both of these approaches are time consuming and prone to error, and should be avoided in practice.

This "sensitivity analysis" is at the heart of why spreadsheets were developed in the first place. While business analysts perform a wide range of calculations, the good ones maintain a healthy disrespect for the numbers upon which they are based, especially those based upon assumptions that can not be verified. Under these conditions, they endlessly permute the numbers and study the results in the development of their project plans. Because of this, spreadsheets include the capability to execute these sensitivity analyses automatically, eliminating the drudgery and opportunity for error that plagued the paper and pencil analysts preceding them. Modern spreadsheets can examine the consequences of varying one, two, and sometimes three model parameters at once, enabling the analyst to examine the impacts of changes in model assumptions and to study their implications upon model results.

General Description and Approach

Using a spreadsheet to perform sensitivity analysis is very simple, and should become a routine part of your spreadsheet analysis. However, if you have never done it before, reading a set of instructions will quickly become bewildering if you fail to keep track of what you're trying to accomplish. Before any descriptions of spreadsheet methods, it pays to think about how you might try to do this analysis without automatic methods. Basically, you would go through a three step process. First, you would select a set of test values for production volume; say 100,000, 200,000, 300,000, 400,000, and 500,000. Second, you would type each test value into the production volume input cell (cell B2). Finally, you would note the resulting Total Cost for each test value (found in cell B6). If you're clever, you would use two columns of the spreadsheet to list the test input values and resulting Total Cost values, so that you could make a graph of the results or just a nice looking table.

The procedure for performing an automated sensitivity analysis includes essentially these same steps. The trick is making sure that you "explain" what you want done, because the computer tends to make very bad guesses on its own!

Step 1: Locate some unused space in our spreadsheet and create a simple list of the possible production volumes that are of interest; say from 100,000 to 500,000 units.

Step 2: We next have to tell the spreadsheet that the Total Cost cell (cell B6) will contain the results that we're interested in; (recall, we want to learn how changes in the Production Volume parameter - cell B2 - will change the contents of the Total Cost cell - cell B6).

(Note: The "+B6" is the Lotus 123 format for a cell formula stating that the contents of the cell containing the formula should be the same as the value in cell B6; in Excel, that same formula is "=B6". Lotus 123 actually allows you to specify that the cell should appear to contain the formula text, rather than the number it evaluates to; hence the representation shown above)

Step 3: You have now laid the groundwork for the sensitivity analysis. *You* know what you want done; now it's time for you to "tell" the spreadsheet Programme what to do.

Excel and 123 have specific menu functions that you use to do this. In Excel, it's Data-Table; in 123 for Windows version 4 and later, it's Range-Analyze-What If Tables (before version 4, it was Data-Table). By invoking these functions, you pass along the following information to the spreadsheet:

1. How many parameters are to be varied in the spreadsheet based upon the data table (one in this case);
2. The location of the data table (the rectangle between cell D3 and E8); and
3. The cell into which the varying values (100,000 to 500,000, in this case) are to be placed before recalculating the spreadsheet (cell B2)

(*Note:* The purpose of this section is to illustrate how sensitivity analyses are generally done; the specifics are given in the next section) Note that you are not limited to a single output column. If you were interested in seeing the contents of another cell, you would just add a new column to the right, headed by a formula pointing to that second cell. In fact, *any* formula, not just these simple ones, can be used.

The differences are small, but significant. First, the formula pointing to the cell of interest (cell B6 - Total Cost) is now located in the top left corner of the table area. Second, the row to the right of the formula contains the potential values for the second input cell, Material Cost. Now, when you invoke the Data-Table function in the spreadsheet, you have to tell the Programme not only what cell the test values in the column belong in, but also the cell the test values in the row should be put into.

Note that you now have no room for a second output variable; only one-way sensitivity tables allow you to examine more than one variable at a time.

Data Tables - Specifics

While each spreadsheet Programme out there today implements sensitivity analysis in one form or another, the actual steps of these tasks varies slightly with each Programme. Although it is not possible to do screen captures of every detail of the process, a couple of them should be helpful. Where necessary, the screen shots are accompanied by a brief note. The Lotus 123 screen shots are taken from Lotus 123 for Windows Version 4.10; the Microsoft Excel screen shots from Excel Version 4. If you are a DOS command-line reprobate, we assume that you are resourceful enough to figure things out from the following hint: / Data Table. If not, then it may be time to give up and move on to a real operating system, like OS/2! Lotus 123 Although Lotus Development was the originator of the "Data-Table" jargon, their more recent Windows versions of their Programme avoids the "Data-Table" menu sequence for a more elaborate sequence starting with "Range-Analyze-What-If Tables." Once you get that far, however, things settle down to the standard sequence described above. This is what you see after getting through the "Range-Analyze-What-If Table" dialog. Note the option to choose the Number of variables, etc. The Input cell is hidden by the dialog box, but the table range is visible to the right of the dialog. Note that the dialog box explicitly covers two of the three pieces of information that the Programme requires in order to perform the sensitivity analysis - where the table is ("Table range "), and where the test values are to be placed.

Input cell 1"). The third piece of information, the cell containing the result to be saved, is implicit in the table definition: the formulas pointing to the desired output cell(s) *must* be in the first row of the table range.

After pressing the "OK" button, you get the following view:

For a two-way table, the screens are pretty similar.

Note that the table layout now only has one function cell (the one containing the +B6, a cell formatted as Text, even though it's a formula). The dialog box now calls for two input cells, corresponding to the column values (100,000-500,000) and the row values (1.2-1.3),respectively.

The resulting output is as follows:

For future reference, the diligent Excel user who is reading this section for completeness should note that cell E5, a part of the data table, is a simple number (21.625). In the next set of screen captures, you will see that Excel data tables are composed of different elements. Microsoft Excel Excel currently holds true to the "Data-Table" expression as the way of defining their sensitivity tables. Unlike 123, however, the user must select the data table region before invoking the Data-Table command; the Data-Table dialog box makes no provision for defining the table range. Here's what you see once you have selected the data table region and selected Data-Table from the command menu.

Note that Excel makes no distinction between one-way and two-way tables in the dialog box. Further, note that Excel requests " Row Input Cell " and " Column Input Cell " rather than Cell 1 and Cell 2 as in Lotus 123. Because the test production volume values are in a column, the Column Input Cell field in the dialog box has been filled. Upon clicking the OK button, we get the following:

As an illustrative point, note that cell E3 contains a formula, not a value (=B6), just as is required in 123. Do not put a number in that cell; you'll get a most uninteresting data table!

The two-way table is not particularly different:

Now you have to supply both Column and Row Inputs. Clicking on OK yields.

Changing other parts of the spreadsheet will change the contents of this data table. If you don't want the values in the table to change, copy the range of values and then do a Paste Special, selecting Values only (not formulas) to be pasted into the spreadsheet.

Distinctions Between Lotus 123 and Microsoft Excel Tables

There is one key difference between Lotus 123 and Microsoft Excel data table entries. In a 123 data table, the calculated values that populate the data table are static numbers; an examination of any particular cell reveals simply a number that does not change until the data table is recalculated. This is most emphatically not the case with Microsoft Excel. In Excel, data tables are actually functional elements of the spreadsheet, as fully active as any other calculated cell within the spreadsheet.

This has two important consequences:

1. First, *every* time that parameters in the spreadsheet are changed, the data table will be updated. As a consequence, no particular analysis can be maintained within the spreadsheet, nor can two data tables coexist easily. There are ways around this, however.

2. Second, think about what it means to have a 10-element data table in an Excel spreadsheet. In the worst case, a change in a single value in the spreadsheet will require not only a recalculation to update the spreadsheet to reflect that change; the 10-element data table will also necessitate a *further* 10 spreadsheet recalculations a total of 11 spreadsheet recalculations. While programmers have managed to teach spreadsheets how to be discriminating about recalculations, it's still going to take longer than it would have without the active data table.

Consequences and Recommended Procedures

Thus, we strongly recommend that users of Excel learn how to do the "Copy... Paste Special..." sequence of commands. By Copying the data table, and then pasting "special" (telling Excel to paste the Values, but not the formulas), you can save yourself a lot of grief, both in terms of saving your sensitivity analyses and keeping your spreadsheet from bogging down with ever-increasing recalculations. Also, an important warning to users of Excel version 5.0: Get an upgrade ASAP! The original version 5 release contains nasty bugs, especially when running macros.

Links To Graphing Concepts

There's not a lot to say here, except to note that these data tables are nicely laid out for generation of graphics – not an accident! As we indicated above, spreadsheets are second only to word processing programs in their endless "feature creep," where each new version introduces Programme capabilities that you probably didn't even know you needed, and that you are unlikely to employ. Not surprisingly, the Programme menus for these programs have become increasingly complex, incorporating whole subsystems that are rarely visited, even by users who employ spreadsheets daily. These include such exotica as "solver" subsystems and direct links to databases external to the spreadsheet. Luckily for you, we view these capabilities with suspicion, and not a little concern. When 90% of a Programme is only used by 10% of the users, one starts to wonder about things like Programme reliability and expense.

One important capability of spreadsheets is the fact that they can be programmed. Known as "Macros," these shortcuts can be used to automate spreadsheet work even further. The DANAL spreadsheet makes extensive use of macros. In Lotus 123, macros are stored as an integral part of the spreadsheet. In Microsoft Excel, the macros are stored in a separate file, with the. XLM extension, that must be loaded before the macros are accessible. Macros can be run from the command menu (usually under the Tools heading, although this can very – use the help system), or with a keystroke (either the Control or the Command key plus a letter from the keyboard - Control-A or Command-X, for example).

FUZZY LOGIC

Fuzzy logic is derived from fuzzy set theory dealing with reasoning that is approximate rather than precisely deduced from classical predicate logic. It can be thought of as the application side of fuzzy set theory dealing with well thought out real world expert values for a complex problem.

Degrees of truth are often confused with probabilities. However, they are conceptually distinct; fuzzy truth represents membership in vaguely defined sets, not likelihood of some event or condition. To illustrate the difference, consider this scenario: Bob is in a house with two adjacent rooms: the kitchen and the dining room. In many cases, Bob's status within the set of things "in the kitchen" is completely plain: he's either "in the kitchen" or "not in the kitchen". What about when Bob stands in the doorway? He may be considered "partially in the kitchen". Quantifying this partial state yields a fuzzy set membership. With only his big toe in the dining room, we might say Bob is 99% "in the kitchen" and 1% "in the dining room", for instance. No event (like a coin toss) will resolve Bob to being completely "in the kitchen" or "not in the kitchen", as long as he's standing in that doorway. Fuzzy sets are based on vague definitions of sets, not randomness.

Fuzzy logic allows for set membership values between and including 0 and 1, and in its linguistic form, imprecise concepts like "slightly", "quite" and "very". Specifically, it allows partial membership in a set. It is related to fuzzy sets and possibility theory. It was introduced in 1965 by Prof. Lotfi Zadeh at the University of California, Berkeley. Fuzzy logic is controversial in some circles, despite wide acceptance and a broad track record of successful applications. It is rejected by some control engineers for validation and other reasons, and by some statisticians who hold that probability is the only rigorous mathematical description of uncertainty. Critics also argue that it cannot be a superset of ordinary set theory since membership functions are defined in terms of conventional sets.

Applications

Fuzzy logic can be used to control household appliances such as washing machines (which sense load size and detergent concentration and adjust their wash cycles accordingly) and refrigerators. A basic application might characterize subranges of a continuous variable. For instance, a temperature measurement for anti-lock brakes might have several separate membership functions defining particular temperature ranges needed to control the brakes properly. Each function maps the same temperature value to a truth value in the 0 to 1 range. These truth values can then be used to determine how the brakes should be controlled.

In this image, cold, warm, and hot are functions mapping a temperature scale. A point on that scale has three "truth values" – one for each of the three functions. For the particular temperature shown, the three truth values could be interpreted as describing the temperature as, say, "fairly cold", "slightly warm", and "not hot".

A more sophisticated practical example is the use of fuzzy logic in high-performance error correction to improve information reception over a limited-bandwidth communication link affected by data-corrupting noise using turbo codes. The front-end of a decoder produces a likelihood measure for the value intended by the sender (0 or 1) for each bit in the data stream. The likelihood measures might use a scale of 256 values between extremes of "certainly 0" and "certainly 1". Two decoders may analyse the data in parallel, arriving at different likelihood results for the values intended by the sender. Each can then use as additional data the other's likelihood results, and repeats the process to improve the results until consensus is reached as to the most likely values.

Misconceptions and controversies

Fuzzy logic is the same as "Imprecise Logic"

Fuzzy logic is not any less precise than any other form of logic: it is an organized and mathematical method of handling *inherently* imprecise concepts. The concept of "coldness" cannot be expressed in an equation, because although temperature is a quantity, "coldness" is not. However, people have an idea of what "cold" is, and agree that something cannot be "cold" at N degrees but "not cold" at N+1 degrees – a concept classical logic cannot easily handle due to the principle of bivalence.

Fuzzy logic is a New Way of Expressing Probability

Fuzzy logic and probability refer to different kinds of uncertainty. Fuzzy logic is specifically designed to deal with imprecision of facts (fuzzy logic statements), while probability deals with chances of that happening *(but still considering the result to be precise)*. However, this is a point of controversy. Many statisticians are persuaded by the work of Bruno de Finetti that only one kind of mathematical uncertainty is needed and thus fuzzy logic is unnecessary.

On the other hand, Bart Kosko argues that probability is a subtheory of fuzzy logic, as probability only handles one kind of uncertainty. He also claims to have proven a derivation of Bayes' theorem from the concept of fuzzy subsethood. Lotfi Zadeh, the creator of fuzzy logic, argues that fuzzy logic is different in character from probability, and is not a replacement for it. He has created a fuzzy alternative to probability, which he calls possibility theory. Other controversial approaches to uncertainty include Dempster-Shafer theory and rough sets.

Fuzzy Logic will be Difficult to Scale to Larger Problems

In a widely circulated and highly controversial paper, Charles Elkan in 1993 commented that "...there are few, if any, published reports of expert systems in real-world use that reason about uncertainty using fuzzy logic. It appears that the limitations of fuzzy logic have not been detrimental in control applications because current fuzzy controllers are far simpler than other knowledge-based systems.

In future, the technical limitations of fuzzy logic can be expected to become important in practice, and work on fuzzy controllers will also encounter several problems of scale already known for other knowledge-based systems". Reactions to Elkan's paper are many and varied, from claims that he is simply mistaken, to others who accept that he has identified important limitations of fuzzy logic that need to be addressed by system designers. In fact, fuzzy logic wasn't largely used at that time, and today it is used to solve very complex problems in the AI area. Probably the scalability and complexity of the *fuzzy* system will depend more on its implementation than on the theory of fuzzy logic.

Examples Where Fuzzy logic is Used

Automobile and other vehicle subsystems, such as ABS and cruise control (e.g. Tokyo monorail)

- Air conditioners
- The MassiveASSIVE engine used in the *Lord of the Rings* films, which helped show huge scale armies create random, yet orderly movements
- Cameras
- Digital image processing, such as edge detection
- Rice cookers
- Dishwashers
- Elevators
- Washing machines and other home appliances
- Video game artificial intelligence

- Language filters on message boards and chat rooms for filtering out offensive text
- Pattern recognition in Remote Sensing

Fuzzy logic has also been incorporated into some microcontrollers and microprocessors, for instance, the Freescale 68HC12.

How Fuzzy Logic is Applied

Fuzzy Set Theory defines Fuzzy Operators on Fuzzy Sets. The problem in applying this is that the appropriate Fuzzy Operator may not be known! For this reason, Fuzzy logic usually uses IF/THEN rules, or constructs that are equivalent, such as fuzzy associative matrices. Rules are usually expressed in the form,

- IF variable IS set THEN action
- For example, an extremely simple temperature regulator that uses a fan might look like this
- IF temperature IS very cold THEN stop fan
- IF temperature IS cold THEN turn down fan
- IF temperature IS normal THEN maintain level
- IF temperature IS hot THEN speed up fan
- Notice there is no "ELSE". All of the rules are evaluated, because the temperature might be "cold" and "normal" at the same time to differing degrees.

The AND, OR, and NOT operators of boolean logic exist in fuzzy logic, usually defined as the minimum, maximum, and complement; when they are defined this way, they are called the *Zadeh operators,* because they were first defined as such in Zadeh's original papers. So for the fuzzy variables x and y:

- NOT x = (1 - truth(x))
- x AND y = minimum(truth(x), truth(y))
- x OR y = maximum(truth(x), truth(y))

There are also other operators, more linguistic in nature, called *hedges* that can be applied. These are generally adverbs such as "very", or "somewhat", which modify the meaning of a set using a mathematical formula. In application, the programming language Prolog is well geared to implementing fuzzy logic with its facilities to set up a database of "rules" which are queried to deduct logic. This sort of programming is known as logic programming. Once fuzzy relations are defined, it is possible to develop fuzzy relational databases. The first fuzzy relational data base, FRDB, appeared in Maria Zemankova's dissertation.

FORMAL FUZZY LOGIC

In mathematical logic, there are several formal systems that model the above notions of "fuzzy logic". Note that they use a different set of operations than above mentioned Zadeh operators.

Propositional Fuzzy Logics

- Basic propositional fuzzy logic is an axiomatization of logic where conjunction is defined by a continuous t-norm, and implication is defined as the residuum of the t-norm. Its models correspond to BL-algebras.
- £ukasiewicz fuzzy logic is a special case of basic fuzzy logic where conjunction is £ukasiewicz t-norm. It has the axioms of basic logic plus an axiom of double negation (so it is not intuitionistic logic), and its models correspond to MV-algebras.
- Gödel fuzzy logic is a special case of basic fuzzy logic where conjunction is Gödel t-norm. It has the axioms of basic logic plus an axiom of idempotence of conjunction, and its models are called G-algebras.
- Product fuzzy logic is a special case of basic fuzzy logic where conjunction is product t-norm. It has the axioms of basic logic plus another axiom, and its models are called product algebras.
- Rational Pavelka logic is a generalization of multi-valued logic. It is an extension of £ukasziewicz fuzzy logic with additional constants.

All these logics encompass the traditional propositional logic (whose models correspond to Boolean algebras).

Predicate Fuzzy Logics

These extend the above-mentioned fuzzy logics by adding universal and existential quantifiers in a manner similar to the way that predicate logic is created from propositional logic.

Effectiveness for Fuzzy Logics

The notions of a "decidable subset" and "recursively enumerable subset" are basic ones for classical mathematics and classical logic. Then, the question of a suitable extension of such concepts to fuzzy set theory arises. A first proposal in such a direction was made by E. S. Santos by the notions of fuzzy Turing machine, Markov normal fuzzy algorithm and fuzzy Programme. Successively, L. Biacino and G. Gerla proposed the following definition where Ü denotes the set of rational numbers in [0,1]. A fuzzy subset $\mu : S \rightarrow [0,1]$ of a set S is recursively enumerable if a recursive map h : S×N Ü exists such that, for every x in S, the function h(x,n) is increasing with respect to n and $\mu(x) = \lim h(x,n)$. We say that μ is decidable if both μ and its complement $-\mu$ are recursively enumerable. An extension of such a theory to the general case of the L-subsets is proposed in a paper by G. Gerla. The proposed definitions are well related with fuzzy logic. Indeed, the following theorem holds true (provided that the deduction apparatus of the fuzzy logic satisfies some obvious effectiveness property.

Theorem. Any axiomatizable fuzzy theory is recursively enumerable. In particular, the fuzzy set of logically true formulas is recursively enumerable in spite of the fact that the crisp set of valid formulas is not recursively enumerable, in general. Moreover, any axiomatizable and complete theory is decidable.

It an open question to give a support for a Church thesis for fuzzy computability and to give Goedel's theorems for fuzzy logic using the notion of recursively enumerable fuzzy subset. To this aim, it is very important to refer to some good definition of fuzzy Turing machines.

Chapter 6

Reporting and Responsibilities

MANAGEMENT ACCOUNTING

Management accounting is concerned with the provisions and use of accounting information to managers within organizations, to provide them with the basis in making informed business decisions that would allow them to be better equipped in their management and control functions. Unlike financial accountancy information (which, for the most part, is public information), management accounting information is used within an organization (typically for decision-making) and is usually confidential and access to which is only available to a select few.

According to CIMA, The Chartered Institute of Management Accountants, Management Accounting is "the process of identification, measurement, accumulation, analysis, preparation, interpretation and communication of information used by management to plan, evaluate and control within an entity and to assure appropriate use of and accountability for its resources. Management accounting also comprises the preparation of financial reports for non management groups such as shareholders, creditors, regulatory agencies and tax authorities" (CIMA Official Terminology)

Aims

1. Formulating strategies;
2. Planning and constructing business activities;
3. Making decisions;

4. Well use of resources;
5. Supporting financial reports preparation; and
6. Safeguarding assets.

Traditional vs. Innovative Management Accounting

In the late 1980s, accounting practitioners and educators were heavily criticized on the grounds that management accounting practices (and, even more so, the curriculum taught to accounting students) had changed little over the preceding 60 years, despite radical changes in the business environment. Professional accounting institutes, perhaps fearing that management accountants would increasingly be seen as superfluous in business organizations, subsequently devoted considerable resources to the development of a more innovative skills set for management accountants. The distinction between 'traditional' and 'innovative' management accounting practices can be illustrated by reference to cost control techniques. Traditionally, management accountants' principal technique was variance analysis, which is a systematic approach to the comparison of the actual and budgeted costs of the raw materials and labour used during a production period.

While some form of variance analysis is still used by most manufacturing firms, it nowadays tends to be used in conjunction with innovative techniques such as life cycle cost analysis and activity-based costing, which are designed with specific aspects of the modern business environment in mind. Lifecycle costing recognizes that managers' ability to influence the cost of manufacturing a product is at its greatest when the product is still at the design stage of its product lifecycle (i.e., before the design has been finalised and production commenced), since small changes to the product design may lead to significant savings in the cost of manufacturing the product. Activity-based costing (ABC) recognizes that, in modern factories, most manufacturing costs are determined by the amount of 'activities' (e.g., the number of production runs per month, and the amount of production equipment idle time) and that the key to effective cost control is therefore optimizing the efficiency of these activities. Activity-based accounting is also known as Cause and Effect accounting.

Both lifecycle costing and activity-based costing recognize that, in the typical modern factory, the avoidance of disruptive events (such as machine breakdowns and quality control failures) is of far greater importance than (for example) reducing the costs of raw materials. Activity-based costing also deemphasizes direct labour as a cost driver and concentrates instead on acitivities that drive costs, such as the provision of a service or the production of a product component.

Development of Throughput Accounting

The most significant recent direction in managerial accounting is throughput accounting, which recognizes the interdependencies of modern production processes and provide managers with a tool that will allow them to measure the contribution per unit of constrained resource for any given product, customer or supplier.

An Alternative View

A seldom expressed alternative view of management accounting is that it is neither a neutral or benign influence in organizations, rather a mechanism for management control through surveillance. This view locates management accounting specifically in the context of management control theory.

In throughput accounting, the cost accounting aspect of Theory of Constraints (TOC), operating expense is the money spent turning inventory into throughput. In TOC, operating expense is limited to costs that vary strictly with the quantity produced, like raw materials and purchased components. Everything else is a fixed cost, including labour unless there is a regular and significant chance that workers will not work a full-time week when they report on its first day.

FINANCIAL ACCOUNTANCY

Financial accountancy (or financial accounting) is the branch of accountancy concerned with the preparation of financial statements for decision makers, such as stockholders, suppliers, banks, government agencies, owners, and other stakeholders. The fundamental need for financial accounting is to reduce principal-agent problem by measuring and monitoring agents' performance and reporting the results to interested users. Financial Accountancy is used to prepare accounting information for people outside the organisation or not involved in the day to day running of the company. Managerial accounting provides accounting information to help managers make decisions to manage the business. Financial Accountancy is governed by both local and international accounting standards.

Basic Accounting Concepts

The accounting equation (Assets = Liabilities + Owners' Equity) and financial statements are the main topics of financial accounting. The trial balance which is usually prepared using the Double-entry accounting system forms the basis for preparing the financial statements. All the figures in the trial balance are rearranged to prepare a profit and loss statement and balance sheet. There are certain accounting standards that determine the format for these accounts (SSAP, FRS, IFS). The financial statements will display the income and expenditure for the company and a summary of the assets, liabilities, and shareholders or owners' equity of the company on the date the accounts were prepared to.

Meaning of the Accounting Equation

The value of a company can be understood simply as the useful assets that ownership of a company entitles one to claim. This value is known as Owners' Equity. Some assets of a company, however, cannot be claimed as equity by the owners of a company because other people have legal claim to them - for example if the company has borrowed money from the bank. The value of a resource claimable by a non-owner is called a liability. All of the Assets of a company can be claimed by someone, whether owner or not, so the sum of a company's equity and its liabilities must equal the value of its Assets. Thus the accounting equation describes what portion of a company's assets can by claimed by the owners.

Various account types are classified as 'credit' or 'debit' depending on the role they play in the accounting equation.

Assets = Liabilities + Equity *or* Assets - Liabilities - Equity = 0

Another way of stating it is:

Equity = Assets - Liabilities

which can be interpreted as: "Equity is what is left if all assets have been sold and all liabilities have been paid".

Managerial Finance

Managerial Finance is that branch of finance that provides tools for a company's financial managers. It encompasses corporate finance and management accounting also known as cost accounting. Financial analysts provide analysis in the corporate finance field. And, cost analysts provide analysis in the cost accounting field. Therefore, the financial-cost analyst provides analysis in the managerial finance arena. These analysts require skills of both the internal corporate financial analyst and cost analyst.

Corporate Finance

Corporate finance is a specific area of finance dealing with the financial decisions corporations make and the tools as well as analysis used to make these decisions. The primary goal of Corporate finance is to enhance corporate value, without taking excessive financial risks. The discipline may be divided among long-term and short-term decisions and techniques. Capital investment decisions comprise the long-term choices about which projects receive investment, whether to finance that investment with equity or debt, and when or whether to pay dividends to shareholders. Short-term corporate finance decisions are called working capital management and deal with the balance of current assets and current liabilities; the focus here is on managing cash, inventories, and short-term borrowing and lending (e.g., the credit terms extended to customers).

The time frames, and the goal of the discipline, are interrelated: value is enhanced when return on capital, a function of working capital management, exceeds cost of capital, a function of previous capital investment decisions. Corporate finance is closely related to managerial finance, which is slightly broader in scope, describing the financial techniques available to all forms of business enterprise, corporate or not.

Capital Investment Decisions

Longer term Corporate finance decisions - generally relating to fixed assets and capital structure - are referred to as *Capital investment decisions*. The decision here will be based on several inter-related criteria. In general, management must "maximize the value of the firm" by investing in projects which are NPV positive, when valued using an appropriate discount rate; these projects must also be financed appropriately. If no such opportunities exist, maximizing shareholder value dictates that management return excess cash to shareholders. Capital investment decisions thus comprise an investment decision, a financing decision, and a dividend decision.

The Investment Decision

Management must allocate limited resources between competing opportunities ("projects") in a process known as capital budgeting. Making this capital allocation decision requires estimating the value of each opportunity or project: a function of the size, timing and predictability of future cash flows.

Project Valuation

In general, each project's value will be estimated using a discounted cash flow (DCF) valuation, and the opportunity with the highest value, as measured by the resultant net present value (NPV) will be selected. This requires estimating the size and timing of all of the incremental cash flows resulting from the project. These future cash flows are then discounted to determine their present value. These present values are then summed, and this sum is the NPV.

The NPV is greatly influenced by the discount rate. Thus selecting the proper discount rate - the project "hurdle rate" - is critical to making the right decision. The hurdle rate is the minimum acceptable return on an investment - i.e. the project appropriate discount rate. The hurdle rate should reflect the riskiness of the investment, typically measured by volatility of cash flows, and must take into account the financing mix. Managers use models such as the CAPM or the APT to estimate a discount rate appropriate for a particular project, and use the weighted average cost of capital (*WACC*) to reflect the financing mix selected. (A common error in choosing a discount rate for a project is to apply a WACC that applies to the entire firm. Such an approach may not be appropriate where the risk of a particular project differs markedly from that of the firm's existing portfolio of assets.)

In conjunction with NPV, there are several other measures used as (secondary) selection criteria in corporate finance. These are visible from the DCF and include payback, IRR, Modified IRR, equivalent annuity, capital efficiency, and ROI.

Valuing Flexibility

In many cases, for example R&D projects, a project may open (or close) paths of action to the company, but this reality will not typically be captured in a strict NPV approach. Management will therefore (sometimes) employ tools which place an explicit value on these options. So, whereas in a DCF valuation the most likely or average or scenario specific cash flows are discounted, here the "flexibile and staged nature" of the investment is modelled, and hence "all" potential payoffs are considered. The difference between the two valuations is the "option value" inherent in the project.

The two most common tools are Decision Tree Analysis (DTA) and Real options.

- The DTA approach attempts to capture flexibility by incorporating likely events and consequent management decisions into the valuation. In the decision tree, each management decision in response to an "event" generates a "branch" or "path" which the company could follow. (For example, management will only proceed with stage 2 of the project given that stage 1 was successful; stage 3, in turn, depends on stage 2. In a DCF model, on the other hand, there is no "branching" - each scenario must be modelled separately.) The highest value path (probability weighted) is regarded as representative of project value.

- The real options approach is used when the value of a project is contingent on the value of some other asset or underlying variable. (For example, the viability of a mining project is contingent on the price of gold; if the price is too low, management will abandon the mining rights, if sufficiently high, management will develop the Ore-body. Again, a DCF valuation would capture only one of these outcomes.) Here, using financial option theory as a framework, the decision to be taken is identified as corresponding to either a call option or a put option - valuation is then via the Binomial model or, less often for this purpose, via Black Scholes; see Contingent claim valuation. The "true" value of the project is then the NPV of the "most likely" scenario plus the option value.

The Financing Decision

Achieving the goals of corporate finance requires that any corporate investment be financed appropriately. As above, since both hurdle rate and cash flows (and hence the riskiness of the firm) will be affected, the financing mix can impact the valuation. Management must therefore identify the "optimal mix" of financing – the capital structure that results in maximum value.

The sources of financing will, generically, comprise some combination of debt and equity. Financing a project through debt results in a liability that must be serviced - and hence there are cash flow implications regardless of the project's success. Equity financing is less risky in the sense of cash flow commitments, but results in a dilution of ownership and earnings. The cost of equity is also typically higher than the cost of debt, and so equity financing may result in an increased hurdle rate which may offset any reduction in cash flow risk. Management must also attempt to match the financing mix to the asset being financed as closely as possible, in terms of both timing and cash flows.

The Dividend Decision

In general, management must decide whether to invest in additional projects, reinvest in existing operations, or return free cash as dividends to shareholders. The dividend is calculated mainly on the basis of the company's unappropriated profit and its business prospects for the coming year. If there are no NPV positive opportunities, i.e. where returns exceed the hurdle rate, then management must return excess cash to investors - these free cash flows comprise cash remaining after all business expenses have been met. (This is the general case, however there are exceptions. For example, investors in a "Growth stock", expect that the company will, almost by definition, retain earnings so as to fund growth internally. In other cases, even though an opportunity is currently NPV negative, management may consider "investment flexibility" and potential payoff and decide to retain cash flows.)

Management must also decide on the form of the distribution, generally as cash dividends or via a share buyback. There are various considerations: where shareholders pay tax on dividends, companies may elect to retain earnings, or to perform a stock buyback, in both cases increasing the value of shares outstanding; some companies will pay "dividends" from stock rather than in cash. Today it is generally accepted that dividend policy is value neutral.

Working Capital Management

Decisions relating to working capital and short term financing are referred to as *working capital management*. These involve managing the relationship between a firm's short-term assets and its short-term liabilities. The goal of Working capital management is to ensure that the firm is able to continue its operations and that it has sufficient cash flow to satisfy both maturing short-term debt and upcoming operational expenses.

Decision Criteria

By definition, Working capital management entails short term decisions - generally, relating to the next one year period - which are "reversible". These decisions are therefore not taken on the same basis as Capital Investment Decisions (NPV or related, as above) rather they will be based on cash flows and / or profitability.

- One measure of cash flow is provided by the cash conversion cycle - the net number of days from the outlay of cash for raw material to receiving payment from the customer. As a management tool, this metric makes explicit the inter-relatedness of decisions relating to inventories, accounts receivable and payable, and cash. Because this number effectively corresponds to the time that the firm's cash is tied up in operations and unavailable for other activities, management generally aims at a low net count.
- In this context, the most useful measure of profitability is Return on capital (ROC). The result is shown as a percentage, determined by dividing relevant income for the 12 months by capital employed; Return on equity (ROE) shows this result for the firm's shareholders. Firm value is enhanced when, and if, the return on capital, which results from working capital management, exceeds the cost of capital, which results from capital investment decisions as above. ROC measures are therefore useful as a management tool, in that they link short-term policy with long-term decision making.

Management of Working Capital

Guided by the above criteria, management will use a combination of policies and techniques for the management of working capital. These policies aim at managing the *current assets* (generally cash and cash equivalents, inventories and debtors) and the short term financing, such that cash flows and returns are acceptable.

- Cash management. Identify the cash balance which allows for the business to meet day to day expenses, but reduces cash holding costs.
- Inventory management. Identify the level of inventory which allows for uninterrupted production but reduces the investment in raw materials - and minimizes reordering costs - and hence increases cash flow; see Supply chain management; Just In Time (JIT); Economic order quantity (EOQ); Economic production quantity (EPQ).
- Debtors management. Identify the appropriate credit policy, i.e. credit terms which will attract customers, such that any impact on cash flows and the cash conversion cycle will be offset by increased revenue and hence Return on Capital (or *vice versa*).
- Short term financing. Identify the appropriate source of financing, given the cash conversion cycle: the inventory is ideally financed by credit granted by the supplier; however, it may be necessary to utilize a bank loan (or overdraft), or to "convert debtors to cash" through "factoring".

FINANCIAL RISK MANAGEMENT

Risk management is the process of measuring risk and then developing and implementing strategies to manage that risk. Financial risk management focuses on risks that can be managed ("hedged") using traded financial instruments (typically changes in commodity prices, interest rates, foreign exchange rates and stock prices). Financial risk management will also play an important role in cash management.

This area is related to corporate finance in two ways. Firstly, firm exposure to business risk is a direct result of previous Investment and Financing decisions. Secondly, both disciplines share the goal of creating, or enhancing, firm value.

All large corporations have risk management teams, and small firms practice informal, if not formal, risk management. Derivatives are the instruments most commonly used in Financial risk management. Because unique derivative contracts tend to be costly to create and monitor, the most cost-effective financial risk management methods usually involve derivatives that trade on well-established financial markets. These standard derivative instruments include options, futures contracts, forward contracts, and swaps.

Relationship with other areas in Finance [ssh]

Corporate finance utilizes tools from almost all areas of finance. Some of the tools developed by and for corporations have broad application to entities other than corporations, for example, to partnerships, sole proprietorships, not-for-profit organizations, governments, mutual funds, and personal wealth management. But in other cases their application is very limited outside of the corporate finance arena. Because corporations deal in quantities of money much greater than individuals, the analysis has developed into a discipline of its own. It can be differentiated from personal finance and public finance.

Related Professional Qualifications

The new internationally recognised Corporate Finance Qualification (CF) is the only directly related professional qualification, although many others traditionally can lead to the field:

- Qualified accountant qualifications: Chartered Certified Accountant (ACCA), Chartered Accountant (CA), Certified Public Accountant (CPA)
- Other non-statutory accountancy qualifications: Chartered Cost Accountant (CCA Designation from AAFM), Certified Management Accountant (CMA), Chartered Management Accountant (ACMA)
- Business qualifications: Master of Business Administration (MBA), Doctor of Business Administration (DBA)

- Finance qualifications: Masters degree in Finance (MSF), Corporate Finance Qualification (CF), Chartered Financial Analyst (CFA), Association of Corporate Treasurers (ACT), Certified Market Analyst (CMA/FAD) Dual Designation, Master Financial Manager (MFM).

FINANCIAL PLANNER

A Financial Planner or Personal Financial Planner is a practicing professional who helps people deal with various personal financial issues through proper planning, which includes but is not limited to these major areas: tertiary education planning, retirement planning, investment planning, risk management and insurance planning, tax planning, estate planning and business succession planning (for business owners). The work engaged in by this professional is commonly known as *personal financial planning*. In carrying out the planning function, he is guided by a process known as the *financial planning process* which should result in creating a detailed strategy for making their clients as wealthy as possible.

Why would people plan their finances with the help of a financial planner? It is because of the complexity of knowing how to perform the following:

- To provide direction and meaning to financial decisions;
- To understand how each financial decision affects the other areas of his finances; and
- To adapt more easily to life changes in order to feel more secure.

This is particularly difficult to cope without professional help as the case in a fast changing environment.

Definition

We may broadly define personal financial planning as a process of determining an individual's financial goals, purposes in life and life's priorities, and after considering his resources, risk profile and current lifestyle, to detail a balanced and realistic plan to meet those goals.

By 'process', it means financial planning is a step-by-step guide that is not specifically attributed to any particular financial product or service. In other words, any content-based practitioner, e.g. life insurance adviser, accountant, investment adviser, etc., can make use of the same steps listed in the process to perform the financial planning function for their client.

The above definition uses the individual's goals and purpose in life as strategic guideposts for mapping a course of action on 'what need to be done' to reach meaningful goals in meaningful ways for him. The goals and purposes in life are the reference points or outcomes to aim at when the financial plan is constructed. Along side the data gathering exercise, the purpose of each goal is determined to ensure that the goal is meaningful in the context of the individual's situation.

Through a process of careful analysis by an experienced financial planner, these goals are then subjected to a reality check by considering the individual's current and future resources available to achieve them. In the process, the constraints and obstacles to these goals are noted. The information will be used later to determine if there are sufficient resources available to get to these goals, and what other things need to be considered in the process. If the resources are insufficient or absent to meet any of the goals, the particular goal will be adjusted to a more realist level or is replaced with a new goal.

To plan for the future would usually require some forms of self-constrains in postponing some enjoyment today for the sake of the future. To be effective, the approach to financial planning should consider the individual's current lifestyle so that the 'pain' in postponing current pleasures is bearable over the term of the plan. It is in times where current sacrifices are involved that the strength of the plan's purpose for each goal is called upon to ensure that the pursuit of the goal will continue. The plan would consider the importance of each goal and prioritized them accordingly for taking action. It should be noted that many financial plans fail because these practical points were not sufficiently considered.

Scope

What does financial planning covers? Financial planning should ideally cover all areas of the client's financial needs and finally to end with the achievement his goals and objectives in each of the targeted areas. Usually, the scope of financial planning would include the following:

- Risk Management and Insurance Planning: To make provision against cash flow risks through sound risk management and insurance techniques:
- Investment and Planning Issues: Planning, creating and managing capital accumulation to generate future capital and cash flows for reinvestment and spending.
- Retirement Planning: Planning to ensure financial independence when one retires.
- Tax Planning: Planning for the reduction of tax liabilities and the freeing-up of cash flows for other purposes.
- Estate Planning: Planning for the creation, accumulation, conservation and distribution of assets.
- Cash Flow and Liability Management: Maintaining and enhancing personal cash flows through debt and lifestyle management.

The Personal Financial Planning Process

The *personal financial planning process* is generally accepted as a six-step process as follows:

Step 1: Setting goals with the client This step (that is usually performed in conjunction with Step 2) is meant to identify where the client wants to go in terms of his finances and life.

Step 2: Gathering relevant information on the client This would include the qualitative and quantitive aspects of the client's financial and relevant non-financial situation.

Step 3: Analysing the information The information gathered is analysed so that the client's situation is properly understood. This include checking whether there are sufficient resources to reach the client's goals and what those resources are.

Step 4: Constructing a financial plan Based on the understanding of what the client wants in the future and his current financial status, a roadmap to the client goals is drawn to facilitate the achievements of those goals.

Step 5: Implementing the strategies in the plan Guided by the financial plan, the strategies outlined in the plan is implemented using the resources allocated for the purpose.

Step 6: Monitoring implementation and reviewing the plan The implementation process is closely monitored to ensure it stays in alignment to the client's goals. Periodic reviews are undertaken to check for misalingment and changes in the client's situation. If there are any deviation or significant changes to the client's situation, the strategies and goals in the financial plan are revised accordingly.

Job Function

Professionally, a financial planner is someone who specializes in the planning aspects of finance, in particular personal finance, as contrasted by a stock broker who is only concerned with the actual investments or a life insurance intermediary who advises on risk products. In today's context, he performs his job guided by the financial planning process, which is usually a six-step process, and considers the client's situation from all relevant angles and recommends solutions that are integrated. The six-step financial planning process has been adopted by the International Organization for Standardization (ISO) and the details can be obtained from the organisation. Financial planners are also known by the title financial advisor in some countries, although these two terms are technically not synonymous, and their roles have some functional differences.

Although, there are many types of 'financial planners', the use of the title today is more lean towards those who mainly consider the whole financial picture of a client and then provide solutions in a holistics and comprehensive manner manner. To differentiate from the other types of financial planners, they are sometimes called 'comprehensive' financial planners. Other financial planners may specialize in one or more areas, such as, insurance planning and retirement planning. There are also a small group of planners who termed themselves as fee-only financial planners. As the name implied, these planners make a living by planning and advising clients on their finance for a fee, which is their only source of earnings.

Licensing, Regulation and Self-regulation

Currently, the title of 'financial planner' is largely an unregulated term in many countries. This has allowed financial services personnel in these countries with no restrictive rules to use the title indiscriminately. Commonly, financial products intermediaries, such as life insurance and unit trusts agents, use the title to project a professional image to their client even when they are not trained in the professional aspects of financial planning. This has often led to abuse. Clients may be deceived to receive financial planning services that are unprofessional and from providers who are unethical.

To promote financial planning as a profession, financial professionals and practitioners from across the globe (starting from the United States) involved in the trade begin to form trade organisations to provide self-regulations and to maintain some orderliness in the industry. Some, such as the FPA, begin to organise high-level training programmes and certify members who successfully completed these programmes. Howerver, the title of 'financial planner' continues to be of common usage among individuals in the financial industry in most countries where the financial planning concept exists at some level as there are little or no legal barriers to prevent them from using the title. Expectedly, the governments in many countries where the financial planning profession is taking roots begin to play an increasingly active role in tasking themselves to ensure the market is orderly. More stringent laws and guidelines were progressively introduced to keep the profession in check.

In Australia, the financial planning services are initially delinated by law by the granting of licence to deal in securities or advise on investments. Licences are issued under the stringent criteria by the Australian Securities and Investments Commission (ASIC), which has evolved these regulations vigourously over the years. Financial planning is now a highly regulated industry in Australia especially where financial advice to the public is involved. Practitioners who offer advice that could influence a client's decision to purchase a financial product must meet minimum training requirements and be licensed by the ASIC. The meaning of 'licenced' refers to Australian Financial Services Licence (AFSL) holders and representatives or authorised representatives of licence holders. Broadly, most people embarking in financial planning will start as an authorised representative of a licence holder.

Becoming a financial planner involves two main steps:

1. Meet the training requirements of Policy Statement 146
2. Select a licence holder to be affiliated with

The licence holder is the authorised representative, and will be ultimately responsible for the advice given by the planner and hence must make sure its representatives meet all compliance and training prerequisites. As at November 2005, there were approximately 4300 licence holders registered with ASIC and over 42,500 authorised representatives in Australia.

Then, in 2001, the Singapore government introduced the Financial Advisers Act (FAA) to regulate the conduct of financial advisory business in the country. However, the FAA do not specifically require a high level qualification before a financial practitioner can use the title 'financial planner'. The Act also defines a financial adviser to mean a firm with a corporate structure which is properly licenced by the Monetary Authority of Singapore (MAS) to perform financial advisory business. In both the Australia and Singapore situation, there is no law specifically on 'holding out' oneself to be a financial planner.

United States

In the United States of America, the NASD regulates and oversees the activities of more than 5,050 brokerage firms, approximately 172,050 branch offices and more than 663,050 registered securities representatives. A financial advisor or stock broker should be licensed to provide any consultation on investment in securities. Typical licenses needed to promote the sale of stocks are the: Series 7 (stock broker exam), Series 63 (state exam), and Series 65 or 66 RIA Registered Investment Advisor Law exam. Generally, any advisor who charges a fee for investment advise would need to also have the Series 65 or 66 license. Thus, anyone can call themselves a financial planner but they would still need NASD licenses to provide advice for a fee or be registered as an investment advisor with the SEC Securities and Exchange Commission in the USA. Many brokerage firms still claim an exemption for their employees who sell fee based products and services.

Licensing

The first country to introduce legislation that require a person to be licensed before he can hold himself out to be a 'financial planner' is Malaysia. This is quite unexpected as the financial planning concept is considered quite a new introduction in the Asian region as compared to those in the west, such as the United States and Australia where the profession is more established. The Securities Commission(SC) of Malaysia introduced legislation through amendments made to the Securities Industry Act in 2003 to regulate financial planning and the use of the title or related-title of 'financial planner' or to conduct activities related to financial planning.

In 2005, amendments to the Malaysian Insurance Act require those who carry out financial advisory business (including financial planning activities related to insurance) and/or use the title of financial adviser under their firm (which, like in Singapore, must be a corporate structure) to obtain a licence from Bank Negara (BNM) Some persons who offer financial advisory services, e.g. licenced life insurance agents, are exempted from licensing for them to engage in financial advisory business.

Among others, one of the basic requirements to apply for a financial planner or financial adviser licence in Malaysia is the key company officers, e.g. directors, must be a RFP designee (most, if not all Malaysian FChFP designees also hold the RFP designation). Subsequently, in Septermber 2006, the CFP qualification is included as one of the alternative that can be used by the financial adviser licence applicant. With this development, the demand for financial planning courses begin to take root in more concrete forms in Malaysia. The licence applicant must also be a member of a self-regulatory organisation (SRO)in financial planning that is recognised by the authorities. For this purpose, the two SROs that are currently recognised by both the Security Commission and Bank Negara is the Malaysia Financial Planning Council (MFPC) and the Financial Planning Association of Malaysia (FPAM). This requirement is to ensure there are some form of self-supervision in place for those practicing financial planning.

In some countries,e.g. United States, financial planners must be registered as an investment advisor first. This requires an employee within a firm to pass the series 65 or 66 Registered Investment Advisor Exam. Or, a private advisor or company can apply to the state and SEC for a RIA Registered Investment Advisor License or Status. It should be understood that being 'licenced' to practice financial planning is not the samc as merely having a professional 'qualification' in financial planning.

A person may be professionally qualified in financial planning, but without a licence required by the law, he cannot practice the trade in that country or call himself a financial planner there. As of now, there are quite a bit of qualifications related to financial planning that can be found in world. The most prestigious financial planning designations are those which are not just of advanced standing and well-known, but are also recognised by the relevant authorities for licensing purpose. The FChFP, RFP,CFP, ChFC, RFC, FFSI, CWM, MFP, or PFS, FPS designations are advanced financial planning or closely related qualifications that are independently offered and regulated by esteemed financial industry organizations but not all are recognised for licensing purpose.

In some palces, individual employees within a licensed and Registered Investment Advisor firm such as a: brokerage, bank or insurance company may be exempt if providing complementary financial planning services in relation to their existing products and services. Moreover, financial planners should be extremely careful in providing estate planning or taxation advise for a fee as these fields are highly regulated by the local bar associations lawyers and public accountants CPAs. "Investment Advisor" also includes any person who uses the title "financial planner" and who, for compensation, engages in the business, whether principally or as part of another business, of advising others, either directly or through publications or writings, as to the value of securities or as to the advisability of investing in, purchasing or selling securities, or who, for compensation and as part of a regular business, publishes analyses or reports concerning securities.

From California Department of Corporations

A financial planner will be registered with the state if they have <25 million in AUM and with the SEC if they have >30 million in AUM, and they are required to present you with their ADV Part II or equivalent before you enter into a contract with them. No certification, tests or training ensure that any planner is suitable for you or any investor, and it is important to read their ADV Part II, interview them, and fully understand any contract that you enter with them.

History of Certifications

As a newly emerged profession, it is quite expected that there will be a lack of regulation in the financial planning industry, especially in the early years of development. The need for some forms of self-regulations and the demand that a financial planner should be competent and trustworthy have prompted several independent financial services organizations to introduce certifications and ethical benchmarks to meet these challenges in accordance to the need in each country. Those who meet the requirement of the certification process and ethical standards will be awarded a professional financial planning designation.

Probably the earliest and the most well-known of the financial planning certification service mark is the Certified Financial Planner(CFP), which has gained global recognition because of its active standard setting activities and worldwide presence. The CFP designation was first introduced in the United States in the earlier 70's to meet the need of the consumers. The CFP mark now belongs to the CFP Board of Standard's ("CFP Board"), USA, which have member association all over the world. CFP Board was founded in July 1985 as the International Board of Standards and Practices for Certified Financial Planners, Inc, (IBCFP) by the College for Financial Planning (College) and the Institute of Certified Financial Planners (ICFP).

The IBCFP became Certified Financial Planner Board of Standards Inc.(CFP Board) on February 1, 1994. As a professional regulatory organization acting in the public interest by fostering professional standards in personal financial planning, CFP Board establishes and enforces education, examination, experience and ethics requirements for CFP® certificants. The CFP service mark is promoted all over the world through its member associations, the FPAs.

Another well-known certification mark with a unique history is the Fellow Chartered Financial Practitioner (FChFP), which is conferred by the Asia-Pacific Financial Services Association (APFinSA). The FChFP designation is the first known professional designation in financial planning that is completely developed in Asia and the programs leading to the designation is tailored to each country's need by local professionals and practitioners who writes these courses. It is also among the earliest to be vigorously promoted in this region. The FChFP designation was pioneered by the National Association of Malaysian Life Insurance and Financial Advisors (NAMLIFA) and was first launched on 31st May 1996 to its members in Malaysia as an 8-module financial planning programme. The FChFP was adopted by APFinSA in 2001 (of which NAMLIFA is a member) as the highest professional financial services designation amongst its member associations in 11 countries. This development effectively made the FChFP designation a regionally recognised designation in financial planning.

Through the Insurance and Financial Practitioners Association of Singapore (IFPAS), Singapore was the second country to successfully introduce the FChFP designation to its practitioners in 2003. It was during this time that the original letters of the designation 'ChFP' was modified to 'FChFP' to prevent the public from confusing it with the CFP mark. The FChFP designation has since spread to all over the Asia-Pacific region and is quick gaining strength in places like Hong Kong, China and Taiwan.

The Registered Financial Planner (RFP)designation is conferred by the Malaysian Financial Planning Council (MFPC)which was registered in 2004. (Note: The MFPC's RFP designation should be differentiated from the RFP designation conferred by the Registered Financial Planners Institute from the United States.) The Malaysian RFP designation and the MFPC was created through the collaborative work of the Life Insurance Association of Malaysia (LIAM), National Association of Malaysian Life Insurance and Financial Advisors(NAMLIFA) and Malaysian Insurance Institute (MII) who also become the founding members of the Association or Charter Promoter Organisations (ChPOs). Since then, other organisations such as the Malaysian Association of Chartered Financial Consultant (MAChFC) have joint the Association as a member.

The Personal Financial Specialist(PFS) credential was established for CPAs in the United States who specialize in personal financial planning. The credential is awarded exclusively to AICPA members who have demonstrated considerable experience and expertise in that area. As of today, the AICPA has granted approximately 3,300 CPA/PFS credentials. In Australia, the financial planning specialisation, CPA (FPS), is available to those members of CPA Australia who can demonstrate their eligibility through experience and education within the financial services industry.

The objectives of the FPS designation is to:

- Achieve public recognition for those who hold the specialisation enhance the quality of financial planning services that members provide
- Increase practice development and career opportunities for CPAs

The FPS is only avail to CPAs and is based on a points system, where a minimum of 100 points must be accrued. It should be noted that while all CPA Australia members who provide financial product advice must be licensed by ASIC, it is not mandatory for a member to be licensed to first obtained the CPA (FPS) designation.

The Chartered Financial Consultant (ChFC) is another prestigious financial planning qualification, which is conferred by American College, USA). Since 1982, the ChFC has remained among the most extensive education available for professionals seeking a designation in financial planning. Todate, more than 41,000 individuals have attained this distinction. This designation has also spread to Asia, where designees are found in countries like Singapore, Malaysia, Indonesia, China and Hong Kong.

In Europe, the European Financial Planner (EFP) designation conferred by the European Financial Planning Association (EFPA) is gaining ground as a financial planning certification mark. The EFPA is the largest professional and educational organisation for financial planners and financial advisors in Europe and is the only Financial Planning Association created solely in the interest of european financial planning consumers and practitioners.

In one of the significant recent developments, several major financial services organisations with international/ regional affiliations have grouped together to form the

Federation of Financial Standards Associations(IFFSA). The organisations that originally initiated the IFFSA concept are the European Financial Planner EFPA and the Asia-Pacific Financial Services Association (APFinSA). It is expected that more organisations will join as associates of this new entity.

The rest of the certification qualifications related to financial planning include: Fellow, Financial Services Institute (conferred by LOMJ, USA); The highest known conditions set for conferment of a financial planning credential seems to be those of the CWM Chartered Wealth Manager (conferred by the AAFM) designation which requires an accredited MBA, PhD or CFA to apply (Note: This entry requirement is not uniform and only applies to some places where the AAFM operates).

Education

In America, more than 150,000 financial services professionals have earned advanced degrees and designations from The American College. Their leading financial planning programs include ChFC programme and courses leading to the CFP certification awarded by the CFP Board of Standards. Another American organisation active in the promotion of financial planning courses is the International Association of Registered Financial Consultants(IARFC), which confers the Registered Financial Consultant (RFC) designation. The IARFC has introduced a financial planning self-study and examination process for Registered Financial Consultant applicants.

In Singapore, the Financial Planning Association of Singapore (FPAS) appoints educational providers to conduct tutorials for students interested in taking the CFP examinations. Two of its active education providers are Financial Perspectives and FTC. The Singapore College of Insurance(SCI) conducts localised courses leading to the ChFC designation which is awarded by The American College. Finally, the Insurance and Financial Practitioners Association of Singapore (IFPAS) uses the educational provider, Professional Education and Consultancy (PEC) to conduct tutorials for its FChFP students. These training companies, i.e.

Financial Perspectives, FTC and PEC, also provide a host of other financial related trainings to the financial practitioners in Singapore.

As for Malaysia, the Financial Planning Association of Malaysia (FPAM) has active education providers such as IMS, IFPA, PNB, KDU and IBBM to conduct its CFP courses. The Malaysian Financial Planning Council (MFPC) also appoints education providers for its RFP courses. Some of them to date are MII, NAMLIFA, MIM-IMS, IBBM, OUM, Kolej Kasturi and Regent School of Economics. For the FChFP, the courses are conducted in-house by the National Association of Malaysian Life Insurance and Financial Advisors (NAMLIFA) and its branches throughout the country. Other Malaysian training providers active in supporting financial planning education in the non-designation domain include BrainStation Academy, AD Capital and Jon Wise.

Globally, cross-recognition agreements are being developed to facilitate the learning of financial planning. The 2 major accrediting agencies AACSB and ACBSP in the west, which accredit over 560 of the best business school programs, provides the Certification of MFP Master Financial Planner Professional from the American Academy of Financial Management, which is available to AACSB and ACBSP business school graduates with finance or financial services related concentrations.

INTERNAL FINANCIAL REPORTING

Management is responsible for establishing and maintaining adequate internal control over financial reporting of the company. Internal control over financial reporting is a process designed to provide reasonable assurance regarding the reliability of financial reporting and the preparation of financial statements for external purposes in accordance with accounting principles generally accepted in the United States of America.

The company's internal control over financial reporting includes those policies and procedures that :

(i) Pertain to the maintenance of records that, in reasonable detail, accurately and fairly reflect the transactions and dispositions of the assets of the company;

(ii) Provide reasonable assurance that transactions are recorded as necessary to permit preparation of financial statements in accordance with accounting principles generally accepted in the United States of America, and that receipts and expenditures of the company are being made only in accordance with authorizations of management and directors of the company; and

(iii) Provide reasonable assurance regarding prevention or timely detection of unauthorized acquisition, use, or disposition of the company's assets that could have a material effect on the financial statements.

Because of its inherent limitations, internal control over financial reporting may not prevent or detect misstatements. Also, projections of any evaluation of effectiveness to future periods are subject to the risk that controls may become inadequate because of changes in conditions, or that the degree of compliance with the policies or procedures may deteriorate.

A primary responsibility of directors and officers is to ensure that the organization is accountable for its programs and finances to its contributors, members, the public and government regulators. Accountability requires that the organization comply with all applicable laws and ethical standards; adhere to the organization's mission; create and adhere to conflict of interest, ethics, personnel and accounting policies; protect the rights of members; prepare and file its annual financial report with the Internal Revenue Service and appropriate state regulatory authorities and make the report available to all members of the board and any member of the public who requests it. The development and maintenance of the organization's internal controls will help to ensure accountability.

What are Internal Controls?

Internal controls are systems of policies and procedures that protect the assets of an organization, create reliable financial reporting, promote compliance with laws and regulations and achieve effective and efficient operations. These systems are not only related to accounting and reporting but also relate to the organization's communication processes, internally and externally, and include procedures for:

(1) Handling funds received and expended by the organization,

(2) Preparing appropriate and timely financial reporting to board members and officers,

(3) Conducting the annual audit of the organization's financial statements,

(4) Evaluating staff and programs,

(5) Maintaining inventory records of real and personal property and their whereabouts, and

(6) Implementing personnel and conflicts of interest policies.

A. Procedures for Monitoring Assets

Every organization should have procedures to monitor and record assets received, held and expended. These financial controls should be described in an accounting policies and procedures manual. The manual should be reviewed with and given to all directors and officers, trustees, employees and volunteers. It should include procedures for:

- Preparing an annual income and expense budget and periodic reports - at least quarterly, preferably monthly - comparing actual receipts and expenditures to the budget with timely variance explanations.
- Writing and signing checks or vouchers and receiving, recording, securing and depositing cash and other receipts. Such procedures should ensure that no single individual is responsible for receiving, recording and depositing funds or writing and signing checks.

Checks and balances are essential to make embezzlement more difficult.

- Ensuring that grants and contributions received are properly recorded, accountings required as a condition of any grant are completed and restrictions on the use of such funds, such as contributions given for a restricted purpose (*e.g.* building fund, scholarships) and prohibitions on the use of the principal of an endowment, are obeyed.
- Requisitioning, authorizing, verifying, recording and monitoring all expenditures, including payment of invoices, petty cash and other expenditures. Such procedures should ensure that no single individual is permitted to request, authorize, verify and record expenditures. For example, the same person should not be responsible for cash disbursements and bank reconciliations. These functions should be assigned to different individuals.
- Accessing, inputting and changing electronic data maintained by the organization.

Preserving electronic records and ensuring data compatibility when systems change and creating an appropriate records retention policy are part of this process.

- Providing for regular oversight by an audit committee or, if there is no audit committee, by the executive committee or by the board of directors itself.
- Reporting to the audit committee or board by employees and volunteers of allegations of fraud or financial improprieties.
- Ensuring that timely and appropriate financial reports are distributed to all directors and officers and reviewed by them, as well as the president, chief executive officer, treasurer and chief financial officer.
- Providing procedures for approving contracts to which the organization is a party, including securing competitive bids from vendors.

- Monitor any legal matters that could impact the financial health and reporting of the organization.
- Institute and oversee any special investigatory work as needed.

In organizations with small boards, the entire board may serve the function of the audit committee. For larger organizations, it is more appropriate to create a separate audit committee that can devote its attention to this area. Whatever form the audit committee takes, at least one member should have an understanding of financial matters and should be comfortable reviewing financial reports and other financial records. No member of the audit committee should ever be involved in any conflict of interest transaction, and no member of the audit committee should be compensated in any manner by the organization other than director's fees paid generally to all directors, if any. The audit committee should be familiar with the organization's internal controls and report to the board as appropriate the adequacy of the internal controls and any concerns raised by the staff or outside auditors.

OPERATING THE MANAGEMENT CONTROL SYSTEM

A financial system supports the financial functions required to track financial events, provide financial information significant to the financial management of the agency, and/or required for the preparation of financial statements. A financial system encompasses automated and manual processes, procedures, controls, data, hardware, software, and support personnel dedicated to the operation and maintenance of system functions. A financial system may include multiple applications that are integrated through a common database or are electronically interfaced, as necessary, to meet defined data and processing requirements.

The term "non-financial system" means an information system that supports non-financial functions of the Federal government or components thereof and any financial data included in the system are insignificant to agency financial management and/or not required for the preparation of financial statements. The term "mixed system" means an information system that supports both financial and non-financial functions of the Federal government or components thereof.

The term "financial management systems" means the financial systems and the financial portions of mixed systems necessary to support financial management. The term "single, integrated financial management system" means a unified set of financial systems and the financial portions of mixed systems encompassing the software, hardware, personnel, processes (manual and automated), procedures, controls and data necessary to carry out financial management functions, manage financial operations of the agency and report on the agency's financial status to central agencies, Congress and the public. Unified means that the systems are planned for and managed together, operated in an integrated fashion, and linked together electronically in an efficient and effective manner to provide agency-wide financial system support necessary to carry out the agency's mission and support the agency's financial management needs.

MANAGEMENT CONTROL AND STAFFING

Although there is a tendency to want a "bright line" to define businesses as small, medium-size or large, this guidance does not provide such definitions. It uses the term "smaller" rather than "small" business, suggesting there is a wide range of companies to which the guidance is directed. The focus is on businesses that have many of the following characteristics:

- Fewer lines of business and fewer products within lines
- Concentration of marketing focus, by channel or geography
- Leadership by management with significant ownership interest or rights
- Fewer levels of management, with wider spans of control

- Less complex transaction processing systems and protocols
- Fewer personnel, many having a wider range of duties
- Limited ability to maintain deep resources in line as well as support staff positions such as legal, human resources, accounting and internal auditing.

None of these characteristics by themselves is definitive. Certainly, size by whatever measure - revenue, personnel, assets, or other - affects and is affected by these characteristics, and shapes our thinking about what constitutes "smaller."

Costs and Benefits

Management and other stakeholders of public companies, particularly smaller ones, have focused great attention on the cost of complying with Section 404, with less attention given to the associated benefits. Although it may be difficult to measure impacts associated with inaccurate financial reporting, market reactions to corporate misstatements clearly signal that the investment community does not readily tolerate inaccurate reporting, regardless of company size. In that respect and with other benefits described below, effective internal control adds significant value.

Among the most significant benefits is the strengthened ability of companies to access the capital markets, providing capital which drives innovation and economic growth. Other benefits include reliable and timely information supporting management's decision-making, consistent mechanisms for processing transactions across an organization enhancing speed and reliability, and ability to accurately communicate business performance with partners and customers.

Meeting Challenges in Attaining Cost-Effective Internal Control

The characteristics of smaller companies provide significant challenges for cost-effective internal control. This particularly is the case where managers view control as an administrative burden to be added onto existing business systems, rather than recognizing the business need and benefit for effective internal control that is integrated with core processes.

Among the challenges are:

- Obtaining sufficient resources to achieve adequate segregation of duties
- Management's ability to dominate activities, with significant opportunities for management override of control
- Recruiting individuals with requisite financial reporting and other expertise to serve effectively on the board of directors and audit committee
- Recruiting and retaining personnel with sufficient experience and skill in accounting and financial reporting
- Taking management attention from running the business in order to provide sufficient focus on accounting and financial reporting
- Maintaining appropriate control over computer information systems with limited technical resources.

While all companies incur incremental costs to design and report on internal control over financial reporting, costs can be proportionally higher for smaller companies. Yet despite resource constraints, smaller businesses usually can meet this challenge and succeed in attaining effective internal control in a reasonably cost-effective manner. This is accomplished in a variety of ways, outlined in this guidance, many of which already exist today in smaller companies and for which management can "take credit" in considering internal control effectiveness.

Wide and Direct Control from the Top

Many smaller businesses are dominated by the company's founder or other leader who exercises a great deal of discretion and provides personal direction to other personnel. While key to enabling the company to meet its growth and other objectives, this positioning also can contribute significantly to effective internal control over financial reporting. In-depth knowledge of different facets of the business - its operations, processes, array of contractual commitments and business risks - enables its leader to know what to expect in reports generated by the financial reporting system and to follow up as needed when unanticipated variances surface. A related downside in terms of ability to override established control procedures can be addressed with specified protocols.

Effective Boards of Directors

Smaller hotels typically have relatively straightforward business operations with less complex business structures, enabling directors to gain more in-depth knowledge of business activities. Directors may have been closely involved with the company during its evolution and have a strong historical perspective. Coupled with what often is exposure to and frequent communication with a wide range of managers, this assists the board and its audit committee in performing oversight responsibilities for financial reporting in a highly effective manner.

Compensating for Limited Segregation of Duties

Resource constraints may limit the number of employees, sometimes resulting in concerns regarding segregation of duties. There are, however, actions management can take in order to compensate for potential inadequacy. These include managers reviewing system reports of detailed transactions; selecting transactions for review of supporting documents; overseeing periodic counts of physical inventory, equipment or other assets and comparing them with accounting records; and reviewing reconciliations of account balances or performing them independently. In many small companies managers already are performing these and other procedures supporting reliable reporting, and credit should be taken for their contribution to effective internal control.

Information Technology

The reality of limited internal information technology resources often can be dealt with through use of software developed and maintained by others. These packages still require controlled implementation and operation, but many of the risks associated with in-house developed systems are avoided. Typically there is a limited need for Programme change controls, inasmuch as changes are done exclusively by the developer company, and generally a smaller company's personnel lack technical expertise to make unauthorized modifications.

Such commercially available packages also bring advantages in the form of embedded facilities for controlling which employees can access or modify specified data, performing checks on data processing completeness and accuracy, and maintaining related documentation. Further advantage can be gained by utilizing software that comes with a variety of built-in application controls that can improve consistency of operation, automate reconciliations, facilitate reporting of exceptions for management review, and support proper segregation of duties. Smaller companies can take advantage of these capabilities, ensuring "flags" or "switches" are properly set to take advantage of the software's capabilities.

Monitoring Activities

The monitoring component is an important part of the Framework, where a wide range of activities routinely performed by managers in running a business can provide feedback on the functioning of other components of the internal control system. Management of many smaller businesses regularly perform such procedures, but have not always taken sufficient "credit" for their contribution to internal control effectiveness. These activities, usually performed manually and sometimes supported by computer software, should be fully considered in designing and assessing internal control. From a different perspective, there is another way monitoring activities can promote efficiency.

After the first year of assessing and reporting on internal control, many companies repeated the assessment process in year two with little if any cost savings. A different approach, however, can be taken to promote efficiency. By focusing on monitoring activities already in place or that might be added with little additional effort, management can identify significant changes to the financial reporting system since the prior year, thereby gaining insight into where to target more detailed testing. While for effective internal control all five components must be in place and operating effectively and some testing of each component is necessary, highly effective monitoring activities can both offset certain shortcomings in other components and sharpen targeting of assessment work with resulting overall efficiency.

Achieving Further Efficiencies

In addition to considering the above, companies can gain additional efficiencies in designing and implementing or assessing internal control by focusing on only those financial reporting objectives directly applicable to the company's activities and circumstances, taking a risk based approach to internal control, right sizing documentation, viewing internal control as an integrated process, and considering the totality of internal control. The COSO Framework recognizes that an entity must first have in place an appropriate set of financial reporting objectives.

At a high level, the objective of financial reporting is to prepare reliable financial statements, which involves attaining reasonable assurance that the financial statements are free from material misstatement. Flowing from this high level objective, management establishes supporting objectives related to the company's business activities and circumstances and their proper reflection in the company's financial statement accounts and related disclosures. These objectives may be influenced by regulatory requirements or by other factors that management may choose to incorporate when setting its objectives. Efficiencies are gained by focusing on only those objectives directly applicable to the business and related to its activities and circumstances that are material to the financial statements.

Experience shows that this can be most efficiently accomplished by beginning with a company's financial statements and identifying supporting objectives for those business activities, processes and events that can materially affect the financial statements. In this way, a basis is formed for giving attention only to what is truly relevant to the reliability of financial reporting for that company.

Focusing on Risk

While management considers risks in several respects, its overarching consideration is the risks to key objectives, including the risks to reliable financial reporting. Risk-based means focusing on quantitative and qualitative factors that potentially affect the reliability of financial reporting, and identifying where in transaction processing or other activities related to financial statement preparation something could go wrong. By focusing on key objectives management can tailor the scope and depth of risk assessments needed. Often risk is considered in the context of initially designing and implementing internal control, where risks to objectives are identified and analyzed to form a basis for determining how the risks should be managed. Another is in the context of assessing whether internal control is effective in mitigating risks to objectives.

In the context of assessing internal control effectiveness, there sometimes is a tendency to consider internal control using generic lists of controls appropriate to a "typical" organization. While these tools in questionnaire or other form may be useful, an unintended result is that management sometimes focuses on "standard" or "typical" controls that simply are not relevant to the company's financial reporting objectives or risks associated with those objectives. A related problem encountered is starting assessments with the details of accounting systems and documenting them in extreme depth without recognizing whether the entirety of processes are truly relevant to achieving reliable financial reporting. This is not to say that such approaches cannot be useful, as they can be. However, whatever approach is followed, efficiencies are gained when attention is directed to the objectives management has established specific to the company's business activities and circumstances.

Right-Sizing Documentation

Documentation of business processes and procedures and other elements of internal control systems is developed and maintained by companies for a number of reasons. One is to promote consistency in adhering to desired practices in running the business. Effective documentation assists in communicating what is to be done, and how, and creates expectations of performance. Another purpose of documentation is to assist in training new personnel and as a refresher or reference tool for other employees. Documentation also provides evidence to support reporting on internal control effectiveness. The level and nature of documentation varies widely by company. Certainly, large companies usually have more operations to document, or greater complexity in financial reporting processes, and therefore find it necessary to have more extensive documentation than smaller ones.

Smaller companies often find less need for formal documentation, such as in-depth policy manuals, systems flowcharts of processes, organization charts, job descriptions, and the like. In smaller companies, typically there are fewer people and levels of management, closer working relationships and more frequent interaction, all of which promotes communication of what is expected and what is being done. A smaller business, for example, might document human resources, procurement or customer credit policies with memoranda and supplement the memoranda with guidance provided by management in meetings. A larger company will more likely have more detailed policies (or policy manuals) to guide their people in better implementing controls.

Questions arise as to the extent of documentation needed to deem internal control over financial reporting as effective. The answer is, of course, it depends on circumstances and needs. Some level of documentation is always necessary to assure management that its control processes are working, such as documentation to help assure management that all shipments are billed, or periodic reconciliations are performed. In a smaller business, however, management is often directly involved in performing control procedures and for those procedures there may be only minimal documentation because management can determine that controls are functioning effectively through direct observation. However, there must be information available to management that the accounting systems and related procedures, including actions taken in connection with preparation of reliable financial statements, are well designed, well understood, and carried out properly.

When management asserts to regulators, shareholders or other third parties on the design and operating effectiveness of internal control over financial reporting, management accepts a higher level of personal risk and typically will require documentation of major processes within the accounting systems and important control activities to support its assertions. Accordingly, management will review to determine whether its documentation is appropriate to support its assertion. In considering the amount of documentation needed, the nature and extent of the documentation may be influenced by the company 's regulatory requirements. This does not necessarily mean that documentation will or should be more formal, but it does mean that there needs to be evidence that the controls are designed and working properly.

In addition, when an external auditor will be attesting to the effectiveness of internal control, management will likely be expected to provide the auditor with support for its assertion. That support would include evidence that the controls are properly designed and are working effectively. In considering the nature and extent of documentation needed by the company, management should also consider that the documentation to support the assertion that controls are working properly will likely be used by the external auditor as part of his or her audit evidence.

There may still be instances where policies and procedures are informal and undocumented. This may be appropriate where management is able to obtain evidence captured through the normal conduct of the business that indicates personnel regularly performed those controls. However, it is important to keep in mind that control processes, such as risk assessment, cannot be performed entirely in the mind of the CEO or CFO without some documentation of the thought process and management's analysis. Many of the examples contained later in this guidance illustrate how management can capture evidence through the normal course of business. Documentation of internal control should meet business needs and be commensurate with circumstances. The extent of documentation supporting design and operating effectiveness of the five internal control components is a matter of judgment, and should be done with costeffectiveness in mind. Where practical, the creation and retention of evidence should be embedded with the various financial reporting processes.

Viewing Internal Control as an Integrated Process

It is useful to view the Framework's five internal control components as comprising an integrated process, which indeed internal control is. A process perspective highlights the interrelationship of the components, and recognizes that management has flexibility in choosing controls to achieve its objectives and that an organization can adjust and improve its internal control over time. As noted, the internal control process begins with management setting financial reporting objectives relevant to the company's particular business activities and circumstances.

Once set, management identifies and assesses a variety of risks to those objectives, determines which risks could result in a material misstatement in financial reporting, and determines how the risks should be managed through a range of control activities. Management implements approaches to capture, process and communicate information needed for financial reporting and other components of the internal control system. All this is done in context of the company's control environment, which is shaped and refined as necessary to provide the appropriate tone at the top of the organization and related attributes. These components all are monitored to help ensure that controls continue to operate properly over time.

The Totality of Internal Control

Each of the five components of internal control set forth in the Framework is important to achieving the objective of reliable financial reporting. Determining whether a company's internal control over financial reporting is effective involves a judgment. Internal control has five components that work together to prevent or detect and correct material misstatements of financial reports.

When the five components are present and functioning, to the extent that management has reasonable assurance that financial statements are being prepared reliably, internal control can be deemed effective. While each component must be present and functioning, this does not mean, however, that each component should function identically or even at the same level in every company. Some trade- offs may exist between components. Accordingly, effective internal control does not necessarily mean a "gold standard" of control is built into every process. A deficiency in one component might be mitigated by other controls in that component or by controls in another component strong enough such that the totality of control is sufficient to reduce the risk of misstatement to an acceptable level.

Applying Principles in Achieving Effective Internal *Control over Financial Reporting*

This guidance provides a set of twenty basic principles representing the fundamental concepts associated with, and drawn directly from, the five components of the Framework.

Control Environment

1. Integrity and Ethical Values - Sound integrity and ethical values, particularly of top management, are developed and understood and set the standard of conduct for financial reporting.
2. Board of Directors - The board of directors understands and exercises oversight responsibility related to financial reporting and related internal control.
3. Management's Philosophy and Operating Style - Management's philosophy and operating style

support achieving effective internal control over financial reporting.

4. Organizational Structure - The company's organizational structure supports effective internal control over financial reporting.
5. Financial Reporting Competencies - The company retains individuals competent in financial reporting and related oversight roles.
6. Authority and Responsibility - Management and employees are assigned appropriate levels of authority and responsibility to facilitate effective internal control over financial reporting.
7. Human Resources - Human resource policies and practices are designed and implemented to facilitate effective internal control over financial reporting.

Risk Assessment

8. Financial Reporting Objectives - Management specifies financial reporting objectives with sufficient clarity and criteria to enable the identification of risks to reliable financial reporting.
9. Financial Reporting Risks - The company identifies and analyzes risks to the achievement of financial reporting objectives as a basis for determining how the risks should be managed.
10. Fraud Risk - The potential for material misstatement due to fraud is explicitly considered in assessing risks to the achievement of financial reporting objectives.

Control Activities

11. Integration with Risk Assessment - Actions are taken to address risks to the achievement of financial reporting objectives.
12. Selection and Development of Control Activities - Control activities are selected and developed considering their cost and their potential effectiveness in mitigating risks to the achievement of financial reporting objectives.

13. Policies and Procedures - Policies related to reliable financial reporting are established and communicated throughout the company, with corresponding procedures resulting in management directives being carried out.
14. Information Technology - Information technology controls, where applicable, are designed and implemented to support the achievement of financial reporting objectives.

Information and Communication

15. Financial Reporting Information - Pertinent information is identified, captured, used at all levels of the company, and distributed in a form and timeframe that supports the achievement of financial reporting objectives.
16. Internal Control Information - Information used to execute other control components is identified, captured, and distributed in a form and timeframe that enables personnel to carry out their internal control responsibilities.
17. Internal Communication - Communications enable and support understanding and execution of internal control objectives, processes, and individual responsibilities at all levels of the organization.
18. External Communication - Matters affecting the achievement of financial reporting objectives are communicated with outside parties.

Monitoring

19. Ongoing and Separate Evaluations - Ongoing and/ or separate evaluations enable management to determine whether internal control over financial reporting is present and functioning.
20. Reporting Deficiencies - Internal control deficiencies are identified and communicated in a timely manner to those parties responsible for taking corrective action, and to management and the board as appropriate.

Index

A

B

C

J

K

L

M

N

O

P

Q

R

S

T

U

V

W

Y

Z